CREATED FOR COMMUNITY
Connecting Christian Belief
with Christian Living

A BRIDGEPOINT BOOK

BridgePoint,
the academic
imprint of
Victor Books, is
your connection
for the best in
serious reading
that integrates
the passion of
the heart with
the scholarship
of the mind.

CREATED
FOR
COMMUNITY

Connecting Christian Belief

with Christian Living

STANLEY J. GRENZ

A
BRIDGEPOINT
BOOK

Editor: Robert N. Hosack
Designer: Andrea Boven
Cover: William Weber, *The Wedding Feast at Cana,* monoprint

Library of Congress Cataloging-in-Publication Data

Grenz, Stanley, 1950–
    Created for community: connecting Christian belief with Christian living / Stanley J. Grenz.
        p.   cm.
    "A BridgePoint book."
    Includes bibliographical references.
    ISBN 1-56476-550-4
    1. Theology, Doctrinal. 2. Christian life. I. Title.
BT78.G75   1996
230 – dc20   95-42911
                                                                                    CIP

BridgePoint is the academic imprint of Victor Books.

© 1996 by Victor Books/SP Publications, Inc. All rights reserved. Printed in the United States of America.

1   2   3   4   5   6   7   8   9   10   Printing/Year 00   99   98   97   96

DEDICATION

To Roger E. Olson

Scholar, Educator, Friend

CONTENTS

FOREWORD

We have strangely mixed attitudes towards theology in the church today. Professors and pastors often tangle over whether seminary education should spend more time in classical theology, or whether the emphasis should be put on practical skills that are needed for leadership in the local church.

Laypersons, too, have different slants—ranging from "don't give me baby food; teach me how to think seriously about my faith and its implications" to "I'm not a theologian; I'm just an ordinary layperson. Just give me something that will help me live day by day."

Part of the problem is that we have such a skewed view about what theology is. The very word "theology" may conjure up the picture of an academic, sitting in an ivory tower, thinking deep thoughts about God that ordinary people can't and shouldn't be expected to understand.

It would help us greatly if we could straighten our thinking on two points. First, *every believer* is a theologian. Second, theology is not about academic affairs, but about life.

Stan Grenz has done the church a great service in *Created for Community: Connecting Christian Belief with Christian Living.* He is convinced that every believer should and can think of and live in the light of God. He believes we need to do this not just as individuals, but as the community of God's people.

And he has done this in a style which will help all of us to be better theologians.

Let me just list a few points I noted that make *Created for Community: Connecting Christian Belief with Christian Living* so helpful.

- It is *biblical*, giving us a clear overview of what Scripture has to say.
- It is *systematic*, covering the major doctrines in Christian theology.
- It is *historical*, giving brief and balanced descriptions of the various views on disputed issues.
- It is *contemporary*, showing, for example, how the doctrine of creation bears on today's environmental issues.
- It is *applied and personal*. When Stan Grenz teaches about the Trinity he goes on to tell us what "Trinitarian praying" and "Trinitarian living" might look like.
- It is *integrated* helpfully around the theme of community—as revealed in the nature of God and demonstrated in the life of the church.
- It tells a *story*—showing us how God's story speaks to a world that has lost its story.

I hope that *Created for Community: Connecting Christian Belief with Christian Living* will be read widely and for a long time. It is my hope that God will use this book to bring renewal to the church—so that our churches will become true communities, truly worshiping God, genuinely caring for others, and effectively reaching out to the world.

Leighton Ford
Charlotte, North Carolina

Peppermint Patty was describing to Charlie Brown the exam she took in school that day. "Get this, Chuck," the girl reported. "She asks us, 'How many angels can stand on the head of a pin?' What kind of a question is that, Chuck? How can you answer something like that?" True to form, Charlie Brown offered an astute, carefully crafted explanation. "You can't, Patty. It's an old theological problem. There really is no answer." Obviously oblivious to her friend's display of theological acumen, Peppermint Patty retorted, "That's too bad. I put down, 'Eight, if they're skinny, and four if they're fat!'"

Many people cringe at the thought of reading a theology book. They are convinced that theologians are stuffy academic types who hang out in "ivory towers" where they discuss obscure, unknowable and irrelevant questions like the one posed to Peppermint Patty. Unfortunately, many theologians provide ample support for this stereotype. They are sometimes content to argue with each other about issues that are of no concern to most people, even to most Christians. And they often give the impression that their discussions have no bearing on life in the "real world." Nothing, however, could be farther from the truth. Theology is by its very nature connected to life. Each of us, regardless of religious affiliation (or lack of it), has a core set of beliefs (a worldview) about God and the world (or ultimate reality). And these beliefs form the foundation for how we live.

This book is about theology, more specifically, Christian theology. It sets forth my understanding of the core beliefs we share as believers. My goal is to make theology accessible to people who are reticent to read a theology text. More specifically, I want to survey the Christian theological landscape with you, so that you might sharpen your core set of beliefs—not for the sake of priming you to win theological arguments, but to assist you to *live* as a Christian in the society in which God has placed us, that is, so that you can connect Christian belief with Christian living.

The theme around which the book revolves is given in the title, *Created for Community*. At the heart of the Christian message is the good news that the Triune God desires to bring us into fellowship with himself, with each other and with all creation. I believe that this biblical vision of community—this core set of beliefs—can provide the foundation for truly Christian living, as we are drawn by the Holy Spirit to live on the basis of this vision.

In a sense, this volume is the distillation of my lengthier book, *Theology for the Community of God*, published in 1994 by Broadman & Holman. In that volume I take the reader through the process by which I arrive at the theological conclusions presented in more summary fashion here. You might view *Created for Community* as an extended "sermon," similar to what a pastor might say in twenty-five minutes. *Theology for the Community of God*, in contrast, represents the diligent work that would occupy the pastor throughout the week of preparation for that Sunday sermon.

Roger Olson represents those theologian-pastors who have devoted their lives to assisting Christians—especially younger Christians—in discovering and clarifying the core beliefs we share. In addition, over the last ten years he has become a close and cherished friend. In gratitude for his partnership in the theological enterprise, for his personal scholarship, but above all for his friendship, I dedicate this book.

Christian Belief and Christian Living

*"We demolish arguments and every pretension that sets itself up
against the knowledge of God, and we take captive every
thought to make it obedient to Christ"*
(2 Cor. 10:5).

"Don't let that theology professor destroy your faith!"

I had worked at the Northwest Church for three years as youth
director during my seminary days. Now I was preparing to leave
for graduate studies in Germany. A dear saint in the congregation
was concerned that further academic training would undermine
the firmness of my Christian convictions and deaden my zeal for
serving the Lord. His concern led him to caution me with this
well-meaning warning about what he feared might be the result
of my desire to pursue further theological education.

Rather than unfounded and misguided, my church friend's caution reflects many tragic experiences. Theological studies are
sometimes the enemy of faith. Yet, his warning strikes at the
wrong target. The problem is not theology itself, but the incorrect conclusions some practitioners of the discipline draw from
their studies.

Contrary to what certain Christians suggest, there are no
"simple believers" who can remain "untainted" by theological
reflection. Whether consciously or unconsciously, each of us has
a set of convictions about ultimate reality. We believe *something*
about God, ourselves, and the purpose of life. And these foundational beliefs surface in what we say and how we live. Every
person is in this sense a theologian.

Although all persons have beliefs, many people give little

thought to how they form their fundamental convictions. And they rarely reflect on how these convictions are affecting the way they live. Christians, in contrast, take convictions seriously. We know that all beliefs are not equal; some are better than others. And certain convictions are true, whereas others are false.

The Bible confirms the importance of convictions. It emphasizes the role of the mind in discipleship. Jesus, for example, reiterated the Old Testament command to love God with all our being, including our minds (Matt. 22:37). Similarly Paul admonished his readers to take captive "every thought to make it obedient to Christ" (2 Cor. 10:5). The attempt to give serious place to this dimension of discipleship—to ask, "What *do* I believe?"—brings us into the realm of theology.

WHAT IS THEOLOGY?

Our English word "theology" arises from two Greek terms, *theos* ("God") and *logos* ("word," "teaching," "study").[1] Hence, "theology" means "the teaching concerning God" or "the study of God." The authors of Scripture constantly engage in this activity. All of their writings speak about God and his dealings with creation.

"Theology" can also carry an expanded meaning. In academic circles, it is a generic term referring to the various aspects of the study of the Bible and the church. Scholars often organize these studies into three major divisions.[2]

☞ *Biblical theology is the study of the doctrine espoused by the individual books or authors of Scripture.*

☞ *Historical theology describes the development of doctrine in the church, whereas systematic theology delineates an understanding of the faith in the contemporary situation.*

☞ *And practical theology applies doctrine to contemporary church life.*

Today, however, Christians often use "theology" in a more specific sense. The word denotes the set of beliefs about God and the world that are uniquely ours. Thus, we may offer this definition:

Theology is the systematic reflection on, and articulation of, the fundamental beliefs we share as followers of Jesus Christ.

Theologians generally organize our foundational beliefs into several major categories. Following their lead, we will arrange the twelve chapters of this book according to a sixfold division of theology:

☞ *God*	*theology proper*
☞ *humankind and the created universe*	*anthropology*
☞ *Jesus and the salvation he brought*	*Christology*
☞ *the Holy Spirit and the Spirit's work in us and in the world*	*pneumatology*
☞ *the church as the fellowship of Christ's disciples*	*ecclesiology*
☞ *the consummation or completion of God's program for creation*	*eschatology*

WHY THEOLOGY?

Theology arises out of an attempt to describe what we believe as Christians and to connect our beliefs with Christian living. But why is this important? Why be concerned to know what we believe?

Since the first century, the church has continually affirmed the importance of theology to its mission. Theology assists the church in at least three ways.[3]

• First, theological reflection helps us sift through the many belief systems that vie for attention. With the help of theology, we are better able to affirm correct doctrine.

As in every era, we are bombarded with the teachings of people who claim to offer a fuller understanding of Christianity. Contemporary claimants carry a variety of labels. These range from the more familiar (e.g., Jehovah's Witnesses) to the more esoteric (e.g., Scientology).

In addition, we find ourselves bombarded with an unprecedented number of competing religious systems and views of the world. These include not only the older world religions (e.g., Hinduism, Buddhism, Islam, Judaism) but also a host of newer proposals. In recent years, "TM," Divine Light, New Age, and countless other cults have challenged the faith of Christians. Each of them appeals to a purported "fuller revelation" from God and promises a "fuller life" to its adherents.

In the midst of this situation, the study of Christian belief can help us differentiate true belief (orthodoxy) from false teachings (heresy). Thereby, theology grounds us in the truth so that we are not "blown here and there by every wind of teaching" (Eph. 4:14).

• Second, theology serves the crucial task of instructing believers in Christian doctrine.

New converts are especially dependent on sound teaching. They may have only a minimal understanding of Christianity. Or their previous conception of the faith may have been ill-informed. For them to become stalwart believers requires that they be instructed in the fundamental beliefs that lie at the heart of the Christian faith. In instructing new believers we are following Jesus' example. Indeed, our Lord commands us not only to evangelize the world, but also to "make disciples of every nation." And this task includes "teaching them" (Matt. 28:19-20).

God desires that we all become mature, stable disciples of our Lord (Eph. 4:11-14). Therefore, we never outgrow the need for instruction. Theological study can deepen our understanding of the distinctively Christian teaching about God and the world.

• Third, theology brings together in summary form what the Bible teaches about God and his purposes.

As Christ's disciples we naturally desire to be biblical Christians. We want our conception of God and our understanding about what God has done for us to reflect that of the prophets and apostles. Theological reflection assists us in this task.

The desire to summarize our faith is not unique to contemporary Christians. Even the biblical peoples capsulized their beliefs. At the heart of the faith of the Hebrews was their belief in the God who had called their forefather Abraham and had rescued their ancestors from Egypt (Deut. 26:5-9). This God was the sole God and the only one worthy of love (Deut. 6:4-5). In a similar manner, the New Testament church summarized what they had come to believe about Christ and the salvation he brought (e.g., 1 Cor. 15:3-8; Phil. 2:6-11; 1 Tim. 3:16).

Theology, then, helps us to

☞ *differentiate true belief from false teaching,*
☞ *gain a firm grounding in the Christian faith,*
☞ *understand what the Bible teaches about God and the world.*

Because it aids us in this manner, the study of theology is vital to every Christian. Rather than undermining the firmness of our convictions, such study should enhance our faith.

Of course, theology exercises a critical function. It leads us to jettison certain beliefs that we thought were true, but which in fact do not square with sound teaching. But even this critical aspect serves to strengthen faith, not destroy it. The study of theology should cause us to become more steadfast in faith and more sure of what we believe.

> ✍ *Your study of Christian belief ought to enhance your faith.*

THEOLOGY AND CHRISTIAN LIVING

Because of this connection to the what and why of our beliefs, Christians generally view theology as a purely intellectual discipline. This perception is, of course, partially correct. Theology can be "heady stuff." And theologians often appear to "split hairs" about seemingly inconsequential matters. But the study of theology includes more than an academic debate about intellectual questions.

While it is an intellectual activity, theology is immensely practical. In fact, theology is among the most practical endeavors of the Christian life!

● First, theology is practical because of its link to our encounter with God in Christ—to that marvelous transaction we call "conversion."

The Bible narrates God's saving activity on behalf of sinful humankind. For us to receive God's salvation, however, we must not only hear the gospel story but also be told the meaning of God's saving acts. Specifically, we must hear not only *that* Christ died and rose again, but also *why* he sacrificed his life and how in him God acted for us.

Theology seeks to understand the significance of the gospel we proclaim. In so doing, it assists the church in declaring the good news in ways that people from varied backgrounds can understand so that they too may encounter God in Christ.

Once we have committed our lives to Christ, we naturally desire to know more about the God who has acted to save us. In this quest, theology also serves the people of God. Through theological reflection we wrestle with how we can best conceive of and speak about the God who is the author and object of our faith. Hence, faith — conversion — naturally leads to theology.

• But theology's purpose is not merely to satisfy our intellectual curiosity. It has another practical goal in view — to provide direction for Christian living.

Regardless of religious orientation, a person's basic beliefs (or "worldview") affect his or her way of life. And the way people live is the best indication of what they *really* believe about reality — in contrast to what they may profess to believe.

The Christian life flows out of a set of beliefs (a worldview) shaped by the Bible. Theology sets forth the uniquely Christian understanding of the world, at the heart of which is the story about Jesus of Nazareth. It explores Christ's significance for all of life. In this way, theology provides the needed intellectual resources for facing the challenges of the historical and social context in which God calls us to live. Our theological orientation — our fundamental beliefs about who God is, who we are as God's people, and what God is seeking to accomplish in the world — offers needed direction as we seek to live as Christ's disciples.

The practical goal of theology stands as a warning against the persistent danger of intellectualism. We pursue theology with the goal of understanding our faith in a systematic manner, of course. But constructing a theological system cannot be our ultimate purpose. Instead, we engage in theological reflection so that our lives might be changed. We desire to become stronger and more effective disciples — to connect Christian belief with Christian living.

> ✍ *Your study of Christian belief ought to enhance your life as a disciple.*

Sound theological reflection will make a difference in how we live. Doctrinal conviction provides the foundation for our attempts to determine the best way to live out our Christian commitment in the midst of the varied situations that confront us. And it motivates us to act continually in accordance with our commitment to Christ. Whenever our theological work stops short of this, we have failed to be obedient to our calling as thinking Christians. Indeed, our goal must always be to link Christian belief with Christian living.

THEOLOGY AND FAITH

What we have said so far suggests that theology is closely connected with faith. Yet we must never confuse the two.

We may characterize the difference by suggesting that biblical faith is "immediate." Indeed, faith comprises our personal response to the God who encounters us in the gospel of Jesus Christ. And this response involves all aspects of our personhood, specifically, our intellect, emotion, and volition.

• Faith includes our intellect. Faith means accepting as true certain specific assertions about reality. For example, we believe that God is our Creator, that humans are fallen, and that Christ died for us. As we acknowledge these truths, we come to view the world in a specific way.

• Faith includes our will. Faith means willingly committing our entire life to the God revealed in Jesus Christ. By faith we cast ourselves on Christ alone to save us.

• And faith includes our emotions. Faith is our heartfelt response of love to the One who saves us. This love for God, in turn, translates into love for others.

If faith touches on all three aspects, what about theology?

Immediately we must note that theology is closely related to faith, because it studies the response to the good news that God desires of us. But theology approaches faith from a unique vantage point. As Christian theologians, we seek to understand faith and to articulate the content of the Christian faith. In this endeavor, we raise certain specifically intellectual questions:

☞ *What statements best express the nature of the God who is the author and resting point of our faith?*

☞ *What is God "up to"—what are God's intentions for creation? And how is God accomplishing these goals?*

☞ *Who are we as participants in God's program?*

But above all, our theological reflection focuses on the significance of Jesus of Nazareth for our understanding of God, creation, and history. By engaging in theology, we seek to assist the Christian community in understanding the importance of Jesus Christ to the divine program. And we seek to understand the significance of our commitment to Jesus for all human life.

In short, therefore, theology probes the intellectual dimension of Christian faith. Consequently, theology is called forth by faith. We engage in theology because we naturally want to articulate the intellectual content of our faith.

We must note as well, however, that theology is likewise subservient to faith. That is, it seeks to serve faith. We engage in theology so that we may better understand our faith. A deepened understanding of faith, in turn, is one means whereby our faith is strengthened.

Because theology is the servant of faith, we must be vigilant against another danger—substitution. People who study theology sometimes allow theologizing to become a substitute for genuine, personal faith. But we cannot fall into this trap. We dare never replace commitment to the Triune God with our doctrines about God. We dare never allow our enthusiasm for our ability to formulate statements about Christ to diminish our love for him. And we must resolutely avoid placing confidence in our abilities to develop a theological system. Our hope for salvation can rest only in the God in whose service we stand.

The danger of substitution is real. Yet when theology truly does its work, the result is the opposite. Our theological reflections will lead to a deeper love for Christ and a deepened trust in the one true God.

OUR RESOURCES AS THEOLOGIANS

Because theology's wider goal is practical—to connect Christian belief with Christian living—theological reflection ought to foster in us a truly godly spirituality and obedient discipleship. What resources or "tools" are available to us as we engage in this?[4]

Central to the theological task are three resources (which theologians often refer to as "sources" or "norms"):[5]

☞ *the biblical message,*
☞ *the theological heritage of the church,*
☞ *the thought forms of our culture.*

By properly using these tools—which includes valuing them in this order—we can construct a helpful theology for our day, a theology that is biblical, Christian, and contemporary.

• Our *primary* resource as we engage in the theological task is the divine message inscripturated in the Bible.

Faith is our response to the God who encounters us in the gospel. Therefore, our articulation of the Christian faith naturally looks to the good news which we find in the Bible. For this reason, our theology must arise from the story of God's saving activity. God has disclosed this saving activity in the history of Old Testament Israel, in Jesus Christ, and in the New Testament church.

Through the pages of Scripture, the Spirit speaks to us about what it means to be the community of those who confess faith in the God revealed in Jesus of Nazareth. And the Bible guides us in our task of verbalizing and embodying our devotion to Christ in the context in which we live.

Some Christians strive to establish the authority of Scripture by elaborate proofs. While these attempts are sometimes helpful, we do not need to prove the Bible in order to begin the theological task. Instead, we may simply assume the Bible's authority.

As we will elaborate in chapter 7, the Bible is the Spirit-produced document through which the Spirit has always spoken to God's people. For this reason, it is the foundational document of the Christian church. Therefore, its message remains the central resource for Christian theology in every age.

• Of *secondary* importance to us in the theological task is the theological heritage of the church.

Throughout their history Christians have joined together to express their faith in the God revealed through Jesus. This has resulted in a rich deposit of theological reflection within the church. The creeds and confessions of the past offer guidance for us as we engage in the same task today.

Past theological statements are instructive in our attempt to set forth a statement of Christian doctrine that is relevant to our contemporary context. They remind us of previous attempts to fulfill the theological mandate. In so doing they alert us to some of the pitfalls to avoid. And they point us in directions that may hold promise for our attempts to engage in the theological calling in our own situation.

Certain past formulations—often called "creeds" or "confessions of faith"—carry special significance. These "classic" statements express what has been the doctrine of the church throughout the ages. Because we are the contemporary expression of the one church, we should take seriously those doctrinal formulations that have engendered broad acknowledgment among Christians of many generations.

Of course, creeds and confessions of faith are not binding in and of themselves.[6] They must be tested by the Scriptures and by their applicability to our situation.

• Theology's *tertiary* resource lies in the thought forms of contemporary culture.

We are called to express the Christian faith within the context of the world in which we live. One aspect of this calling is the task of articulating Christian doctrine in a manner that speaks to people today.

Engaging in this task requires that we understand our culture.[7] We must become aware of the longings of people today. And we must be thoroughly acquainted with the ways people around us view their world and speak about life. Only then are we equipped to express Christian belief in a way that connects with life—in a way that can address the problems, felt needs, and valid aspirations of people today.

We can discuss the resources for theology in isolation from each other. However, when we engage in the theological enterprise, we discover that they are inseparable. In seeking to express the faith of the people of God we must look simultaneously to the biblical message, the theological heritage of the church, and our contemporary cultural context. At the same time, we keep our focus on the Bible as our "norming norm," as the one authoritative standard for Christian belief and Christian living.

> ✍ *In exploring Christian belief use the tools of the Bible, Christian heritage, and contemporary culture.*

THEOLOGY AND THE CONCEPT OF "COMMUNITY"

The pages of this volume seek to build from these three resources. Our goal is to offer a systematic statement of the faith of the church in a manner that can speak to contemporary culture. To this end, we will order our theological reflections around the concept of "community" understood as the goal of God's program for creation. God is at work in our world, we declare. And God's purpose in this activity is the establishment of "community"—a reconciled people who enjoy fellowship with him, with one another, and ultimately with all creation.

Why community?—because the focus on community encapsules the biblical message, it stands at the heart of the theological heritage of the church, and it speaks to the aspirations and the sensed needs of people in our world today.[8] In short, as we realize that we are created for community, we are in a position to connect Christian belief with Christian living.

The following chapters describe the Christian faith by speaking about "community." Our discussion opens with the central doctrine of the Christian faith—God (theology proper). In chapters 1 and 2 we explore the nature of the Triune God who is at work in establishing community in the highest sense.

> ✍ God's goal for creation is "community"— a redeemed people dwelling on a renewed creation, enjoying the presence of the Triune God.

Standing in relationship with the sovereign, community-building God are God's moral creatures. The discussion of who we are as those God has designed for community forms the subject of chapters 3 and 4 (anthropology).

Chapters 5 and 6 focus on the Second Person of the Trinity, Jesus the Christ (Christology). In this section we reflect on what it means to confess that the man Jesus is the eternal Son whose earthly vocation was to initiate community between God and sinful humans.

In chapters 7 and 8 (pneumatology) the third person of the Trinity, the Holy Spirit, comes into our purview. We explore the Spirit's role in Scripture and in effecting personal salvation, which we will view as community with God and others.

Chapters 9 and 10 (ecclesiology) and 11 and 12 (eschatology) view the Spirit's corporate and consummative work. In these chapters, we explore the activity of the Holy Spirit as God at work establishing community in history and ultimately in eternity. The bringing about of the eternal community brings to completion the divine goal for creation.

A CLOSING CONNECTION

Each of us is a theologian, just as God intended. Consequently, our question is not "will we be theologians?" but "will we be good theologians?" Will we develop a worldview that is biblically sound and theologically correct? And will we translate theology into life, thereby showing ourselves to be disciples of the one we acknowledge as Lord? The following pages are intended to sharpen our theological knowledge so that we may connect Christian belief with Christian living—that is, so we may love God more completely and serve Christ more effectively.

Songwriter Mark Pendergrass got the order correct. In his poignant musical prayer, "The Greatest Thing," he articulates the earnest desires of his heart.[9] The three verses of his prayer express the yearning first to know, then to love, and finally to serve God more. Indeed, as we come to know God more—which is the direct task of theology—our love for God ought to deepen. And a deeper love for God ought to flow into greater service. Only then have we truly connected Christian belief with Christian living.

FOR CONNECTION AND APPLICATION

1 How would you define "theology"? Why is theology as you defined it important?

2 Do you agree that we are all theologians? How are our real beliefs reflected in the way we live?

3 Think of a specific situation in which you have consciously connected Christian belief with Christian living. What process did you go through to make the connection? Can you think of other areas of your life where God is calling you to translate your faith into "good works"? (cf. James 2:14-17)

4   If Christianity is true, then our beliefs as Christians can make a real difference in our lives. Your Christian belief should lead you to a greater commitment to Christ and a deeper love for God. How have your studies of Christian belief strengthened you spiritually? Who can you share this discovery with, in order to encourage them?

ONE

Knowing the God of the Bible in the Contemporary World

"And this is eternal life: that they may know you,
the only true God and Jesus Christ, whom you have sent"
(John 17:3).

"We no longer need to *prove* the existence of God to the people living around my church." The pastor's remark grabbed my attention. "The people living in this 'yuppie' neighborhood in the heart of Toronto," he explained, "all *assume* the reality of the supernatural."

The pastor's observation is confirmed by opinion polls which consistently indicate that the vast majority of people in the United States and Canada claim to believe in God or to acknowledge some divine reality. Yet, this does not mean that these people enjoy a personal relationship with the living God.

At the heart of our faith is the testimony that through Jesus Christ we have come to know the only true God. We declare that to know God means more than merely asserting that a vague, generic Supreme Being exists. We likewise cannot assume that all religious traditions automatically lead their devotees to the God of the Bible.

On the contrary, we assert that biblical faith entails a personal relationship with the God who encounters us in Jesus. Knowing this God, in turn, leads us to see all of life in a special way. Our faith commitment motivates us to live for the glory of the Father of our Lord Jesus Christ. And faith provides the foundation for knowing how to live for God's glory. Theology assists in this process, for it facilitates us in our quest to know the God of the Bible.

GOD AND THE CONTEMPORARY WORLD

But how can we continue to proclaim the ancient message about the God of Jesus our Lord in the contemporary context? Does our Christian confession still remain credible in today's world? And can we truly anticipate that people will listen when we declare that God has encountered us in Jesus Christ?

In responding to these questions, we must remind ourselves that our world is populated by people with many differing opinions about, and attitudes toward, religious matters. Therefore, our claim that the Christian faith is true may take several forms.

Is There a God? — Our Response to Atheism

Certain people today deny the existence of any God whatsoever. "There is no God," they firmly assert. We may call this denial "atheism," a word which means literally "no God." Atheists argue that the universe is not the creation of a purposeful God. Rather, it is shaped by blind, random natural forces. Or they see in the presence of evil in the world conclusive proof that a benevolent God cannot exist.

An atheistic spirit has filtered into our general cultural ethos. Pressured by a scientific worldview that leaves no room for religion, many people have discarded the concept of God. For them, God has become either the God-of-the-gaps for whom no gaps are left or a debilitating limitation on human freedom.

What can we say to people who do not acknowledge the reality of God?

Intellectual atheism is a relatively new development in the history of humankind. It did not gain a widespread following until long after the church expanded into the world dominated by Greek culture. In fact, it is in one sense a result of the rejection of the Christian gospel by intellectuals standing in the tradition of the Greeks.

Let's look at this historical development, for it provides a window on our world today.

The Greek philosophers loved to engage in intellectual argumentation. Above all, they debated whether or not we could devise philosophical proofs for theological beliefs, including the existence of the one God, understood as the First Cause of the world.

Influenced by the Greeks, Christian philosophers devised arguments which they thought actually proved God's existence. These Christian thinkers intended to provide intellectual confirmation of faith in God. Apologists such as Anselm of Canterbury (1033–1109) thought that they were simply living out Augustine's famous dictum, "I do not seek to understand that I may believe, but I believe in order to understand."[1] Like other thinkers, Anselm was convinced that intellectual proofs for God's existence offered the "understanding" — the logical persuasion — which Christian faith naturally evokes.

Christian philosophers developed three basic types of arguments for God's existence:

☞ *the ontological proofs,*
☞ *the cosmological and teleological proofs,*
☞ *the moral proofs.*

● A first type of argument — the ontological approach — claims to demonstrate God's existence by considering the idea of God itself.

Ontological proofs begin with a commonly held definition of God. They then show that there must be a Being (God) who corresponds to the definition. These arguments claim that by definition God cannot merely be an idea in our minds, but must also actually exist.

In his classical ontological proof, Anselm defined God as "that than which no greater can be conceived."[2] He then offered two possibilities: either God exists only in human minds, or God exists both in human minds and in reality. But if we conceive of God as existing only in our minds and not in reality, Anselm added, this God is not "that than which no greater can be conceived." Indeed, we could conceive of a God that exists both in our minds and in reality. The God who we conceive of as existing both mentally and actually is obviously greater than the God who we believe exists only in our minds. Therefore, Anselm concluded, by definition God *must* exist.

Several centuries later, the French philosopher René Descartes (1596–1650) argued in a somewhat similar manner. God, he said, is the "supremely perfect Being."[3] Now if God does not exist in reality, Descartes reasoned, he lacks one perfection — existence. But the God so conceived — as perfect in every way but not existing in reality — is not the most perfect being.

In the 1800s, Georg Hegel (1780–1831) offered a quite different ontological proof. He defined God as the infinite one, who stands as a contrast to finite beings. The idea of such a God, Hegel argued, is necessary to our human thinking process. The mind, he noted, cannot conceive of finite reality without at the same time thinking of an "infinite" that lies beyond the finite.[4]

More recently Norman Malcolm (1911–) asserted that God must exist because by his very conception he cannot not-exist. Malcolm believed that God's existence is by definition *necessary* existence.[5] That is, God necessarily exists or exists by necessity.

• The second type of philosophical proof — the cosmological and teleological arguments — seeks to demonstrate the existence of God by drawing on evidence provided by sense experience.

Cosmological and teleological arguments build from our observations of the world. They conclude that God must exist as the explanation for certain aspects of the universe which we readily observe.

Thus, *cosmological* proofs purport to demonstrate that God must exist as the ultimate cause of the universe itself. The world must have come from somewhere. And this Somewhere is God.

Teleological arguments, in contrast, look to more specific details of the universe. They claim that God must exist as the cause of some specific characteristic we observe in the natural world. The aspect philosophers most often cite is the apparent design or order in the universe. The design of the universe declares the existence of a cosmic Designer.

Already in the thirteenth century, the great Catholic theologian Thomas Aquinas (1225–1274) developed a series of cosmological and teleological arguments, which are often called "the five ways."[6]

Perhaps more widely known is the teleological argument proposed by William Paley (1743–1805). Paley's proof draws an analogy from the common watch, which in his day was an impressive array of springs and wheels, rather than the electronic timepiece we wear today. Paley noted that a precise mechanical instrument such as a watch declares the existence of its designer (the watch-maker). In a similar manner the intricate construction of the natural world bears witness to the existence of its Designer. We call this cosmic Architect "God."[7]

Early in the twentieth century F.R. Tennant (1866–1957) offered an updated version of the teleological argument. Unlike many thinkers for whom Darwin's theories were a stumbling block to faith, Tennant saw the evolutionary development of the universe as a pointer to God's existence. Specifically, he found a "wider teleology" within evolutionary nature. Many strands have worked together in the production of higher and higher levels of creatures, he declared. The evolutionary process climaxed in the appearance of humankind, the moral creature. This grand cosmic cooperation, Tennant claimed, provides ground for reasonable belief that God must exist. God is the One who gave direction to evolution.[8]

Recently the cosmologist Robert Jastrow has offered a restatement of the cosmological proof. He argued that the widely held "big bang" theory once again makes the postulate of God intellectually respectable.[9] God is the One who set off the "big bang" which started the universe.

• A third philosophical proof begins with the human experience of being a moral creature.

Immanuel Kant (1724–1804) offered a classic formulation of this approach. Each human, he noted, lives out of an unavoidable sense of duty. Kant did not mean that all humans share a specific moral code. Rather, he argued that behind the various and differing codes of conduct humans devise is a common feeling of being morally conditioned, or held responsible by the sense of duty.

Kant concluded that God must exist, if this experience of moral obligation is to have any meaning. In a truly moral universe virtuous conduct must be rewarded and wrongdoing must be punished. But for this to occur, there must be a Supreme Lawgiver. This God guarantees that ultimately moral justice will be done.[10]

Hastings Rashdall (1858–1924) devised a somewhat different formulation of the moral proof. He noted that ideals — standards and goals toward which people strive — exist only in minds. But, he added, certain ideals are absolute. These can exist only in a mind adequate for them, namely, in an absolute or divine mind. Therefore, he concluded, God must exist.[11]

Perhaps the most well-known contemporary formulation of the moral argument came from the pen of C.S. Lewis in his widely read book, *Mere Christianity*.[12] All human societies reflect a universal code of morality, Lewis claimed. In all cultures certain conduct is praised, while certain other actions are universally condemned. According to Lewis, this phenomenon indicates that behind the universe lies something that is conscious, has purpose, and prefers one type of conduct to another. Hence, this "something" is more like Mind than like anything else we know. Consequently, Lewis concluded, the "Something" at the foundation of the world is God.

Each of these classical proofs for God's existence has elicited a corresponding criticism. Nevertheless, many people find them intellectually compelling. For this reason, some Christians continue to use such arguments in the attempt to prove to modern skeptics that belief in God is intellectually credible. These Christian apologists believe that such proofs provide ammunition in the war against atheism. In addition, they add, intellectual arguments assist in evangelism. The classical proofs remove the intellectual misgivings that hinder some people from coming to faith.

How should we respond to this? Are such proofs helpful? Yes and no.

The various proofs for God's existence may provide some assistance in speaking to contemporary skeptics. But we ought not to be surprised to discover that few people can be "argued into the kingdom."

> ✍ *You can seek to demonstrate that faith is intellectually credible, but you cannot argue anyone into the kingdom.*

Nevertheless, the classic proofs remind us that in every age we have an apologetic role to fulfill, a role in explaining and defending the faith. As believers, we are convinced that only when we acknowledge God's existence can we truly understand the universe and ourselves as humans. As John Calvin declared, "it is certain that man never achieves a clear knowledge of himself unless he has first looked upon God's face, and then descends from contemplating him to scrutinize himself."[13]

Which God? — Christian Faith within the Competition of the Gods

We find ourselves living in a complex situation. Not only does our world include skeptics who deny the existence of God, many other people retain some semblance of belief in God while living as "practical atheists." Like the "fool" the psalmist mentions (Ps. 14:1; 53:1), they go about the tasks of life with little apparent need for God. For them God has become at best an innocuous postulate or perhaps even totally irrelevant to life.

But this does not exhaust our situation. Our society is also rapidly becoming a fertile field for a myriad of old and new religions. For some people, this proliferation of rival beliefs is merely another indication that Christianity cannot be true. For others, however, the spiritual aridness of contemporary life has produced a new thirst for the divine. As a result, we are witnessing a rebirth of interest in the supernatural. Yet people are not necessarily gravitating to the Christian faith. Rather, many are being enticed by the gods proclaimed by the messengers of other religions.

The proliferation of gods in our society suggests that we may be living in a situation similar to that faced by the biblical community. The first-century Christians were steadfastly loyal to Jesus in a society which worshiped a pantheon of pagan gods (1 Cor. 8:5-6). Like the ancient Hebrews, the early believers proclaimed that the God of Abraham and the Father of Jesus Christ is the only true God. Their response to their situation stands as an example of how we can set forth Christian belief today.

In the ancient world, everybody acknowledged one or more deities. As a result, during the biblical era rival gods competed with each other for the loyalties of people. And the crucial religious question of the day was "Which god is worthy of homage and service?"[14]

But how could this question be answered? The people of the ancient Near East believed that events in the world revealed the relative strength of the various tribal deities. The strong god was the one who could perform mighty acts.

In keeping with the ancient understanding, the Book of Exodus presents the plagues as signs indicating that Yahweh was stronger than the Egyptian gods. Israel's God could do wonders which the deities of Egypt could not imitate.[15] The deliverance of the fleeing Hebrews at the Red Sea became a further sign of Yahweh's power (Ex. 15:11-16). Forty years later, Yahweh parted the waters of the Jordan River so that the children of Israel could enter the land of Canaan. This demonstration of power struck terror in the hearts of the Canaanites (Josh. 5:1). And at a subsequent low point in Israel's history, Yahweh once again vindicated himself, together with Elijah the prophet, against the company of Baal worshipers on Mount Carmel (1 Kings 18).

For the ancient peoples, one mighty act stood above all others — the provision of victory in battle.[16] They viewed military conflicts not merely as contests of rival armies, but as struggles between rival deities. A military venture succeeded only because the god of the conquering tribe had vanquished the deity worshiped by the defeated people.

For example, when the army of Assyria surrounded Jerusalem, the invading general taunted not only Israel but also Israel's God. The haughty commander reminded his dispirited opponents that the gods of the nations had been unable to protect their devotees from the conquering Assyrian army (2 Kings 18:32-35).

A grave crisis of faith unfolded when foreigners finally devastated the kingdoms of Israel and Judah. Could it be that Yahweh had been vanquished by other gods? In response, the prophets declared that the captivity of God's people did not mean that Yahweh was unable to protect his own. Instead, they were signs of his judgment on their sin. God had allowed foreigners to take his people into captivity so that they might return wholeheartedly to him.[17]

The Old Testament prophets knew that Yahweh alone was the true God. This, however, meant that idolatry — paying homage to any other god — was a grievous sin. There is only one God, they adamantly asserted. And he alone is to be worshiped.[18]

The prophets posed another far-reaching question as well: Is Yahweh merely Israel's tribal god, or is he also the God of all humankind? Could the Hebrews alone worship Yahweh? Or was their God the only true God, so that all the nations of the earth should join in the worship of the Holy One of Israel?[19]

Prophets such as Zechariah anticipated the answer. He pointed to a day when all nations would worship in Jerusalem (Zech. 14:16). Zechariah's vision of an international congregation of worshipers announced that Yahweh is the God of the whole world. He is to be worshiped by all the peoples of the earth.

At the Jerusalem council (Acts 15) the church ratified Zechariah's conclusion. They declared that Gentiles do not need to become Jews in order to join the community of faith. Through Jesus Christ we know that there is only one God, who is God over all (1 Cor. 8:4-6; 10:18-22).

The way the biblical community of faith responded to the conflict of the gods offers a model as to how we can declare our faith in a situation in which many gods are increasingly pervading society.

Their example reminds us that we cannot limit our response to intellectual argumentation, especially an argumentation that focuses on the proofs for God's existence. Instead, ours must be a living demonstration. We must embody—live out—our faith commitment in the midst of life.

> ✍ *There is only one God. This God is not merely your personal God. Rather the God you know in Christ is the God of the whole world.*

Nor in the context of the many "gods" that vie for the loyalties of people today can we merely proclaim the existence of some generic god. As Christians, we assert that the only true God is the one disclosed in Jesus of Nazareth and who raised Jesus from the dead. One day this God will publicly demonstrate Jesus' lordship, for our Lord will return in glory and judgment.

Until that great day, we must continue to proclaim the good news about the God of the Bible, who alone can give meaning to life. In so doing, our claim that "God exists" flows into a humble declaration that in Christ we have come to know God. In the end, we believe that "God is" because we have encountered the only true God in Jesus Christ. And ultimately our claim to know the one God only gains credence in the contemporary world as he demonstrates the divine presence through the way we live—through our lives as we connect our Christian belief with true Christian living.

This is our most powerful apologetic in a world of many "gods."

> ✍ *Your claim to know God gains credibility as you connect belief in God with life as a Christian.*

KNOWING GOD

As Christians, we declare that the only true God has made himself known to us in Jesus of Nazareth. In Jesus, we have come to know God. But what does it mean to know God? Can we make such a claim today? And how does this encounter with God occur?

We Know the Incomprehensible God

Many people today respond with skepticism when we claim to know God. As we have seen, some deny God's existence (atheism). Others, however, assert that even if God exists no one can ever come to know the deity. We may call this viewpoint *agnosticism*, a word which means literally "no knowledge."

We, however, boldly testify that we have come to know the living God. Yet in voicing our claim we dare not miss the valid reminder agnostics offer us. We must humbly acknowledge with the biblical authors that God is *incomprehensible* (e.g., Job 11:7-8; Pss. 97:2; 145:3; Isa. 40:28; 45:15; 55:8-9; 1 Cor. 2:11).

But what does this admission mean?

• To acknowledge that God is incomprehensible means that no human being can fully comprehend God.

We cannot fathom the depth of the divine reality. Whatever knowledge we have about God is at best only partial. Nor can we ever claim to know everything about him. Rather, God always remains partially hidden, beyond our gaze. God declared through Isaiah: "As the heavens are higher than the earth, so are my ways higher than your ways and my thoughts than your thoughts" (Isa. 55:9).

• To acknowledge that God is incomprehensible means that our knowledge of God is limited.

Nevertheless, we also adamantly maintain that God can be known. Although our knowledge of God is always partial, we know God as he actually is. Our Lord himself has declared that through him we truly come to know God (John 17:3).

But how does this "knowing God" come about?

We Know the Self-revealing God

We know God ultimately only as God comes to us—only as he gives himself to be known—only as God *reveals* himself to us. We know God, therefore, because God takes the initiative. Jesus explains, "All things have been committed to me by my Father. No one knows the Son except the Father, and no one knows the Father except the Son and those to whom the Son chooses to reveal him" (Matt. 11:27; cf. 1 Cor. 2:9-16).[20]

• This means that we can never make God the object of our human scrutiny.

We do not approach God like we engage in the study of things around us. We do not scrutinize God in an objective, scientific manner or at our own whim. Rather, in our knowing God, God gives himself to be known.

• This means as well that there is a great difference between knowing God and possessing knowledge about God.

When we know God, we have gained more than a body of truths. Rather than merely possessing a list of statements about God, we enjoy fellowship with the living, personal God. From this relationship, lofty declarations about God take on new meaning. They describe God's character and greatness as we have experienced the living One.

• This likewise means that ultimately when we know God *we* are the known object, not the knowing subject.

We do not actively come to know God. Instead, God grasps and knows us. As Paul remarks to the Galatian believers: "But now that you know God or rather are known by God" (Gal. 4:9). The apostle finds an echo in J.I. Packer's declaration, "What matters supremely therefore is not in the last analysis the fact that I know God, but the larger fact which underlies it—the fact that *He knows me.*"[21]

How does this occur? Where does God come to us with the result that we know him?

Of course, this occurs in conversion, the point at which we

encounter God personally. We will explore this more thoroughly in chapter 8. Here we need only note that through conversion the Holy Spirit links us with a larger story that begins in the past and will be completed in the future.[22] This story has purpose or goal, for it is leading to that great day when God will reveal the fullness of the divine glory (1 Cor. 13:12; 1 John 3:2). The revelation of God's glory is not merely future, however. It has already invaded our world in Jesus of Nazareth (1 John 5:20). Consequently, it is in Jesus Christ that God confronts and apprehends us.

And what is the goal of knowing God?

According to the Bible, God's ultimate desire is to create from all nations a reconciled people living within a renewed creation and enjoying the presence of the Triune God. This biblical vision of "community" is the goal of history. But it is also the present — albeit partial — experience of each person who has come to know God.

In the final analysis, therefore, we know that we have encountered God in that we have been brought to share in community, that is as we enjoy fellowship with God and participate in the people of faith.

In subsequent chapters we will explore the implications of our encounter with God and the fellowship or community which it inaugurates. One conclusion, however, is crucial to the present discussion. The participation in community with God, each other, and creation offers a final answer not only to the question about the possibility of knowing God but also the question of God's existence.

The contemporary world challenges our claim that we have come to know the only true God. We must meet this challenge on many fronts. Our answer includes demonstrating that the Christian faith is intellectually credible. But our response cannot end there. We must also embody our commitment to God by the way we live. We must connect Christian belief with Christian living.

> ✍ *Your life together with other believers stands as the best confirmation that you know God.*

This includes living now in fellowship with God, others, and creation. Only Christian living on this plane can confirm our testimony that we know the only true God, the "God who is."

FOR CONNECTION AND APPLICATION

1   Which — if any — of the classical proofs for God's existence do you find intellectually compelling? What about it do you find appealing?

2   Although it is true that "few people can be argued into the kingdom," what role did intellectual arguments play in your experience of coming to faith?

3   How did you come to know God personally? Looking back on your experience, how was this event actually God's own initiative in coming to know you?

4   What attracted you to the Christian faith? Did the consistency of life you observed in other Christians play a role? If so, how?

5   Do our lives as Christians really affect how others respond to our public testimony? Cite an example that you have experienced where your witness made a difference.

6   Why are both intellectual credibility and consistent living important dimensions of the Christian faith?

The God Whom We Know

"May the grace of the Lord Jesus Christ, and the love of God,
and the fellowship of the Holy Spirit be with you all"
(2 Cor. 13:14).

Linus and Lucy were watching the rain through their living room window. "Boy, look at it rain," Lucy exclaimed with a frown. "What if it floods the whole world?" To this, the ever confident Linus replied, "It will never do that. In the ninth chapter of Genesis, God promised Noah that would never happen again, and the sign of the promise is the rainbow." Upon hearing these reassuring words, Lucy broke out in a big grin. Looking again at the torrential downpour outside, she noted, "You've taken a great load off my mind." Linus seized this teachable moment. "Sound theology has a way of doing that!" he announced to his young companion.

Indeed, an understanding of God and his purposes for creation does take a great load off our minds. And it affects the way we live as well.

At the heart of the Christian faith is a unique understanding of God. This picture of God is marvelously sublime—intellectually eloquent, yet retaining a deep sense of mystery, because our intellectual capabilities can never bring us to understand the fullness of God. What we have come to know about God provides solace for our hearts and a motivation for our conduct. Theology, therefore, appropriately begins with a discussion of God.

In this chapter, we explore three grand affirmations central to the Christian conception of God:

☞ *God is triune.*
☞ *God is relational.*
☞ *God is creator.*

These affirmations help clarify the mystery of the God we have come to know in Christ.

THE TRIUNE GOD

A theologian once said, "Deny the doctrine of the Trinity and you'll lose your salvation; try to comprehend it, and you'll lose your mind."

No dimension is closer to the heart of the mystery of our faith than our confession, "I believe in the Father, Son, and Holy Spirit." Above everything else, this conception of God sets Christianity apart from the religious traditions of the world. Consequently, no teaching lies closer to the center of Christian theology than does the doctrine of the Trinity.

The Foundation for Our Affirmation of the Triune God

We must be clear at the beginning of our discussion that the doctrine of the Trinity is not explicitly spelled out in the Bible. There is no single verse of Scripture that reads, "The one God is three persons." Instead, this doctrine is the product of a lengthy process of theological reflection that arose from the experience of the early Christians.

The first followers of Jesus inherited from their Old Testament background the strict allegiance to the one God—the God of Abraham, Isaac, and Jacob. But they had also come to confess Jesus as the risen and exalted Lord. In addition, they were conscious of the ongoing divine presence within their community, a presence provided by the Holy Spirit.

Christians throughout the ages share this experience of the early believers. Therefore, three nonnegotiable aspects of Christian faith and experience provide the building blocks for the understanding of God as triune:

☞ *the belief in one true God,*
☞ *the acknowledgment that Jesus is Lord,*

☞ *the experience of the indwelling Holy Spirit.*

One true God. At the heart of the Old Testament faith was the belief in one God. This monotheistic belief entailed the rejection of the worship of many gods found among the surrounding nations. The Old Testament prophets asserted unequivocally that there is but one God. And this God demanded total loyalty (Deut. 6:4-5; cf. Deut. 32:36-39; 2 Sam. 7:22; Isa. 45:18).

As Christians we view ourselves as the spiritual descendants of the Old Testament people of faith. Consequently, we resolutely remain loyal to the theological treasure inherited from the Hebrews. The God we worship is none other than the God of the patriarchs — the one and only true God.

The Lord Jesus. Like the early Christians, we also believe that God has revealed himself in Jesus. Because he is the Christ, Jesus is both the head of the church and the Lord of all creation. For this reason, we confess that he is the Lord of the cosmos (e.g., John 1:1; 20:28; Rom. 9:5; Titus 2:13).

At the First Ecumenical Council (Nicea, 325), the church unequivocally affirmed the full deity of Christ. And we today affirm that decision. At the same time, Jesus is not the Father, for he clearly distinguished between himself as the Son and the one whom he called his Father (e.g., Rom. 15:5-6).

The indwelling Spirit. Beginning with Pentecost, the church has enjoyed the ongoing presence of the personal, divine reality within the fellowship. This reality is neither the Father nor the Son, however. He is yet a third person, the Holy Spirit whom Jesus promised to send to his followers (John 14:15-17).

The church officially acknowledged the full deity of the Holy Spirit at the Second Ecumenical Council (Constantinople, 381).

The integration of the three. Their confession of God as Father, Son, and Spirit demanded that the early believers integrate these foundational aspects of their understanding of God into a unified picture.

After many years of debate, the efforts of three theologians — Basil, Gregory of Nyssa, and Gregory of Nazianzus (the "Cappadocian fathers")—gave birth to what became the classic formulation of the doctrine of the Trinity.[1] These thinkers declared that God is one "essence" *(ousia)* but three "centers of consciousness" or "independent realities" *(hypostaseis)*. The three trinitarian persons share the same will, nature, and essence. Yet each also enjoys special properties and engages in unique activities.[2]

Aspects of the Doctrine of the Trinity

Christians have repeatedly sought to understand the mystery of how God is triune by devising analogies from the natural realm. Some suggest that just as the one chemical formula H_2O can occur in three forms—ice, water, or steam—so also the one God is three persons. This analogy, however, falls short. Ice, water, and steam are simply three modes in which the one chemical formula can appear. Father, Son, and Spirit, in contrast, are not merely three appearances of a God who stands behind them; they *are* the one God.

Other Christians may point to such physical objects as trees or eggs. The one tree consists of three—root, trunk, and branch. And an egg is yolk, egg white, and shell. In a similar manner, the analogy declares, the one God is three persons. But as we will see, these analogies fail to reflect the dynamic movement by which the three trinitarian persons form the one God.

As helpful as they sometimes can be, analogies can only take us so far. In the end, we cannot adequately visualize the doctrine of the Trinity. Nevertheless, we can declare what it entails.

Four statements summarize the contents of the trinitarian understanding of God:

☞   *God is one.*
☞   *God is three.*
☞   *God is a diversity.*
☞   *God is a unity.*

God is one. Christians are not polytheists—we are neither bitheists nor tritheists. Rather, we are monotheists; we confess that the God whom we know through Christ is the one God whom the Old Testament people called "Yahweh." Indeed, there is no other God.

God is three. Yet this one God is three persons—the Father, the Son, and the Holy Spirit. Each of the three is divine, for they share together in the one divine nature or essence.

The one God who revealed himself in the Old Testament, therefore, is not an undifferentiated, solitary oneness. Instead this God is a multiplicity—the three members of the Trinity. In fact, God is none other than Father, Son, and Spirit.

The divine threeness is not simply a declaration about how we experience God. Nor is God's threeness merely the way God appears to us. Rather, the one God *is* eternally three persons. God actually *is* the Father, Son, and Spirit. Just as God is characterized by oneness, therefore, threeness also belongs to the way God actually is.

"Three-in-oneness" also indicates the way God acts in the world. The three persons together comprise the one God throughout all eternity. In the same manner Father, Son, and Spirit are at work—and work together—in the divine program for creation.

God is a diversity. The doctrine of the Trinity means that the one God is a diversity-within-unity. The Father, Son, and Spirit are eternally different from each other. And the three carry out different tasks in the one divine program for creation as well.

The early church theologians explained the differentiations among Father, Son, and Spirit by relating them to a double movement within the one God. They described this movement by two picture words, "generation" and "procession." "Generation" provides a means to distinguish the Father and the Son: the Father generates the Son, and the Son is generated by the Father. "Procession" leads us to distinguish the Spirit from the Father and the Son: the Spirit is the one who proceeds from the Father (and from the Son).

These two words, therefore, help us understand the multiplicity within the eternal God:

☞ *The Father* generates.
☞ *The Son is* generated.
☞ *The Spirit* proceeds.

Similarly, each of the three trinitarian persons fulfills a specific role in the one divine program. The Father functions as the source or ground of the world and the originator of the divine program for creation. The Son functions as the revealer of God, the exemplar and herald of the Father's will for creation, and the redeemer of humankind. And the Spirit functions as the personal divine power active in the world, completing the divine program. Hence, we can summarize the role of each in the work of the one God in the universe:

☞ *The Father is the* originator.
☞ *The Son is the* revealer.
☞ *The Spirit is the* completer.

God is a unity. Finally, the doctrine of the Trinity affirms that the three trinitarian persons comprise a unity. Despite their varying functions in the one divine program, all are involved in every area of God's activity in the world.

Although the Father is the ground of creation, the Son and the Spirit act with the Father in the task of creating. The Son is the Word, the principle of creation, the one through whom the Father creates (John 1:3). And the Spirit is the divine power active in bringing the world into existence (Gen. 1:2).

Likewise, the Son is the redeemer of humanity, yet the Father and the Spirit are involved with the Son in the program of reconciliation. The Father is the agent at work through the Son (2 Cor. 5:18-19). And the Spirit is the active divine power effecting the process from the new birth to the final resurrection.

And although the Spirit is the completer of the divine program, he is joined in this work by the Son and the Father. The Son is the Lord who will return in glory. And the Father is the one who will be "all-in-all" (1 Cor. 15:28).

In our theological reflections, we will be exploring these central aspects of God's work in the world. As these examples indicate, the work of the triune God follows a specific order. In each divine work

☞ *the Father acts,*
☞ *through the Son,*
☞ *by the agency of the Spirit.*

The unity of the three trinitarian members in the world points to the parallel truth about the eternal God. The three members of the Trinity build an eternal unity-in-diversity. Father, Son, and Spirit together comprise the one divine reality and share the one divine essence.

The Loving God

Throughout all eternity God is none other than the Father, Son, and Spirit bound together in an eternal dynamic relationship. But what is the bond that unites the Triune God we have come to know? The key to the answer to our query lies in the biblical declaration, "God is love" (1 John 4:8, 16).

God is love. The New Testament word "love" *(agape)* speaks about the giving of oneself for the sake of another. Jesus, for example, spoke about the good shepherd who gives his life for his sheep (John 10:11).

Active, self-giving love builds the unity within the one God. The unity of God is nothing less than each of the trinitarian persons giving himself to the others. This unity is the dedication of each to the others. Through all eternity the Father loves the Son, and the Son reciprocates that love. This love is the Holy Spirit, who is the Spirit of the relationship of the Father and the Son.[3] Through all eternity, therefore, God is the social Trinity, the community of love.

The dynamic within the one God has a glorious implication for our understanding of salvation. When we become believers, the Spirit makes his abode in our hearts. But this indwelling Holy Spirit is none other than the Spirit of the relationship between the Father and the Son. When he comes to live within us, therefore, the Spirit brings us to share in the love the Son enjoys with the Father. No wonder Paul exclaims, "Because you are sons, God sent the Spirit of his Son into our hearts, the Spirit who calls out, *'Abba,* Father' " (Gal. 4:6).

"Love" describes God's nature throughout eternity. But "love" also characterizes the manner in which God responds to the universe. Indeed, the God who is love naturally acts toward the world in accordance to the eternal divine essence, which is love. With profound theological insight, therefore, John bursts forth, "For God so loved the world that he gave . . ." (John 3:16).

There is a "dark" side to God's love. God always responds to creation in accordance with the divine nature, which is love. But his love is not a soupy sentimentality that indulges creatures to do as they please. Rather, God is characterized by "tough love." God's love has a "dark" side. Or to use the older theological term, God's is a *holy* love. In this sense, our God is also a jealous, wrathful God. Our God is an awesome God!

One cautionary note is in order here. In our reflecting on God's holiness, we ought not to separate God's love and wrath as if they were two contrary characteristics. Instead, "wrath" is the best description we have for the way in which God's love encounters sin. It is our description of the way sinful creatures experience God's love. Simply stated, the presence of sin transforms the experience of the divine love from the bliss intended by God into wrath.

To understand this, consider how wrath naturally arises out of the nature of love itself. Bound up with love is a protective jealousy. Genuine love is positively jealous or protective, for a true lover seeks to defend the love relationship whenever it is threatened by disruption, destruction, or outside intrusion.[4]

Perhaps we can understand this dimension of God's love by thinking about human marriage: I love my wife. But being a loving husband does not mean that I would simply stand idly by and watch should another man seek to lure my wife into a relationship with him. On the contrary, in such a situation the meddling third party would experience the "dark," jealous, protective side of my love. He would see my love in the form of wrath.

In a similar manner, those who would undermine the love God pours forth for the world encounter the dark side of the divine love. They experience the wrath of the divine Lover.

There is another aspect of the dark side of God's love as well. As we have noted previously, God's ultimate goal for his creation is "community." God desires that we enjoy fellowship with him, with each other, and with all creation. Whoever rejects the divine design and seeks to undermine the community God wants to establish suffers the outworking of this wayward course of action. God continues to love them. But if they spurn that love they experience God's love in the form of wrath. And the spurning of the love of God eventually leads to the irrevocable, never-ending experience of the wrath of the eternal Lover. We call this situation, "hell."

The Trinity and Christian Discipleship

The doctrine of the Trinity is not merely a theological construction that we acknowledge with our intellects and confess with our words. It also forms a vital foundation for true Christian living. Our understanding of God as the triune one ought to transform the way we pray, for example, and it ought to revolutionize the way we act in the world.

Trinitarian praying. The way we pray ought to reflect that we know the Triune God. In fact, our realization that the God who calls us to pray and who responds to prayer is the Father, Son, and Spirit is one key to the enjoyment of renewed meaning and power in our prayer life.

Some Christians simply address all prayer to Jesus. After all, we naturally sense a closeness to our Lord, because he walked the earth and experienced life as a human. Other believers address all prayer to "God." This too is understandable, for prayer is communication with God. But our knowledge of the Triune God ought to motivate us to address our prayers to the Father, Son, and Spirit, in accordance with both the purpose of the specific prayer we are voicing and our understanding of the activities in which each trinitarian person engages.

Let's look more closely at how this works. As the New Testament itself confirms, we generally address the Father in prayer. Jesus instructed his disciples to pray, "Our heavenly Father." And James reminds us that "every good and perfect gift is from . . . the Father" (James 1:17). Indeed, as we have noted, the Father functions as the originator of the divine plan. He is the ground and source of creation and of salvation. Consequently, we ought to bring our praise and our requests to him (Rev. 4:8-11).

Yet, we may also want to address certain prayers to the Son. It is only right that we would praise our Lord for who he is. We also thank him for the salvation he has won (Rev. 5:11-14), for his ongoing intercession on our behalf (Rom. 8:34; Heb. 7:25), and for his soon return, which we anticipate. In so doing, we become the advance chorus of all creation that will one day publicly pay him homage as the Lord of all (Phil. 2:9-10). While bringing prayers of adoration and thanksgiving to Jesus, we do well to address most of our petitions to the Father. In so doing, we follow the pattern our Lord himself taught us (Matt. 6:9-13).

The Spirit is the completer of God's program. His activity in the divine work spans the ages from creation to Christ's return. Therefore, we can also properly address prayer to him. Of course, because he is divine, we may offer him our praise and thanksgiving. In addition, however, we may petition the Spirit in areas of his work in the world. We may invoke his presence to comfort, strengthen, illumine, or convict of sin. Or we can petition the Father to send the Holy Spirit to engage in such work.

> *Breathe on me, Breath of God,*
> *Fill me with life anew,*
> *That I may love what Thou dost love,*
> *And do what Thou wouldst do.*[5]

While we may want from time to time to address the Spirit, we must keep in mind that the Spirit acts as the "silent" member of the Trinity. Rather than drawing attention to himself, the Spirit shows his presence by exalting the Son and the Father. Spirit-filled prayer, therefore, moves from the Spirit through the Son to the Father. The Spirit prompts us to address our heavenly Father in the name of Jesus.

> *When you pray, come before the Father in the name of the Son and by the prompting of the Spirit.*

In short, trinitarian prayer generally addresses the Father, in the name of the Son, by the prompting of the Spirit.

Trinitarian living. Knowing the Triune God should not only affect the way we pray. It should also influence the way we act. Indeed, the Triune God is the ultimate model and the standard for Christian living (Matt. 10:39).

As the doctrine of the Trinity indicates, the one God is the social Trinity, the community or fellowship of the Father, Son, and Spirit. Because God is a plurality-in-unity, the ideal for humankind does not focus on solitary persons, but on persons-in-community. God intends that we reflect the divine nature in our lives. This is only possible as we move out of our isolation and into godly relationships with others. Consequently, true Christian living is life-in-relationship or life-in-community.

The doctrine of the Trinity also reminds us that God is love. The God who is love within the relationships of Father, Son, and Spirit also loves all creation. This God is concerned about all creatures and wills the best for each of them.

Knowing that God is love ought to motivate us to seek to reflect God's loving concern for all creatures. Consequently, Christians ought to be at the forefront in both practicing and promoting the genuine stewardship God has entrusted to humankind (Gen. 1:28; 2:15).

Stewardship according to God's own example includes living in fellowship with our environment, of course. But humans are the special recipients of God's love. Therefore, modeling our lives after the example of the loving God leads us to focus on other humans. Because God loves each human being, God demands that we act justly. And God calls us to be instruments in bringing about the divine vision of love, justice, and righteousness for all humankind.

THE RELATIONAL GOD

Knowing the Triune God lies at the heart of our Christian experience. *Affirming* the doctrine of the Trinity—the one God is Father, Son, and Spirit united in love—forms the heart of the Christian understanding of God. God's triune nature means that God is social or relational—God is the "social Trinity." And for this reason, we can say that God is "community." God is the community of the Father, Son, and Spirit, who enjoy perfect and eternal fellowship.

We must take this central Christian doctrine a step farther, however. The God who is relational within the eternal divine being enters into relationship with creation.

How should we understand this great Christian affirmation? And how does God enter into relationship with us? To this divine relational dynamic we now turn.

God Relates to the World as the Transcendent and Immanent One

From the beginning, Christian theology has used the terms, "transcendence" and "immanence" to characterize the foundational aspects of the manner in which God enters into relationship with creation. Unfortunately, these words are often misunderstood. Therefore, let's look more closely at them.

First, God is *transcendent* over the world. Transcendence means:

☞ *God is self-sufficient in relationship to the world. God does not need the world to be who he is. God is the eternal Lover prior to, and apart from, creation.*

☞ *God is not fully immersed in creation. Rather, God is "above" or "beyond" the universe.*

☞ *God enters into relationship with the world freely. Nothing, not even God's own nature, compels God to do so.*

The Scriptures forcefully declare God's transcendence. The Preacher cautions, "God is in heaven and you are on the earth" (Ecc. 5:2). Likewise, the Prophet Isaiah saw the Lord "seated on a throne, high and exalted" (Isa. 6:1).

But God is also *immanent* in the world. This means:

☞ *God is fully present to creation.*

☞ *God is active within the universe. God is involved with the natural processes. Above all, God works in human history.*

The Bible celebrates this dimension of God's relationship to the world as well. The Old Testament writers repeatedly sound the theme that God is the sustainer of creation through the divine Spirit (Job 27:3; 33:4; 34:14-15; Ps. 104:29-30). Jesus credited the natural processes such as sunshine and rain, the feeding of the birds, and the beauty of the flowers to the agency of his Father (Matt. 5:45; 6:25-30; 10:29-30). And in his well-known speech to the Athenians, Paul declared that God "is not far from each one of us. 'For in him we live and move and have our being' " (Acts 17:27-28).

God is both transcendent and immanent. These two aspects of

God's relationship to the world carry far-reaching significance for the way we think about God. On the one hand, we dare not place God so far beyond the world that we devise a God who cannot enter into relationship with creatures. Our God is not a distant deity who cannot see, hear, or know what happens in the universe.

On the other hand, we also dare not collapse God so thoroughly into the world processes that our God cannot stand over the creation which he made. God cannot be reduced to the "divine spark within each of us" nor to the great "Matrix" which connects all living creatures together.[6]

God Relates to the World as Spirit

The God who is both transcendent and immanent is also "spirit" (John 4:24). This, too, refers to how God relates to the world.

Basically the biblical word "spirit" means "breath" or "wind." Because breath is the sign of life, "spirit" also refers to the life principle in all living creatures, but especially in humans. The biblical writers consistently acknowledge that God is the source of life in each human. Indeed, when God breathed into Adam's nostrils "the breath of life . . . man became a living being" (Gen. 2:7). Because God is the source of life, as "Spirit" God is able to create and sustain life.

By declaring "God is Spirit," therefore, we are affirming a vital dimension of the relationship of God to creation. We are acknowledging that God is the source of life. God bestows life on us. And we in turn are dependent upon God for our very lives.

Yet "God is Spirit" carries a deeper meaning as well. At the foundation of His relationship to the world as the Giver of life stands a more fundamental, eternal relationship within the Triune God. "God is Spirit" means that the God we worship is no static being. Rather, God is the Living One. Throughout all eternity God is alive; God is dynamic, active.

Jesus himself spoke about the vital internal divine activity: "For as the Father has life in himself, so he has granted the Son to have life in himself" (John 5:26). The divine life is the eternal activity of the Father who as the fountain of deity generates the Son to share in his own deity. The Father's love for the Son, in turn, is reciprocated in the Son's love for the Father. This relationship between the Father and the Son is the third trinitarian member, the Holy Spirit.

To say "God is Spirit," therefore, is to speak about the relational God. Throughout eternity the Triune God is a vital dynamic. This vitality, in turn, overflows to creation. The God who is dynamic activity within the eternal trinitarian life is the source and sustainer of the creaturely life he freely creates.

God Relates to the World as Person

The God we have come to know is also "Person." Indeed, God enters into relationship with creation as "Person."

• We speak of God as person because we experience God as one who is incomprehensible, willful, and free.[7]

First, we acknowledge that God is person, because God relates to the world as the incomprehensible one.

We use the word "person" to describe humans, because we experience each other as incomprehensible beings. No one is totally transparent to the knowing eyes of another. Nor can we ever fathom the depths of another's being. In the end, we all remain mysterious or hidden from each other.

In an even greater sense, the God who enters into relationship with us remains ultimately mysterious to us. God lies beyond our ability to understand completely (Rom. 11:33-34). In his relationship to the world, God remains incomprehensible; God is therefore "person."

Second, we acknowledge that God is Person, because God relates to creation as "will."

We speak of each other as persons, because we are self-determining, active agents. We have goals, purposes, and plans which color how we act in the world.

To an even greater extent God is "will." God has a goal for creation. And God acts in the world to bring his purposes to completion. God, therefore, is person.

Third, we declare that God is Person because he relates to the universe in freedom.

We designate each other as persons, in that we are all free to act. Our actions are beyond the total control of others. In fact, those who are controlled by another (such as through forced slavery) often cease to be persons in our eyes.

God is free in relationship to the world. God is totally beyond our control. In fact, God is the source of our finite human freedom. For this reason, we speak of God as "person."

• In addition to being incomprehensible, willful, and free, God's personhood surfaces in the divine name.

God confirmed his personhood when he announced his name — Yahweh — to Moses (Ex. 3:14-15). This name speaks of God as the great "I Am," that is, the "one who will be."[8] The God who called Moses into his service is the one who will show his identity by being active in human history.

Jesus invoked this divine name when he boldly declared, "Before Abraham was born, I am" (John 8:58). Although his enemies took our Lord's assertion to be blasphemous, we know that the Master's claim is true. In Jesus of Nazareth we do indeed encounter the great "I Am," the ultimate reality who is active in history from beginning to end. In Jesus, we see God as fully personal.

• God's Personhood confirms us as persons.

The fact that God relates to the world as "person" means that God is personal. But this has important implications for us as well. By relating to each of us as persons, God affirms us in our own unique personhood. And by relating to us as Person to persons, God confirms the distinction between him and us.

• You are person, because God is Person.

This aspect of Christian doctrine forms a striking contrast to religions which acknowledge an impersonal deity. Because they view God as impersonal, they denigrate human personhood as well. They teach that the ultimate goal of life is to lose one's personhood and merge into an all-encompassing Absolute. The God we know, in contrast, enters into a person-to-person relationship with us. In so doing, God eternally honors our unique personhood.

God Relates to the World as the Eternal One

The God we know is not only the personal source of life, he is also eternal. Theologians often characterize the "eternality" of God by appeal to the three great "omnis": God is omnipresent

("present everywhere"), omniscient ("all-knowing"), and omnipotent ("all-powerful"). Although easy to state, these theological concepts are difficult to understand and therefore open to misunderstanding.

The Greek philosophers contrasted the changeable realm of time with a static, changeless domain above the flow of events. These thinkers viewed static changelessness as more "real" than change. Consequently, for them God's eternality meant that he exists totally beyond the temporal realm and therefore remains untouched by events in time. This Greek conception of a timeless, static God does not square with the God we know.[9] The biblical God sees, knows, cares, and responds to the plight of creatures. The Bible speaks of a God who is not untouched by time, but who is faithfully present through time.

This leads, however, to a difficult question. How does the God who is faithfully present through time relate to time? Our experience of time offers a beginning point in speaking about God and time.

> ✍ Eternality means "God is faithfully present through time."

To us, time has three aspects — past, present, and future. Although we can speak of events that are past and future, we are immediately cognizant only of present events. Our awareness of the past is limited to memory. And our only connection to the future is our ability to anticipate events. Because we directly experience only what is immediately present to us, we live in a realm we call the "present."

Our experience of direct cognition of the present provides us with a limited participation in eternity. And by extension, this experience of our relationship to our world gives us a window into God's relationship to the processes of the universe. Just as we are aware of present events in our own personal world, so also God is cognizant of what occurs in the universe. God is immediately and simultaneously aware of all events. Whether they be in what we call "past," "present," or "future," they are all in God's "present."

Perhaps an analogy can help us understand this concept. Supposing I want to see the Rose Bowl parade. On January 1, I make my way to Pasadena, California and successfully find a curbside spot along one of the streets on the parade route. My limited height and the size of the throng crowding around me means that my view of the parade consists in watching each individual float as it passes by the point where I am standing. But supposing I had a friend who invited me to join him in the Goodyear Blimp. Traveling high above the ground would give me a far more encompassing view of the parade. Rather than being limited to a direct citing of each passing float, I could see the entire parade in one breathtaking look.

Without pressing the analogy too far, we might suggest that we view time from a position "on the curb." We experience each event that moves through our present. But God sees all of time from a cosmic "Goodyear Blimp." All events are simultaneously in God's encompassing "present."

This understanding of God's eternality provides a context in which to speak about his omnipresence, omniscience, and omnipotence.

• Let's start with *omnipresence.*

Often Christians declare that God is near or present to all things. But it would be better to turn the definition around: all things are present to God. God enjoys a direct "view" of every occasion in the universe.

• Omnipresence naturally leads to God's *omniscience.*

Some Christians speak of God's omniscience as if it were a statement about the divine being, rather than about God's relationship to the world. Consequently, they debate whether God knows not only all *actual* events, but also all *possible* events.

Omniscience, however, refers to God's perfect and complete cognition of the world. God knows all occasions in the universe. God knows all things because God perceives all events simultaneously.

• Omniscience and omnipresence mean that God is *omnipotent.*

Some Christians suggest that omnipotence, like omniscience, refers to God's being apart from the world: God is able to do anything he chooses. But speaking about God's omnipotence in an abstract sense, as referring to some theoretical power, only leads to nonsensical problems and apparent dilemmas. It leads people to debate whether God could make a rock so heavy that even he could not lift it.

In contrast to such misguided discussions, to say "God is omnipotent" is to acknowledge that God is able to bring to completion the divine design for creation.

God is not a disinterested observer of the world. Instead, God relates to the universe as the Eternal One, the one who is faithfully present to the world throughout time. God acts in the world as the one who knows all events from the perspective of the final purposes for creation. And all God's actions in human history contribute to that final outcome. Cognizant of his own purposes, God is able to overcome every evil for the sake of the good that he intends to do for creation. And the omnipotent God is able to replace the old order with the new, which he will do completely at the end of the age when Jesus returns in glory.

• Our acknowledgment of God's eternality provides a firm foundation for faith.

Because God is omniscient, we can be confident that our God knows what is best for us. Because God is omnipotent, we can trust our God to do what is best for us. And because God is omnipresent, we can entrust ourselves to him in every moment of life, knowing that he is with us en route to the end.

• Knowing the eternal God should also lead us to bold prayer and confident action.

The God who is faithfully present through time invites us to cooperate with him in the completion of the divine program for history through fervent petition and obedient action. In both of these activities we "rebel against the status quo"—that is, we refuse to acknowledge that the present state of affairs in our world is wholly in keeping with the divine plan. Through prayer and action we seek to allow ourselves to be instruments of the hands of the Holy Spirit to open the present to the in-breaking of the power of the future kingdom.[10]

> ✍ *Because God is eternal, pray boldly and live confidently.*

God Relates to the World as the Beneficent One

Finally, the eternal God we know is completely good in all he does. That is, God is morally upright in the ways he relates to creation.

We can pinpoint two aspects of God's goodness.

☞ *God is holy.*
☞ *God is compassionate.*

In this context "God is holy" means that God is completely upright, fair, just, and righteous in his treatment of creatures. Not only is God morally perfect, he is the standard for morality. God's disposition toward creation is the standard by which he will judge us and, therefore, by which we are to appraise all human conduct.

"God is compassionate" means that God is gracious, benevolent, and long-suffering with us. The authors of Scripture glory in this dimension of God's relationship to the world (e.g., Ex. 34:6; Neh. 9:17; Pss. 86:15; 103:8; 111:4; 116:5; 145:8; Isa. 54:10; Joel 2:13; Jonah 4:2). According to the New Testament, the supreme act of divine compassion is the coming of Jesus Christ for our salvation (Eph. 3:4-5; Titus 3:5). And awareness that God is compassionate provides a biblical foundation for faith in him.

Knowing a God who is holy and compassionate ought to lead to joyful and awe-filled praise to this glorious God. But in addition it ought to revolutionize the way we live.

God's holiness has crucial considerations for human living on both the personal and the social levels. It means that we must look to God and how God acts, rather than to human opinions, if we would gain a clear understanding of such foundational concepts as "justice," "fairness," and "righteousness."

But above all, the God of all compassion calls us to emulate him in our relations with others. John, the apostle of love, reminds us of the connection between God's character and our conduct: "This is how we know what love is: Jesus Christ laid down his life for us. And we ought to lay down our lives for our brothers" (1 John 3:16).

THE CREATOR GOD

The Bible opens with the simple yet profound declaration, "In the beginning God created the heavens and the earth" (Gen. 1:1). This statement boldly declares the glorious truth that the Triune God brings the cosmos into existence and enters into relationship with what he makes. In so doing, the eternal God becomes the

Creator of the universe, and the world exists as the creation of God.

The declaration that the biblical God is the Creator of the universe means that Christians espouse a unique understanding of the cosmos which we inhabit. Because the God we know is the Creator of the world, the universe did not come into being on its own. Instead, it exists by the will and action of God.

But what kind of "act" is God's creation of the world? In raising this question we are not intending to investigate any specific scientific hypothesis about the beginning of the universe, such as the "big bang" theory. Rather, we are looking into the implications of our confession "God is the Creator" for the relationship between the Creator and creation.

Let us pursue five lines of response to our query:

☞ *Creation is a free act of God.*
☞ *Creation is a loving act of God.*
☞ *Creation is an act of the Triune God.*
☞ *Creation is an act of a sovereign God.*
☞ *Creation is God's future act.*

God Creates the World by an Act of Freedom

The God we know as Creator creates the world freely. This means that God is not driven to bring the universe into existence. Were God forced to create, God would need the world to be who he is. But the God we know is transcendent, complete in the divine reality apart from the world. God remains eternally God, whether or not the universe exists.

God's triunity helps us understand how this is so. As we saw earlier, God is the social Trinity bound together by mutual love. Consequently, God is fully who he is—the loving God—within the eternal, divine life. God does not need the world to be the God of love. Instead, throughout all eternity the Father loves the Son, the Son reciprocates that love, and the love they share is the Holy Spirit.

The universe exists, therefore, because God graciously chooses to create a cosmos with which to share God's own existence.

God Creates the World by an Act of Love

Not only does God freely choose to create, the act of creation arises out of God's love.

Here again, God's triunity assists us in seeing this. As we have seen, God is love — a love manifest between the Father, Son, and Holy Spirit. The act of creation, in turn, is the "outflowing" of this eternal love relationship within the heart of God. Because it is created as an outflow of God's own nature (love), creation exists as both the recipient and the mirror of God's eternal love.

The Triune God Creates the World

The Father, Son, and Spirit are all involved in the act of creation. Specifically:

☞   *the Father creates the world,*
☞   *through the Son,*
☞   *by the divine Spirit.*

● The Father fulfills the primary role in the act of creation.

The Father is the direct creator of all that exists (1 Cor. 7:6). His will forms the foundation for the existence of all things (Rev. 4:11). Hence, all creation owes its existence to the Father (Acts 17:28).

In addition, the Father's glory is the goal of all things. The purpose of every creature is to praise him. Creation around us quite naturally fulfills this divine intention (Ps. 19:1). But the Father invites humans, his highest creatures, to glorify him willingly and consciously, and therefore most fully.

● The Son is the principle of creation.[11]

The Son is the Word or ordering principle through whom the Father creates (John 1:3, 14; Col. 1:16a). This means that only by their connection with Jesus and his story do all things in our world find their meaning (Col. 1:16b). This means as well that Jesus exemplifies the way creatures ought to relate to the Creator, namely, by living in humble dependence on, and obedience to, the one whom Jesus called "Father" (John 5:26).

● The Holy Spirit is the divine power active in creating the universe.

As the one who broods over the void (Gen. 1:2; cf. Job 26:13), the Spirit is the power who gives form to the universe. And he is also the power who gives life to all living creatures (Gen. 6:17; 7:22; Ps. 104:30), but especially to humans (Gen. 2:7; 6:3; Job 33:4).

The role of each of the trinitarian persons in creation is not arbitrary. Rather their involvement in this act arises out of their function in the eternal dynamic within the one God. The Father who eternally loves the Son creates the world so that creatures might reciprocate his love after the pattern of the Son's love for the Father. As the Spirit of the relationship between the Father and the Son, the Holy Spirit is the power by whom the one God fashions the world.

Creation Is an Act of a Sovereign Creator

As Creator, God rightfully enjoys a special status in relationship to the universe. Specifically, God is *sovereign* over creation. Sovereignty means that ultimately God alone has the right to declare what creation should be. God's will alone should be universally obeyed. We must keep in mind, however, that the sovereign God always acts in accordance with the divine character, which is love. In all he does, God seeks only what is best for the universe that he fashioned as the outflow of the divine love.

Yet the undeniable presence of evil in the world leads us to wonder to what extent is God truly sovereign over creation. Two vantage points provide us with a response.

> 📖 *Sovereignty means that God alone ultimately has the right to declare what creation should be.*

☞ *Present and future sovereignty.*
☞ De jure *and* de facto *sovereignty.*

● The first vantage point looks at the world from the perspectives of the present and the future.

Strictly speaking, sovereignty refers to God's ability to bring to pass the divine goal for the world. Seen from this perspective, we anticipate the glorious display of God's sovereignty when Jesus returns. Then God will be fully and clearly sovereign.

In the meantime, however, there is much which calls God's

sovereignty into question (e.g., Ps. 73:3-14). Yet, according to the Bible God is not idle; God is at work in all of history directing creation to its intended purpose. Because God will be sovereign when he completes the divine program, we can also affirm that God is sovereign each step of the way. Even before the end of the age, God is at work directing creation and overcoming evil for good.

• A second vantage point looks at the situation from the perspective of *de jure* ("in principle," or "by right") and *de facto* ("in fact") sovereignty.

When viewed from the perspective of God's status as Creator, God alone may rightfully both claim and exercise sovereignty. Only God is sovereign *de jure*. In the actual situation in the present moments of history, however, God's complete will is not always evident. Nor do God's human creatures always live in accordance with God's design or will for them.

Yet, this is not the end of the story. One day God will bring all creation into conformity with its glorious design. Then God will not only be sovereign *de jure* but also *de facto*. In the meantime, God is actively bringing creation to its intended goal. And many creatures do acknowledge, reflect, and obey the divine will. Whenever this occurs God becomes *de facto* sovereign in our present moments.

> ✍ *Is God not only* de jure *but also* de facto *sovereign of your life?*

Creation Is a Future Act

Finally, we raise another crucial question. When does God create the world?

• In a sense, the answer seems obvious: "in the beginning."

After all, the world obviously exists. And the Bible begins with the clear declaration, "In the beginning God created the heavens and the earth" (Gen. 1:1). Therefore, creation was an event in the distant past.

Of course, the creation of the world did occur in the primordial past, "in the beginning." In this sense, "creation" refers to God's free act in calling the world into existence.

● In another sense, however, creation is a future event.

"Creation" can also refer to God's completion of the divine work in bringing the universe to its destined goal. "Creation" is God's act in shaping the cosmos according to its design. In this sense, the creation of the world does not merely begin the temporal sequence, but stands at the end of history. The act of creation, in other words, is not yet completed. Instead, God remains active in history bringing about God's world-creating work.

This understanding of creation lies at the heart of the Bible. Prophets in both Testaments anticipated a day when God will transform the present universe into the perfect reality God plans for it. Through Isaiah, for example, God announced this intention: "Behold, I will create new heavens and a new earth. The former things will not be remembered, nor will they come to mind. But be glad and rejoice forever in what I will create" (Isa. 65:17-18). Centuries later John reiterated Isaiah's prophecy. In his vision of the glorious future, he saw "a new heaven and a new earth" (Rev. 21:1).

One day God will fashion the universe in accordance with the divine design and purpose. In the meantime, the world eagerly anticipates that great day (Rom. 8:19-25).

● This focus on the future as the ultimate point of God's creative work has profound implications for how we view the world and ourselves in the world.

If creation is God's future act, then we must look to the future and not to the past to determine who we are. Our true nature is not given through our connection to Adam in the primordial past. Rather, it lies in our future participation in the resurrection, as our risen Lord has disclosed to us (1 Cor. 15:48). Our ultimate identity, therefore, is the complete Christlikeness which will be ours when through the resurrection we come to "bear the likeness of the man from heaven" (v. 49).

> ✍ Be who through Christ you will one day become.

One future day we will share completely in the glorious goal the Creator God has for his handiwork: community on the highest plane. On that day, as we have emphasized, we will enjoy eternal fellowship with our God, with each other, and with the new creation that

God is bringing to pass. This alone is our true home and our ultimate identity.

Our hope that one day the Triune God will complete the divine work in fashioning the world and us as children of God ought to move us to renewed praise for the triune, relational, creator God whom we have come to know. And it ought to challenge us to live even now in the light of that glorious future reality.

FOR CONNECTION AND APPLICATION

1   How does the Christian understanding of God differ with the conceptions of the divine reality proposed by other world religions?

2   How does the doctrine of the Trinity differ from the conceptions propagated by so-called "Christian cults"? Should a group call itself "Christian" if it denies this doctrine? Why or why not?

3   Is a person's conception of the nature of God all that important? What difference does his or her understanding of God make in the way people live?

4   How do you understand the "triunity" of God? How would you explain the Trinity to someone else?

5   Why is the Christian teaching that God is Person so crucial for our understanding of who we are?

6   Is God "in charge" of the world? Explain the distinction between *de jure* and *de facto* sovereignty.

7   Describe what bold praying and confident living in the light of God's eternality mean to you.

8   How ought the command, "Be who through Christ you will one day become," affect you and the way you live today?

THREE

Our Identity As God's Creatures

" 'For in him we live and move and have our being.'
As some of your own poets have said, 'We are his offspring' "
(Acts 17:28).

In one episode of the comic strip "Betty," the main character and two of her work colleagues, Bea and Alex, were staring at a "find Waldo" picture. Suddenly Alex announced to the amazement of the others, "There he is—behind that column." As she and Betty walked away, Alex mused, "Yep, I have no trouble finding Waldo. It's myself I can't find."

Alex's candid confession rings a responsive chord because it reflects our own feelings. On the surface we may appear to "have it all together." But in the deep recesses of our innermost self, each of us wonders, "Who am I?" And left to ourselves, we cannot find a satisfying answer to this query. In the end, we don't have a clue who we really are. As a result, we spend our lives vainly searching for an identity.

You and I are not the first humans to wonder, "Who am I?" Long before Christ was born, the Old Testament psalmist contemplated the vastness and majesty of the universe and cried out in amazement, "What is man that you are mindful of him, the son of man that you care for him?" (Ps. 8:3-4)

Like people in every age, the psalmist wondered who we human beings are. Yet the ancient writer sought the answer in a direction far different from what most people pursue today.

The Hebrews derived human identity from the unique position they believed we enjoy within an orderly creation. Hence, the psalmist declared, "You have made them [humankind] a little lower than God and crowned them with glory and honor. You have given them dominion over the works of your hands; you have put all things under their feet" (Ps. 8:5-6, NRSVB). The psalm suggests that the sense of bewilderment we all share is at its core religious in nature. Our search for an identity is ultimately a religious or spiritual quest. And according to the ancient view, our identity derives from a fixed place we enjoy in the cosmos: We stand above the material universe, but under the angelic hosts who also belong to the created order.

Amid the bewilderment and confusion people today sense about who we are, the gospel stands as truly good news. The Christian faith proclaims that we are God's creatures. We belong to the one whom Jesus declared to be our Heavenly Father. Because we are the creatures of God, we can know both where we come from and where we are going. In God we find our origin and our destiny. And as we realize we have in God an origin and a destiny, we can begin to understand who we are.

The acknowledgment of God, then, offers a foundation for the human quest for identity. In this chapter, we pursue the answer Christian faith provides for this universal human quest. We boldly declare that we can know who we are. With the psalmist we claim that we have an identity which arises from our place in God's creation.

☞   *We are God's handiwork.*
☞   *We are God's image.*
☞   *We are related to other beings in the universe.*

WE ARE GOD'S HANDIWORK

"What is man?" wondered the author of the beautiful reflective prayer of Psalm 8. And the biblical writer concluded that humans are made "a little lower than the heavenly beings and crowned . . . with glory and honor" (8:5).

Like the ancient Hebrew psalmist and the entire Old Testament tradition, the Christian faith responds to the human search for an identity by declaring that we are God's handiwork. But what does this mean? What are we saying when we acknowledge that we are God's handiwork, the creatures of the divine Creator?

To acknowledge that we are God's handiwork entails realizing that

☞ *we are dependent on God,*
☞ *we find our origin solely in God,*
☞ *we have a special purpose from God.*

We Are Dependent on God

In contrast to the ancient peoples, we do not generally view our status as creatures as the foundation for our identity. Rather, we see ourselves as active creators, and we view the world around us as the material for our transforming activity. In a sense, this contemporary understanding fits well with modern biology's findings and its concern to pinpoint what sets humans apart from other living species.

One current understanding focuses on the relationship of living organisms to their environment. Animals are bound to their world by limitations set by heredity. Humans, in contrast, are not so closely restricted by inherited factors. Instead, we are characterized by what one biologist calls "plasticity and adaptability." This endowment enables us—more so than any animal—to alter and even control our environment.[1]

Linked to our adaptability is another uniquely human characteristic—"self-transcendence." Unlike other living things, we are able to stand back from ourselves. We can place ourselves "above" the here-and-now. We can reflect on ourselves and scrutinize ourselves as living persons.

Our adaptability and self-transcendence work together to rob us of any sense of identity that can be derived from the world. Plasticity means that we lack a biological "home" in the cosmos. Other living beings have a discoverable "niche" in the biological framework. But biologists have yet to discover a set role for humankind that explains our purpose for existence.

At the same time, our adaptability and self-transcendence mean that we enjoy the unique possibility of continually experiencing our environment in new ways. We can project, envision, and plan for an existence "beyond" any "world" we create.

But for this reason, we are never completely fulfilled by any one achievement or by any one "world" we fashion as a "home" for ourselves. Rather than being at home in the world, we are continually on the move to something yet undefined. We are always seeking the new, the "future," the not yet. We continually chase that illusive "something" which surpasses the here-and-now or the status quo. We are continually shaping and reshaping our environment in an unfulfilled attempt to create a "home" for ourselves.

Some scholars label this aspect of our human situation "openness to the world."[2] They find in this general human characteristic great theological importance.

These thinkers argue that because we are "open to the world," we are "infinitely dependent." We remain dependent on the world for our sense of identity. But we can find no ultimate fulfillment in any one "world" we create for ourselves. Our fulfillment, therefore, must lie "beyond" the world. For the goal of our quest, they conclude, we are dependent on Something other than the world. In short, if we are to discover any truly satisfying sense of identity, it must come from a relationship to a Source of identity beyond our world.

This very contemporary conclusion reminds us of what Augustine so eloquently declared in the fifth century: "Our hearts are restless until they find rest in thee, O God."[3]

We Find Our Origin Solely in God

Our "openness to the world" indicates that ultimately we too are creatures. That is, we are beings who are dependent on a reality beyond the universe. In this way the modern biological understanding of humankind returns us to the Christian faith. We acknowledge that the God of the Bible is the Creator of the universe.

To acknowledge God as Creator means that we look to God as the origin not only of the universe but of ourselves as well. Indeed, as Christians we humbly declare, "Our origin" — or perhaps better stated *"my* origin" — "lies in God the Creator."

To say that God is our origin is to acknowledge at least two significant dimensions of our lives. This confession speaks about

☞ *our existence as persons, and*
☞ *the human essence or nature we share.*

God and our personal existence. We do not create ourselves. I am not the source of my own existence, nor are you the author of yours. This seems to be obviously true, for we owe our lives to a host of other people whom we call our parents and ancestors.

But there is a deeper sense in which we do not create ourselves. Ultimately, we owe our existence to God the Creator. We are not in this world simply because our parents decided to have children. More importantly, we are here because God has freely and graciously bestowed existence on us.

"God is our origin," therefore, means that he is the author of our existence. This does not merely refer to our physical existence, however. Rather, "we find our origin in God" is a statement about the meaning of our lives. God freely and graciously gives meaning to our existence. And this meaning arises from the goal, purpose, or destiny he intends for us.

> ✍ *You are here because God wills that you exist.*

People today are frantically searching—hoping to discover some meaning for their fragmented and frantic existence. But according to the gospel, our lives *already* have meaning. God has created us for a purpose. As the Westminster Shorter Catechism states with simple eloquence, the aim of our lives "is to glorify God, and to enjoy him forever."[4] We exist in order to experience the glorious fellowship God intends for us to enjoy. We are created for community.

God and our human nature. Acknowledging that God is our origin also has implications for the human nature we share in common with each other. Above all, it means that we realize that God alone has the prerogative to declare what it means to be human.

In chapter 5, we will explore human nature as revealed in Jesus Christ. Here we need only remind ourselves of the important practical implications of this confession. If *God* declares what it means to be human, then our lives are not the meaningless collections of unrelated events they so often appear to be. On the contrary, God has designed us with a purpose in view. And our lives have true meaning as they reflect this divinely given design. Further, if God declares what it means to be human, then all creatures have value insofar as God gives them value. This affirmation stands contrary to the thinking that permeates contemporary society. People today tend to see themselves as the determiners of value. Things — even other people — have value insofar as they serve our ends. But if God declares what it means to be human, then it is no longer our prerogative to decide what is valuable and what is not. Rather, our task is to view all creation and every creature from God's perspective and, as a result, to value as God does.

> ✍ *As we commit ourselves to God and by the power of the Holy Spirit live to God's glory, we discover true meaning for our lives.*

This is especially applicable to the realm of human value or the worth of individual persons. We spend so much time and expend so much energy trying to gain a sense of worth from others. We scrutinize how others treat us and seek to determine what they think of us. In the end, however, our value is not based on how others perceive our worth. Ultimately, only God's opinion of us matters. And the gospel declares that each of us has value because God ascribes worth to us. This good news should cause us to stand tall in the face of every challenge of life.

> ✍ *You are valuable because God values you.*

In addition to bestowing great value on us, God commands us to acknowledge the value he graciously gives to each other person. We can do this as we give up the struggle to gain our own value from other persons. When we come to see ourselves as truly valuable apart from our position in any "pecking order," we can freely acknowledge the value of each person we meet. We then can realize that God bestows value on them, just as God values us.

Valuing as God values also indicates how we should respond to many contemporary ethical questions. For example, this conviction ought to shape how we deal with the grave ecology crisis we now face. Because God values creation for itself, we must be concerned for the environment as God's stewards. God calls us to value the earth not for its utility, but in accordance with the value he places on it.

In the same way, our understanding of value should affect our approach to life and death issues, such as abortion and euthanasia. In contrast to the widely held view today, we know that a fetus does not become valuable only when he or she is "a wanted child" or when society chooses to acknowledge the unborn child as a person. Nor is life worth living only so long as we sense we are enjoying "quality of life." Rather, God values all human life. And we must do so as well.[5]

Through Adam We Have a Special Purpose from God

We have an identity because we are God's handiwork. We are dependent on God, who is our origin. God is the source of our existence, and God determines what it means to be human. Also connected to our identity is a special purpose we have from God.

The first human. The good news that we are God's handiwork naturally leads us to inquire about our connection to the beginning of humankind. Many people raise this issue by inquiring, If humankind began with a first person whom the Bible calls "Adam."

Christians have struggled at length about how certain scientific theories about human origins fit together with the Genesis narratives that place the beginnings of humankind in the Garden of Eden. The Bible does not speculate about the actual physical process by which humans appeared on the earth. Nevertheless, it consistently treats Adam as the first human. This carries great theological importance in our quest to understand who we are.

To declare that Adam is the first human means that with humankind God's purposes for creation reach a new, special plane. Adam appears on the earth as a special work of God, for the Creator had a unique goal for Adam and entered into a special relationship or "covenant" with him. This covenant marks a new intention for the developing cosmos. God desires that in Adam creation should come to be related to the Creator in a new way.

But God's purposes for Adam are not limited to a historical individual. Rather, with Adam the Creator enters into a special relationship with creation. God's covenant is directed toward Adam and his offspring. Consequently, as Adam's descendants we share in his special role in God's program and his special responsibility before God.

The unity of humankind. The biblical declaration that Adam marks the beginning of humankind means that every human is the offspring of Adam. This has great importance for our faith. It means that all humankind forms a unity in the presence of God.

The unity of humankind in Adam is a glorious affirmation of each human being. In entering into covenant with Adam, God bestowed value upon all Adam's descendants. And God desires that all humans share together in the purposes God has for us.

Because God intends that all persons share in the one purpose for Adam's descendants, we must be concerned to promote justice and to denounce all forms of racism.

The unity of humankind in Adam as the recipients of a special purpose from God has a dark side as well. It means that we all participate in the universal human failure we call "sin," which we will discuss in the next chapter.

WE ARE GOD'S IMAGE

With the psalmist we ask, "What are human beings that you are mindful of them?" (Ps. 8:4, NRSVB) To this question, the Bible offers a second profound answer: "So God created humankind in his image, in the image of God he created them; male and female he created them" (Gen. 1:27). Or as the psalmist responds to his question about humankind, "You have . . . crowned them with glory and honor" (Ps. 8:5, NRSVB).

We are not only God's handiwork, we are also God's own image. But the divine image is no simple idea. Instead, this declaration, "We are God's image," raises several crucial questions: What does it mean to be the image of God *(imago dei)?* And how is it that we are God's image?

Ultimately, the "image of God" is connected with God's design for humankind. It speaks of God's goal for us. It is a way of viewing God's intention, or the role God desires that we fulfill in creation. In short, being "the image of God" describes our identity as God's special creatures. We are the image of God in that we have received, are now fulfilling, and one day will fully live according to the special calling God has given us. And this calling (or design) is that we mirror for the sake of creation the nature of the Creator.

> ✍ *We are the image of God as we mirror in creation the nature of the Creator.*

Let us now expand this statement. Being in the divine image involves:

☞ *a special standing,*
☞ *a future goal,*
☞ *a glorious fellowship in community.*

Being in the Divine Image Involves a Special Standing

The foundation for our being in the image of God lies in the grace of the Creator. God has graciously given us a special standing. This unique status has several dimensions.

● Our special standing entails being the recipients of God's special love.

God loves the entire universe, of course. But humans are the recipients of his love in the highest sense. Indeed, love for humankind led the Father to give his only Son to be our Savior (John 3:16).

● Our special standing entails a special worth in God's sight.

God values all creation, of course. But God places special value on us. Jesus pointed to this special value when he encouraged his disciples to trust in the gracious heavenly Father rather than to worry about the cares of physical life: "Look at the birds of the air, they do not sow or reap or store away in barns, and yet your heavenly Father feeds them. Are you not much more valuable than they?" (Matt. 6:26)

● Our special standing entails a special responsibility.

The animate creatures and inanimate things around us quite naturally fulfill their responsibility to bring honor to God. Indeed, as the psalmist noted, "The heavens declare the glory of God" (Ps. 19:1).

But there is something special about the human response to the Creator which sets us apart from the rest of creation. As the prohibition to Adam in the Garden of Eden indicates (Gen. 2:16-17), God desires that we reciprocate the divine love by actively obeying our Creator. God places in us the privilege of fulfilling our divinely given design willingly.

This desire endows us with a great responsibility. The Bible connects our responsibility with our task of exercising "dominion" within creation.

Unfortunately, we too often interpret the idea of dominion against the background of modern industrial society. Dominion, we erroneously conclude, indicates that the natural world exists solely for our benefit so that we can exploit it as we choose. And we even claim biblical support for this view, finding the license for exploitation in God's instruction to the first humans: "Rule over the fish of the sea and the birds of the air . . . and over all the creatures that move along the ground" (Gen. 1:26). Indeed, in answering the question "What is man?" the psalmist concluded, "You make him ruler over the works of your hands; you put everything under his feet" (Ps. 8:6).

The Bible does declare that as God's image-bearers we are to enjoy dominion over the earth. But the foundation for what this means lies in a quite different direction than the modern industrialist model suggests. Its source is a certain practice of ancient sovereigns.[6]

The kings of the ancient Near East often left images of themselves in those cities or territories where they could not be present in person. Such images served to represent their majesty and power.[7] In a similar manner, God placed humankind upon earth to live as representatives of the Creator.[8] Therefore, God — and not humankind — is sovereign over creation. Our mandate is only that of acting as God's representatives.

But how do we represent the Creator to creation? Central to our role as God's representatives is the responsibility of managing creation. The Genesis narrator declares, "The Lord God took the man and put him in the Garden of Eden to work it and take care of it" (Gen. 2:15). This suggests that our managerial role comes from no lesser source than the Creator. It means as well, however, that we do not manage creation for our own purposes, but as God's stewards. And this management entails caring for creation, not exploiting it for our own ends.

Caring for creation or managing it for its own good points us toward the correct understanding of what it means to be God's image. We do not exercise "dominion" over creation for our sakes, as if the natural world existed merely to sustain human existence. Instead, our role serves a higher goal. God has designated us as his representative so that through us creation might experience what God is like. We are to mirror the divine character and thereby reflect God's own nature.

Consequently, as we care for the natural world, love each other, and worship God, we reveal the compassionate, loving character of the Creator who alone is worthy of worship. In so doing, we function as God's image.

Being in the Divine Image Involves a Future Goal

This conclusion suggests that being in the divine image may be somewhat more complicated than the common assertion, "Each of us is created in the image of God," indicates. It raises some important questions. In whom is the image present? And in what sense is the image of God present in all humans?

We tend to speak of all humans and each human individually as created in the divine image. In a sense, this is correct. Even the Bible itself speaks in this manner (Gen. 9:6; James 3:9).

Declaring that we are all in the image of God reminds us that God loves each of us and that we are all recipients of worth from the Creator. Further, it is a reminder that each human is personally responsible before God to live according to the Creator's design for us. Each of us is accountable to respond to God in love and obedience and thereby to live out the purpose of our existence. In short, all persons are "in the image of God" in that they are all called to mirror God's nature to creation.

Although in one sense we may declare that all persons are created in the image of God, the New Testament teaches that only Jesus Christ is fully the divine image (2 Cor. 4:4; Col. 1:15). Christ is the image of God, because he alone reveals to us what God has created humankind to be (2 Cor. 4:6). And he alone brings us to participate in that destiny so that we may live as true human beings.

Christ's position as the divine image carries a wonderful implication for us: through Christ, believers are participants in this glorious privilege.

Our participation in the divine image affects us in the present. Even now we are being transformed into the image of Christ (2 Cor. 3:18). This renewal carries implications for how we should live: we must "put on the new self, created to be like God in true righteousness and holiness" (Eph. 4:24; cf. Col. 3:9-10).

Although we enjoy a foretaste in the present, our full participation in the divine image lies ultimately in the future. Conformity to Christ as the likeness of God is the glorious destiny that awaits us when Jesus returns (Rom. 8:29). By bringing us to share in Christ's resurrection (1 Cor. 15:50-53), God will transform us to become just like our Lord (1 John 3:2). This good news ought to inspire us to hopeful anticipation of the day when we will "bear the likeness of the man from heaven" (1 Cor. 15:49).

Christians, therefore, are the image of God in a special way. We who are united to Christ share in the divine image that he bears. Or perhaps better stated, as we are being made like Christ, we are being transformed into the image of God. Therefore, being created in the divine image is a process which begins with conversion and continues until the great future day when God brings us into full conformity with the divine goal for us. Then we will truly be the image of God as revealed by Christ.

> ✍ *Live as the divine image bearer that God intends you to be.*

Being in the Divine Image Involves Fellowship and Community

Our divinely given destiny to be the image of God begins with his gracious gift of a special standing before the Creator. It reaches its goal in the glorious renewal of our lives which awaits us in the future. But it focuses on a special fellowship—a special enjoyment of community—which we can experience in part even now.

At the heart of the enjoyment of community, of course, is the fellowship with God we experience as we respond to his love. In so doing, we find the fulfillment of the search for a "home" that arises out of our fundamental "openness to the world," as we described it earlier in this chapter. As we enjoy the fellowship God intends for us, we *are* the image of God.

But ultimately the enjoyment of fellowship is no mere private, individual experience. On the contrary, the fellowship God intends for us is a shared experience. And therefore, the divine image is likewise a shared, corporate reality. It is fully present only as we live in fellowship. It is ours only as we enjoy "community."[9]

The narrative of creation in Genesis 1 highlights the community aspect of the image of God.[10] God declared, "Let us make man in our image" (Gen. 1:26). Then the Creator fashioned humankind in his own image by creating *them* male and female (Gen. 1:27). This aspect of the biblical narrative suggests that humans in relationship with each other reflect the divine image in a way that the solitary individual human being cannot.

The narrative of Adam and Eve in Genesis 2 deepens the biblical theme of the social nature of the divine image. God created the first human pair in order that humans enjoy community with each other. More specifically, the creation of the female was designed to deliver the male from his isolation. This primal community of man and woman then became expansive. It produced the offspring that arise from the sexual union of husband and wife and eventually gave rise to the development of societies.

What began in the Garden of Eden finds its completion at the end of history. The Bible envisions a day when God's will for creation will come to completion. One day God will bring to pass a human society in which God's children enjoy perfect fellowship with each other, the created world, and the Creator (Rev. 22:1-4).

Our discussions in chapter 2 ought to alert us as to why the image of God can only be expressed in human community. The God we know is the triune one — the Father, Son, and Holy Spirit united together in perfect love. Because God is "community" — the fellowship shared among the Father, Son, and Spirit — the creation of humankind in the divine image must be related to humans in fellowship with each other. God's own character can only be mirrored by humans who love after the manner of the perfect love which lies at the heart of the Triune God.

Because God himself is triune, we are in the image of God only as we enjoy community with others. Only as we live in fellowship can we show forth what God is like. Ultimately, then, the "image of God" is a social reality. It refers to humans as beings-in-fellowship.

As we live in love—that is, as we give expression to true community—we reflect the love which characterizes the Creator himself. And as we reflect God's character which is love, we also live in accordance with our own true nature. Only by being persons-in-community do we find our true identity—that form of the "world" toward which our "openness to the world," our restless shaping and reshaping of our environment, is intended to point us.

Our Lord himself articulated this truth in his call to radical discipleship: "For whoever wants to save his life will lose it, but whoever loses his life for me will find it" (Matt. 16:25). The way to true life leads through the giving of one's own life in relationship to Christ. Indeed, <u>we come to find our true identity only as we participate together with others in the community of the followers of Christ</u>. In so doing, we bring honor to our Creator by reflecting the very character of the Triune God.

Indeed, we are created for community.

WE ARE RELATED TO OTHER BEINGS IN THE UNIVERSE

"What is man?" the psalmist wondered. Musing on this question led the biblical writer to consider the relationship between humankind and other spiritual beings. Our identity arises from our position in the universe "a little lower than the heavenly beings" (Ps. 8:5).

We are not alone in the universe. Our world is populated by other physical life forms, of course. But in addition, the biblical authors indicate that other spiritual realities—commonly called "angels" and "demons"—also participate in God's created realm.

Two aspects about these realities and our relationship to them are especially illuminating.

☞ *Spiritual beings are creatures of God.*
☞ *Spiritual beings are connected to structures of human existence.*

Spiritual Beings Are Creatures of God

Like humans, spiritual beings are God's creatures. Although they are not physical beings, they nevertheless possess powers of will and reason. More importantly, they are moral—beings whose actions are either right or wrong.

Angels. Some spiritual beings fulfill their God-given role. These are God's holy angels.

As the entourage of God, the primary duties of these heavenly beings is to praise and serve their Monarch (Isa. 6:1-8). As God's servants they assist God in governing the world (1 Kings 22:19), standing ready to be dispatched to protect God's earthly people (2 Kings 6:17) or to carry out divine judgments.

Angels are interested in the unfolding drama of salvation (1 Peter 1:12). They were active participants in the story of Jesus, the incarnate Son. And they will once again become prominent when Jesus returns (Matt. 13:39; 25:31; Mark 8:38; 13:27; Luke 12:8; 2 Thes. 1:7; Rev. 7:1; 8:1–9:21; 16:5).

The angels worship Christ who is their Lord (Heb. 1:5-14). In fact, through our union with Christ we are also above the angels (Heb. 2:5-9). One day we will even judge the heavenly beings (1 Cor. 6:3). Until that day, the angels minister to us at God's bidding in ways that are largely unknown to us.

According to the Bible, the creaturely status of the heavenly powers indicates that to worship them or to look to them for guidance is actually idolatry. One obvious abominable practice is soothsaying or necromancy (the attempt to gain contact with the dead or with spirits for the purpose of obtaining guidance concerning the future). This practice leads humans to substitute faith in lesser powers for faith in the one true God who alone is sovereign over the future and to whom alone we are to look for guidance.

In a similar manner, dabbling in astrology and divination are idolatrous. These practices also mark a turning away from the God of the future in a vain attempt to gain access to the future. Astrology mistakenly supposes that the heavenly bodies, which are actually only creatures of the one true God, can affect our lives. And divination assumes that through certain acts we can get in touch with powers that know the unknown. In neither case, however, do the participants seek guidance from the only source of wisdom. Instead they ascribe to lesser powers what belongs to God alone.

The demons and their leader. The danger of idolatrous involvement with the heavenly beings reminds us that not all of these creatures are willingly serving God (2 Peter 2:4; Jude 6). In addition to the good angels, the Bible speaks of demons which form a unified kingdom of evil under the leadership of their chief, Satan, "the accuser." Demons are agents of Satan's will and are locked in conflict with God's kingdom (Dan. 10:12-13; 10:20–11:1).

Satan and the demons seek to undermine God's work in the world. They attempt to blind unbelievers to the truth of the gospel, they tempt believers to sin, and they foment persecution of Christians. Demons also seek to harm the well-being of God's creation and to destroy community. Hence, these rebellious beings try to incite human agents to injure the natural environment, God's creatures, other humans, and even themselves. If given opportunity, demons can even take possession of a human person and thereby impair or distort the personality.

The good news of the gospel, however, is that despite their rebellion Satan and the demonic hosts remain under God's ultimate control. In addition, the incarnate Son, Jesus, has been victorious over the powers of evil. Consequently, he is Lord of the entire cosmos. And because our Lord shares his victory with all who are part of his community, we need not fear the powers of evil. One glorious day God will completely destroy all the demonic forces, banishing Satan and his hosts from the eternal community of the new creation.

Spiritual Beings and Structures of Human Existence

Generally when we think about our relationship to the spiritual beings, our minds are drawn to the possibility of individual contact with angels and demons. Thus, we are all too aware that the devil tempts us. We know about demon possession, at least that it occurred in "Bible days." And our contemporary media seems filled with people's stories about their personal encounters with angels.

A "Calvin and Hobbes" comic strip captures well this contemporary cultural fascination with angels. Calvin, sitting on a rock with Hobbes, muses, "I think angels are everywhere." Hobbes questions, "You do?" Calvin responds, "They're on calendars, books, greeting cards . . . almost every product imaginable." Hobbes then simply but keenly observes, "What a spiritual age we live in."

But our relationship to angels and demons moves far beyond Hobbes' wry observation. Nor is it limited to the more familiar areas mentioned above. Instead, the Bible provides the foundation for an additional, broader understanding of the activity of the cosmic forces. The spiritual beings function in connection with what we may call "structures of human existence."

Structures of existence are the various dimensions of social interaction which form the inescapable context for human life together. By providing parameters for human interaction, these structures "govern" human affairs. They make human social existence in its various dimensions possible. They give cohesion to life. And they undergird human society, preserving it from disintegration and chaos.[11]

Structures of existence operate in many dimensions of human life. Religious structures include the various myths, traditions, and practices which provide a cosmic or transcendent reference point for society. Important as well are intellectual structures, that is, the various ideologies by means of which we perceive the nature of reality. Moral structures encompass the codes and customs which facilitate and organize interactions among us as people. And political structures include the systems of politics by means of which we govern ourselves.[12]

These structures are a means through which God orders creation for our benefit. The Creator desires that we live together in harmony, and structures of existence promote harmonious social life (or community). For example, cultural mores (such as a friendly handshake and a polite "How are you?") expedite fellowship among people who otherwise might remain strangers.

God intends that the heavenly beings work through these structures of existence. The angelic hosts are to guide these structures so that they foster true human community.

Consider, for example, the moral law as a structure. God desires that the law orient our existence toward God-honoring actions. To this end, the moral codes of our society should show the parameters in which truly loving relationships can emerge. The task of angels is to enhance the governance of human affairs by promoting wholesome social morality.

However, the demonic hosts often press the structures into service against God, humankind, and creation. Through the diabolical misuse of structures, evil realities bring humans into bondage (Eph. 6:12). Rather than aiding people in the task of building community, the powers enslave them, demanding rigid obedience to traditions and forms which in themselves cannot be the objects of our loyalty.

Demons seek to co-opt the structures into advancing the will of Satan rather than God's will. God desires that the structures of existence foster the kind of human interaction that embodies biblical principles, such as justice, righteousness, and love. Whenever these principles no longer govern human social life, the structures have failed to operate according to their God-given purpose of promoting fellowship with God, harmony within creation, and rich interpersonal relations.

The New Testament presents human government as an example of the ambiguous possibilities of the structures. Paul speaks of the civil magistrate as God's servant sent to punish the wicked and reward the good (Rom. 13:1-7). But according to the Book of Revelation, the same civil structure can be manipulated by Satan in his attempt to injure the church through persecution. Indeed, even today Satan may exploit the legal and policing agencies of civil government as a vehicle for his attack on the people of God. Think of how many governments blatantly persecute believers. Or the devil may subvert legislative structures, leading them to encode laws that are destructive of the community God intends for creation.

The religious dimension of life is another example of the ambiguity of the structures. Demons can use religious or moral codes as a means to bring people — including Christians! — into bondage (Col. 2:20-23). Even the Old Testament law, which God intends to bring us to Christ, can fall victim to this manipulation and misuse, becoming an imprisoning power over us (Gal. 3:23-24). The misuse of the moral law occurs as Satan and his cohorts lead believers to seek stability for their lives through a scaffolding of laws,[13] which rather than drawing us to God, actually becomes a false god—that is, the source of a false sense of meaning, security, and identity.

In a similar manner, "seducing spirits" can manipulate human religious traditions in order to propagate false teaching (1 Tim. 4:1).

The structures can be manipulated by demonic forces. But because Christ has punctured Satan's power, structures of human existence ultimately lie under Christ's lordship. As a result, the structures will one day conform to God's reign. And even now the structures of human existence can be agents for fostering the community for which we were created. For this reason, under the leadership of the Holy Spirit we can boldly seek to bring the structures into closer conformity with the will of God. Knowing that Jesus is Lord of all, we dare not abandon any dimension of human social life to the enemy. Instead, in Jesus' name, we can bring a Christian presence to all spheres of life, whether it be politics, economics, or even the arts.

WHO ARE WE?

The central question of the ages is "Who are we?"—or "Who am I?" To this human quest for identity the gospel speaks as good news: we are God's handiwork; we are God's image; and we are related to the heavenly beings.

The fullness of this lofty identity, however, is ultimately ours only in Christ. He is the one who brings us into true community according to God's purpose for creation. But before we look more deeply into the face of our Lord, we must survey the bad news. We must speak about the sad human condition of failure which the Bible calls "sin," and the next chapter provides this opportunity.

FOR CONNECTION AND APPLICATION

1 When asked to introduce yourself before a group, what kinds of things do you say about yourself? In what sense do such introductions indicate who you really are?

2 What difference ought an acknowledgment that God is our Creator make in how you see yourself?

3 How are humans different from the rest of creation, including the animals? How are we similar?

4 Do you think it is important to believe that we are all descendants of a literal first human (Adam)? How would this belief affect the way we live?

5 What difference does it make whether the image of God is primarily a social or an individual reality?

6 How should we feel about "guardian angels" and "spirit guides"?

7 How should we relate to angels? What should be our response to Satan and his demons?

8 Should Christians read their horoscopes? Why might this be a dangerous practice?

9 If the "structures of human existence" can be agents for good and foster community, list some tangible ways in which you can "boldly" and actively seek to bring these structures into conformity with the will of God. For example, what are some implications for politics and government?

FOUR

Our Human Failure

"For all have sinned and fall short of the glory of God"
(Rom. 3:23).

An illuminating installment of the comic strip "Peanuts" pictured Charlie Brown comfortably in bed with Snoopy snoozing on his lap. The lad mused out loud: "Sometimes I lie awake at night and I ask, 'Where have I gone wrong?' " A forlorn look came over Charlie's round face as he added, "Then a voice says to me, 'This is going to take more than one night.' "

Charlie Brown's comment humorously expresses feelings that surface in us as well. Deep inside, we sense that we are a strange paradox. Sometimes we find ourselves doing things which make us genuinely proud. We act unselfishly. We care and even sacrifice for others.

But other times we seem so self-centered and mean-spirited. We constantly promote ourselves, even at the expense of others. We destroy what others have constructed. And we plunder the good earth that nourishes us. Living with ourselves leads us to a sad realization. We are a mixture of good and evil—of godly beauty and demonic hideousness—of great potential and awful failure. We are sinners on one hand and saints on the other.

Our Christian faith speaks of this paradox as well. We are God's good handiwork. Yet something has gone tragically awry. We are not what we should be; we are characterized by failure. This dark side of the human situation is what the biblical authors call "sin."

In this chapter we seek to make sense out of our human failure. To do so, we raise three crucial questions.

☞ *What is sin?*
☞ *How did we become involved with sin?*
☞ *What are the results of the presence of sin?*

SIN IS FAILURE — "MISSING GOD'S MARK"

The Scriptures uncompromisingly assert what we know from personal experience: we have failed, and we continually fail. That is, we are sinners. What is sin? The Bible understands sin fundamentally as failure.

Sin Is a Failure of the Human Heart

The biblical word "sin" means primarily "missing the mark" or "falling short."[1] It refers to our inability to be what God desires us to be. It speaks of our failure to fulfill God's intention for us.

Our human failure is radical. Rather than being some inconsequential defect on the surface of our lives, sin has found lodging within us — in our personal "control center." Sin infects the core of our being, the nucleus of our existence or, to use the biblical word, the "heart" (Mark 7:14-23; Matt. 12:33-37). In fact, so pervasive is this plague that the Bible declares that sin infects our *hearts* (e.g., Rom. 7:18; Eph. 2:3; Jer. 17:9). And as a result, our attitudes and actions are polluted.

Paul describes this corruption of the heart in vivid terms. He declares that sin causes "our foolish hearts" to be "darkened" (Rom. 1:21) and our minds to be "corrupt" (1 Tim. 6:5). Because of sin, our thinking has become "futile" (Rom. 1:21). We cannot understand spiritual truth (1 Cor. 2:14; 2 Cor. 4:4). Indeed, our minds are actually hostile to God (Rom. 8:7-8).

As an infection in the human heart, sin likewise corrupts our affections. Paul writes that we are "enslaved by all kinds of passions and pleasures" (Titus 3:3). And Jesus observes that rather than abhorring our situation, we actually *love* darkness instead of light (John 3:19).

So pervasive is sin's sway that the Bible speaks of us as *slaves* to it. Jesus, for example, declares, "I tell you the truth, everyone who sins is a slave to sin" (John 8:34).

Our first reaction upon hearing this may be to protest. "Nonsense!" we object. "This makes us out to be despicable and wicked. Talk of sin pervading our hearts fails to note how often people do good deeds."

The biblical authors do not deny that we occasionally do what appears right. On the contrary, they hold out the prospect that we can indeed engage in good acts (Rom. 2:14-15). Yet the claim that we are able to do good must be tempered. Repeatedly we discover that beneath our seemingly good acts are at best mixed, and often purely selfish, motives.

How often do we discover that we are like the "pious" Jew in Jesus' parable: "Two men went up to the temple to pray, one a Pharisee and the other a tax collector. The Pharisee stood up and prayed about himself: 'God, I thank you that I am not like all other men — robbers, evildoers, adulterers — or even like this tax collector. I fast twice a week and give a tenth of all I get' " (Luke 18:9-12).

I recall one of my seminary professors telling how he was once asked to pray in a large Christian gathering. He articulated a fervent, eloquent prayer. But the first thought that entered his mind when he finished was, "My, but you did a good job!"

How often do we — like the seminary professor — find mixed motives at work in even our best conduct? And like the Pharisee's habitual praying, even our apparently good acts regularly arise out of a self-righteous attitude or self-serving motivations. So easily we grow smug about how much more "self-sacrificial" and "giving" we are than most "other people" we know. And how often do we carefully measure the kindness we show toward others according to the personal profit we hope to gain in return?

In these and many other ways, we show how deeply ingrained sin is in our hearts. We fail — we fall short of God's standard.

Sin, we have suggested, is failure. But we must press this a step farther. To do so, we ask, What kind of failure is this?

Sin Is a Failure of Community

Sin, of course, refers to what we do. Our actions are often evil. And even our apparently good deeds are tainted with evil motives.

The Bible does not limit sin to our conduct, however. As we have seen, at a deeper level sin also encompasses who we are. Sin is a failure to *be*. But, we wonder, *what* or *who* have we failed to be?

> ✍ *"Sin" refers to any attitude or action that fails to radiate God's own character.*

To answer this question, we must return to the image of God we spoke about in chapter 3. There we noted that God created us to be his image-bearers. And at the heart of the *imago dei* is God's desire that we show forth the divine character. "Sin," therefore, is the failure to reflect the image of God.

But we cannot stop here. As we saw in chapter 2, the God who is love is the triune one, the community of Father, Son, and Spirit. Because God desires that we reflect the divine community—because we are created for community—sin is a failure of "community."

> ✍ *Sin is the failure to live in fellowship with God, each other, and all creation.*

This failure displays its presence in what we do. We see it in our active rebellion against God, our quarreling with each other and our misuse of creation. But it is equally present in what we don't do. It permeates our passive apathy toward God and others. And it is visible as we avoid our responsibilities as stewards of creation.

By not participating in the fellowship God intends for us, we "miss the mark."

Again, we may respond with a protest: "Isn't all this merely outdated theological talk?" "Isn't the idea of sin passé in the contemporary world? And have we not simply evolved beyond the consciousness of sin?"

We Know Sin Only through the Gospel

Indeed, we live in a society that avoids the label "sin." We don't like to think of ourselves as sinners.[2] Oh, we willingly acknowledge our shortcomings. But we don't attach *blame* to them. We excuse our foibles and even our despicable deeds as the product of some illness. Or it is due to the treatment we endured as children or the social environment in which we live. "Yes, I am not what I should be," we readily admit. "But this is because I am a *victim*. Don't call me a sinner."

The contemporary denial of sin ought not to surprise us. Ultimately, a true sense of sin only comes as we hear the gospel.[3] We cannot see the radical depth of our human failure until we come to see the depth to which God suffered on our behalf.

The Bible narrates the story of the suffering God. God's suffering the burden of human sin began in the Old Testament. In the face of the faithlessness of Israel, the compassionate God remained faithful. But the story reached its climax in the sufferings of the innocent Jesus. Our sin — our breach of community — is so serious that it could only be overcome through the sacrifice of Jesus, in whom God suffered in our behalf.

> *Alas! and did my Savior bleed,*
> *And did my Sov'reign die?*
> *Would he devote that sacred head*
> *For such a worm as I? . . .*
> *Was it for crimes that I have done,*
> *He groaned upon the tree?*
> *Amazing pity! grace unknown!*
> *And love beyond degree!*[4]

"Sin" denotes the tragic human failure which cost Jesus his life. But how did we become caught up in this deplorable situation? To this question we must now turn.

SIN HAS BEEN WITH US "FROM THE BEGINNING"

The Bible declares that we are God's handiwork. Yet, we are not what God desires us to be. We fail to live in accordance with God's purposes. And each of us shares in this failure.

If "all have sinned and fall short of the glory of God," when did this "falling short" begin? How did sin enter our world? And why did it spread to me?

The Book of Genesis indicates that failure has characterized us "from the beginning," from the first human pair onward. This does not mean that God created us sinful — sin was not present "in the beginning." Rather, sin entered the world through a willful human act. We speak of this event as the *Fall*.

Humans "Fell" into Sin

The story of our descent into sin begins with Adam and Eve in the Garden of Eden. Humans began their existence in seemingly perfect innocence. As the divine image-bearers, they enjoyed fellowship with God, who walked in the Garden in the cool of the day (Gen. 3:8). They savored community with each other; indeed, they were naked and felt no shame (Gen. 2:25). And they experienced harmony with the rest of creation; they ate fruit from the trees (Gen. 2:16) for which they cared (v. 15) and lived among the animals Adam had named (Gen. 2:19-20).

Despite the bliss of the Garden, the first human pair chose to disobey a divine prohibition. Thereby they plunged humankind into sin (Gen. 3:1-7).

This downward plummet began with mistrust. As innocent creatures, Adam and Eve had not yet been confronted with the awful distinction between good and evil. Nor did they personally know the sting of sin. In this sense, the forbidden act did promise them something they lacked—access to knowledge of good and evil.

The serpent exploited this situation. He subtly raised doubts about God's goodness, suggesting that through his prohibition God intended to withhold some good from them. The serpent set before Adam and Eve the possibility of a heightened knowledge he claimed God had maliciously reserved for himself.

God's intent, of course, was not to deprive creatures. Rather, the prohibition was given for their own good—to protect them from the adverse consequences of eating the forbidden fruit. But the beguiling words of the serpent worked their charm. They led Adam and Eve to question God's goodness—just as we so often do.

At the same time, the command served as a test. It would determine whether or not the first humans would fully obey the Creator. In this sense, the possibility of sin originated with the divine prohibition. God's command gave birth to choice—a choice between trusting obedience or faithless disobedience—the same alternatives that face us. Yet the presence of choice was not itself sin. Evil arose only when Adam and Eve opted for rebellion. So today, the fact that we face choices is not the problem. Rather, our failure lies in the path we choose to follow.

The Genesis story concludes with the sad reality of the consequences of their act (Gen. 3:8-19). Once they disobeyed God, the first humans no longer reflected the grandeur of the divine image. The idyllic community was shattered. Through this act, Adam and Eve destroyed the fellowship with God, each other, and creation that had characterized life in the Garden.

When they heard God's footsteps in the Garden, Adam and Eve grew fearful and sought to hide from God. This response indicated that the pristine fellowship with the Creator had been broken. They likewise covered themselves from the gaze of the other, indicating that their sense of guilt and shame had marred the fellowship they had once known. And through their act, the first humans introduced enmity into a creation that had only known harmony (Gen. 3:14-15, 17-19).

As a result of their act, Adam and Eve could no longer anticipate unending bliss. God had warned Adam, "when you eat of it [the forbidden fruit] you will surely die" (Gen. 2:17). Their sin brought its tragic outworking. They were banished from the Garden of Eden (Gen. 3:23), and the principle of death invaded their lives. God told Adam that he would now toil "until you return to the ground, since from it you were taken; for dust you are and to dust you will return" (Gen. 3:19).

Fallen humans experience the sting of death in stages. It begins as spiritual deadness in the present: we are "dead through the trespasses and sins" (Eph. 2:1, NRSVB). At the end of our life on earth, we face physical death and the uncertainty it inaugurates. One day—at the judgment—death will come in its fullness, as sinful humans experience final separation from the source of life, eternal banishment from God's community (Rev. 20:14-15).

Adam's Sin — Our Sin

The Book of Genesis answers the question, "How did sin come into the world?" with the story of the Fall. Paul echoes the primordial narrative when he declares, "sin entered the world through one man" (Rom. 5:12) so that "in Adam all die" (1 Cor. 15:22).

But left unanswered is the question as to how *we* became involved. Hence, we wonder how Adam is related to us. Why do the effects of Adam's sin extend to all his descendants? And above all, how is it that I am a sinner? Theologians have offered several possible ways in which we could understand our connection to Adam. Let's summarize their suggestions in chart form before launching into our discussion.

	FEDERAL HEADSHIP	NATURAL HEADSHIP	NON-HEADSHIP
Adam's person and us	Adam is our representative	Adam is our progenitor	Each of us is Adam
Adam's act and us	Adam chose for us	We chose in Adam	Each chooses as Adam

Adam is our representative. Perhaps God appointed Adam as the representative, the "federal head" of humankind and through him entered into a legal agreement with all humans.[5] The terms of the agreement were simple: If Adam obeyed the command not to eat from the forbidden tree, he would enjoy continued life (cf. Rom. 7:10); but his disobedience would result in death.[6] As the designated representative—the federal head—of all humankind, Adam not only acted for himself, but also on behalf of us all.[7]

At first glance, the idea of federal headship appears to violate our individualistic sensibilities. Are we not each responsible solely for ourselves? Is not my sin *mine* alone?

Yet at many levels of contemporary life we actually see this principle at work. One obvious area is human government. Governmental officials repeatedly act on behalf of, or in the name of, all the citizens of the land. For example, the President and the Congress are the designated representatives of the people of the United States. Their decisions have grave implications for each citizen, even for future generations of Americans. Indeed, if our lawmakers choose to live beyond our government's income or if our leaders declare war on a foreign power, we are all affected.

Perhaps in a similar fashion God designated Adam to act on behalf of all his descendants, whether for good or for ill—for life or for death.

Adam is our progenitor. Rather than seeing Adam as our legal representative, perhaps we should look to Adam as the progenitor of humankind. He is our "natural head." Maybe this forms the bridge between his sin and our sinfulness.

Adam's status as our natural head suggests that we were all present in him when he sinned. Each of us actually acted in Adam, and thus his sin is literally our sin.

Our first response to this suggestion, however, might be to demure. "Nonsense!" we may be inclined to say. "All this happened centuries before I was conceived. How then can anyone assert that I was present in Adam?"

There is a biblical answer to our objection: you were indeed in the Garden. Specifically, you were in Adam's "loins" at the time of the Fall. You were there in the same way Levi was in the loins of Abraham when he paid the tithe to Melchizedek (see Heb. 7:4-10). Hence, the scriptural authors have a profound sense of the unity and solidarity of humankind. They held to a literal connection between us and our progenitors.

If we were in the Garden with Adam, then we can easily understand how we are implicated in his debilitating deed.

We are Adam. But perhaps the Book of Genesis is not reporting the story of one man in prehistory at all. Suppose the "Fall" is not an event in the primordial past but a tragedy that we all experience in the present.[8] What if the Genesis story is a description of what happens when we move from innocence to death through our own sinful choice?

Understood as *our* story, the narrative of the Fall describes what happens when we sin. "In the beginning"—prior to committing a sinful act—we are innocent. The deed is only a possibility, a choice we are considering. In addition, "in the beginning" we may be blissfully ignorant of the evil consequences that will follow from the mistaken choice we are contemplating. Indeed, the proposed act seems to promise so much at such little cost!

Once we've yielded to the impulse, however, its hidden sting emerges. Only then do we experience the full force of the detrimental aspects of the action. Once this occurs, we feel remorse, and we regret our mistake.

How often has this scenario repeated itself in our own lives? A little act of treachery, a little lie (such as claiming to be sick when in fact we are leaving early on a trip), a little secret illicit sexual encounter—it seems to be the way to get ahead. The contemplated act appears to offer great benefit at no cost. But once we've done it, we feel its sting. In the end, we discover to our dismay that the benefit was so small and the cost in terms of loss of integrity and hurt inflicted on others was so great.

Whatever else it may be, the biblical story is about us. It describes our experience.[9]

Adam's sin and us. Although the narrative of the Fall offers valuable insights into our situation, the Genesis story is not *simply* about us. It also speaks about a "first" sin, the sin of Adam.

Indeed, there are important differences between Adam's sin and ours. The first temptation came *to* Adam, for it was instigated by the serpent. But our plight is different. Because sin lies at the core of our being, temptation already has a foothold *within* us. As James notes, "Each one is tempted when by his own evil desire he is dragged away and enticed" (James 1:14).

In addition, Adam's sin occurred in a pristine community. In the Garden our first parents enjoyed fellowship with God, each other, and all creation. We, in contrast, find ourselves in a quite different situation when we sin. As those who are "dead in trespasses and sins" (Eph. 2:1), we act in the context of a prior failure and loss of community.

Perhaps this observation provides a clue to the mystery of our involvement in Adam's sin. In the Garden of Eden, humankind enjoyed a universal community unparalleled in subsequent history. But the first sin shattered this glorious fellowship which existed at the infancy of our corporate story.

Once destroyed, the primordial community remains forever lost. Just as we cannot return to any prior era in history, so also we cannot return to "the beginning." Just as the evil we do carries far-reaching consequences, so also we simply can never restore the fellowship that our ancestors squandered. Instead, we are forced to start in the present. And we can only begin with the conditions of the world as they now are.

In this sense, the first sin is in a class by itself. And for this reason its effects always remain with us. Adam's sin has permanently tainted the world. And it has irreparably altered us, earth's human inhabitants. We no longer know creation, our co-pilgrims, our Creator, and even ourselves solely as friends. Instead, the pristine community — fellowship without flaws, wholesomeness without a history of hurt — has been destroyed.

Perhaps we can better understand this if we think of what often results from a breach of friendship. When a close friend has severely injured you, you may immediately be able to speak sincere forgiving words. But even though you have forgiven your friend, a wound remains. It may take a long time before you are able to trust her again. In fact, you may never trust completely. Your friendship may continue to flourish, but you will carry the memory of the hurt throughout your life.

In a much greater way, the sin of our first parents marred the pristine fellowship of the Garden for all time.

The Fall lies in the distant past. Yet, in a certain sense, we continually repeat it. Adam's disobedience decimated the pristine experience of community. But the destruction of fellowship that marked the error of our parents characterizes our attitudes and actions as well. We too are guilty of destroying the semblances of community that here and there emerge among us. Nations break the peace through war. Families quarrel and feud. Marital bliss becomes the casualty of abuse. And the list continues. As we find ourselves guilty of undermining fellowship, we gain a glimpse of the awfulness of the primordial human sin and of God's righteous judgment on us all.

As we noted already, the temptation that drew our first parents into sin was external. But our sinful attitudes and actions flow from the inner core of our being — from the human heart. We find ourselves involved in a radical failure that encompasses our very being. But we have not yet fully answered a still pressing question. What is the source of the corrupt nature that plagues each of us?

Our experience confirms what Christian theology has declared for centuries. Our corruption is not merely the result of what we ourselves do. Rather, it comes to us through our participation in humankind.

Sinfulness invades our heart in several ways. In part it comes through our social surroundings. Simply stated, we *teach* each other to sin.

But there is an additional aspect of the invasion of sin as well. To see this, we must look at another connection between Adam's sin and us that arises from his status as our natural head. The sin of our first parents irreparably altered—corrupted—the human nature they passed on to us. As a result, we inherit what theologians often call a "depraved nature" or a "fallen disposition" from our ancestors.

The depraved nature comes to us in the same way as do the other basic human characteristics we all share. We may say that it lies in our gene pool. In a sense, sin is now a part of our common human genetic makeup. This is not to suggest that we carry a specific "sin gene" that scientists might someday discover and eradicate. Rather, our total inheritance is morally defective. And this defect is passed from parents to children. No wonder we seem to sin so easily!

The Outworking of Our Defective Human Nature

Because the humanity we inherit is corrupted, each of us will and does sin. We commit sinful acts once we are in a position to act out what is present within our nature by heredity and socialization.

This leads to further questions. When does this happen? When do we begin to participate in the common human failure?

The connection to heredity indicates that the potential for our involvement in the breakdown of community is present in us already at birth. Perhaps we can best understand this if we seek to describe how it works.

All who have observed infants know that these innocent beings are largely unaware of anything outside their own little world. Infants are naturally egocentric and self-absorbed. What is natural in infancy, however, later becomes malicious. God's intention is that the growing human develop wholesome, healthy attitudes that balance personal independence and a sense of self-worth with a full awareness of an interdependence with creation, other humans, and ultimately the Creator. But instead of developing as God desires, our egocentricity and self-absorption grow unchecked. This results in a breach in community.

In short, the self-absorption of infancy carries the potential to develop into a community-destructive force within each of us — a depraved nature. Eventually this depraved nature expresses itself in moral choices that are either overly egotistical or overly self-abasing, and hence are displeasing to God. In this way, what ought to drive us to a quest for God and the fulfillment of his intention that we participate in the community of God degenerates into a search for a humanly devised substitute.

When this happens, we "miss the mark," and sin's awful consequences follow.

SIN CARRIES CONSEQUENCES

We, of course, have no firsthand awareness of inheriting a corrupted nature. Nor is it likely that we remember the day we committed our first sinful act. Yet we continually experience the sad reality of sinning. We see how sin invades, colors, and even controls our attitudes, motives, and actions. And we repeatedly observe the terrible results of sin. We realize that sin ruins lives, destroys families, undermines societies, and even threatens life on planet Earth.

The Christian faith acknowledges these disastrous effects of human sin. But its chief concern is to place them in a broader context. The presence of sin in our lives affects how we live in the world because it undermines, as we have emphasized, our fundamental relationships — with God, others, and creation. In this manner, sin thwarts God's intentions for us.

We can describe our plight through four words, which provide poignant pictures of the awful consequences of sin:

☞ *alienation,*
☞ *condemnation,*
☞ *enslavement,*
☞ *depravity.*

We Are Alienated

The presence of sin carries adverse effects in the realm of interpersonal relations. Viewed from this perspective, we discover that sin leads to alienation.

We experience sin's alienation in our relationship to God. God created us to be his friends—even his children. But we have chosen to live as God's enemies (Rom. 5:10a).

> ✍ *Our failure robs us of the enjoyment of community God intends for us and leaves us isolated and alone—alienated.*

As the narrative of the Garden of Eden indicates, God desires that we be able to enjoy the divine presence. But instead, we flee from God. We live in fear, presuming that he is hostile toward us. In fact, however, we are the hostile ones and project our hostility on God. We run from the only one who can overcome our fear, brokenness, and hostility. We seek to get away from the only one who can fulfill our deepest needs.

Because we are alienated from God, sin alienates us from other humans as well. God designed us to enjoy wholesome, enriching relationships with each other. But we find ourselves exploiting and being exploited. We jostle with each other for power, influence, and prominence. Or we allow others to rob us of our dignity and sense of worth.

We are also alienated from creation. God intended that we live in harmony with what he has made. But rather than seeing ourselves as divinely mandated stewards of creation, we seek to enslave it and make it serve our wants. We no longer see the earth as an organic whole which we manage on God's behalf. Instead, in our insatiable but misguided quest for a "home," we view creation as the raw material for our industrious activity or as an untamed foe that we must conquer. Our sin has introduced destruction into creation. As Paul declares, creation itself now exists—yea, "groans"—under the bondage caused by human sin, awaiting the liberation of the new creation (Rom. 8:19-22).

The alienating effects of sin reach even to our personal existence. We do not fulfill God's design for us. As a result, we are alienated from our own true selves. We simply are not who we were created to be. And we sense within ourselves this disruptive loss. For this reason, we are our own worst enemies.

We Are Condemned

Viewed from the perspective of God's tribunal, sin carries adverse legal implications. Our plight as sinful creatures standing before a holy God entails "condemnation."

The presence of sin means that we stand condemned by a righteous Judge.

This sad situation is the opposite of what God intended. God designed us to live as righteous bearers of the divine image, as those who mirror the divine holy character. Instead, as our fallen nature expresses itself through our actions, we commit sins. The presence of sin in our lives leaves God, the righteous Judge, no alternative except to view us as guilty (John 3:18).

Although God could destroy us immediately, in grace he spares us the full implications of our sin. We are guilty and therefore deserving of death. And although the sentence hovers over us, the gracious Judge has ordered a temporary "stay of execution."

> ✍ *"Condemnation" refers to the sentence or judgment which hangs over us because of our sin.*

One day, however, this will change. At the final judgment the Judge of all humankind will pronounce the verdict we deserve. All guilty human beings will be banished from God's presence (Rev. 20:11-15; Matt. 25:31-34, 41).

Unfortunately, some people use this gracious reprieve as an opportunity to slip into even greater depths of sin (Rom. 1:18-32). Despite appearances to the contrary, however, sinful humans are headed for destruction. The hell that awaits them is but the natural outworking of their failure to live in accordance with God's intention.

The Bible clearly teaches that one day we will all appear before God our Judge. Scripture also indicates that we will be judged according to our *deeds* (2 Cor. 5:10; Rev. 20:12-13). That is, the basis for God's final verdict will be our *actions*.

This biblical teaching has important implications. It means that ultimately we are not condemned because we have inherited a sinful nature. It is this disposition that the Holy Spirit will one day root out of us, when he completes his work of making us like Christ. What brings the sentence of death are the wrong moral choices through which we give *expression* to the fallen nature within us.

The biblical teaching about judgment according to our deeds suggests that normal human development includes a threshold we may call the "age of accountability."[10] When we are very young, God does not yet hold us accountable for what we do (Num. 14:29-31; Deut. 1:39; Isa. 7:15-16; Matt. 18:1-14; 19:14), because we are not yet in a position to make moral choices. But at some point we move from innocence to responsibility and begin to carry full accountability as moral agents.

This means that we can entrust to God those who never develop into responsible moral agents (e.g., persons who die in infancy and the severely mentally challenged). Although they inherit the fallen human nature from their parents, such persons do not make moral choices—decisions which are morally right or wrong. And therefore they have no deeds which demand eternal condemnation before the righteous God.

We Are Enslaved

Not only does sin leave us alienated and condemned, it is an alien, evil force that holds us in its grasp. Consequently, the presence of sin brings "enslavement."

When the New Testament speaks of "enslavement" to sin, it borrows an image from the first-century practice of slavery. Whenever the conquering Roman armies returned from their escapades, they brought with them the most talented from among the subjected peoples as slaves to serve Roman citizens.

> ✍ *Enslavement means we are in bondage to a hostile, alien force that has overwhelmed us.*

Sin is like an enslaving army which takes us captive. As slaves to this power we cannot choose not to sin. Rather, sin rules over us, so that we find that we must sin (Rom. 7:21-23).

Once again, we may be inclined to lodge a protest: "What about 'free will'? I thought we are free moral agents. How then can we speak about enslavement to sin?"

Our protest against this biblical teaching is often generated by an understanding of "free will" derived from the everyday experience of choosing among alternatives. In the morning we wonder, "Should I wear my black or my brown shoes?" Then at lunch we choose again, "Should I order the chicken sandwich or the shrimp salad?" And on it goes.

Everyday choices lead us to picture ourselves as self-motivated choosers, standing before decisions unencumbered by any overpowering inclination to decide in one direction or another. And we tend simply to extend this experience to the realm of moral decision-making. We assume that we approach moral decisions with the same freedom that we bring to the selection of our daily apparel from among the clothes in our closets.

This is not what the Bible means by freedom. The biblical ideal is not the neutral decision-maker who chooses from among the alternatives that present themselves. In fact, no such person has ever lived; this ideal is an illusion. Rather, the ideal the Bible presents is the person who lives as he or she *should.*

As we know from personal experience, in any situation our options are limited. A host of influences and circumstances narrow our range of possible actions. But there is yet a more significant dimension limiting our "freedom." We never approach the moral decision-making process as neutral choosers. Instead, we are already predisposed. And the presence of sin leaves us predisposed toward evil.

> ✍ *True moral freedom is the ability to live according to God's purposes.*

Given this tragic situation, "freedom" means to be released from the predisposition toward evil in order to be able to choose the good. True freedom, therefore, is God's gift given through Christ. This is what Jesus meant when he said, "if the Son sets you free, you will be free indeed" (John 8:36).

We Are Depraved

We can sum up our plight by acknowledging that the presence of sin is debilitating. It leaves us depraved. Our innate resources are simply too meager to pull us out of the mire. But we may wonder why this is. The answer lies in what we have already discussed.

- "Depravity" refers to our inability or powerlessness to remedy our dire situation.

As we noted earlier, sin is not some mere surface blemish on what is otherwise a beautiful human face. Instead, it is radical; it infects the very core of our being. It has corrupted *all* aspects of our lives. No dimension of our existence has withstood the onslaught of the alien power we call "sin."

If sin is a radical problem, it requires a radical cure. If sin has penetrated to our heart, it cannot be remedied by heartfelt action. If sin holds us captive, we are powerless to escape from our plight. The cure for our disease must come from outside us, and it must go to the core of our being. In short, if our human condition is to be altered, we require the help of a power outside ourselves, a power greater than sin.

Many people refuse to admit the radicality of our human failure. For them "depravity" is too strong a word for our human condition. For example, certain theologians of the medieval Roman Catholic Church concluded that as bad as it was, the Fall left our natural human powers, especially the power of reason, intact. This means that human reason remains capable of attaining some knowledge about God.

The Protestant Reformers, however, rejected this idea. They recovered the biblical truth that the effects of sin extend to all dimensions of human existence. Even our reason falls under sin's power and consequently can lead us astray. This predicament is what the Reformers meant by "total depravity." We simply lack the ability to remedy our plight. We have no righteousness to offer, we must rely on what Martin Luther termed an "alien righteousness." If salvation from sin is to come, it must come from God.

The message of depravity is equally scandalous to people today. We want to find some aspect of human life that is untainted by the consequences of sin. We desperately search for some realm to which we can escape to find the purity and innocence that we know is sadly lacking in our world.

Today many people — enticed by the media, especially the movie industry—look to sex for that place of pristine purity. They long for the perfect sexual encounter which for one brief moment will transpose them back to the lost Garden of Eden.

Others scurry off to self-help programs. Or they flock to New Age and Eastern religions whose teachers promise to release a power they claim lies within each of us. Still others seek to ease the ache by throwing themselves into their careers.

But the gospel speaks the truth of our situation to a people caught up in the lie of our era. There is no return to Eden: not through sex, money, pleasure, "success," nor the release of an internal power, which in the end is merely our own human frailty.

Let's simply admit it; we are helplessly and hopelessly depraved.

This then is our situation. Created by God, we are good. God intends that we reflect the character of the Triune Creator. But we are caught in a failure that has characterized human existence from the beginning. Our failure is a radical problem, for it infects even the core of our being. This failure leaves us alienated, condemned, enslaved, and depraved. Within ourselves we have no answer. If there is a solution, it must come from beyond ourselves.

> ✍ There is no "realm" into which you can retreat to escape the grim reality of human sin.

The good news of the Christian faith meets us in our abject spiritual poverty. Help is available! God has intervened radically in this situation. The grace of God has come. In Christ, God has made provision to rescue us from sin. And through the Holy Spirit, God seeks to lead us into the community for which we are created.

We may summarize the effects of sin and God's antidote by a chart, which we will later complete in chapters 6 and 8:

HUMAN CONDITION	CHRIST'S PROVISION	SPIRIT'S APPLICATION
Alienation		
Condemnation		
Enslavement		
Depravity		

Now as we turn to the next chapter, we gladly move from our human problem to God's gracious solution.

---

1 How would you describe sin in a manner that people today could grasp this concept?

2 Is it "fair" that Adam's transgression affects us? Given that Adam is the father of all humankind, would it have been possible that his Fall would "not" affect his children? How do our sins affect others? Can we ever really sin alone?

3 In what everyday ways do seemingly "good" people "miss the mark"?

4 How do people today seek to escape the biblical teaching about sin?

5 In what ways do contemporary people admit the reality of sin, even though they may use some other word to describe it?

Jesus Christ—
"God with Us"

"Therefore let all Israel be assured of this:
God has made this Jesus whom you crucified, both Lord and Christ"
(Acts 2:36).

The cover of the December 1994 issue of *Life* magazine sports an ancient picture of Jesus of Nazareth with the caption, "Who Was He? Solving the Mystery of Jesus and Why It Matters for Today?"

Who was—no, who is—Jesus? Indeed, the identity of the man from Nazareth has been the most perplexing question of all history. Already during Jesus' earthly life speculation abounded as to his identity (Matt. 16:13, 16). Rather than dying out, the debate about Jesus is as intense two millennia later as it was while he walked the paths of Palestine. The question remains as crucial and provoking today as it was on the day Jesus stunned his disciples with the query, "Who do people say I am?" (Mark 8:27)

On that day the disciples recounted the opinions of the people. But then Peter burst forth with the insightful assertion, "You are the Christ" (Mark 8:29).

Peter's Spirit-inspired confession lies at the heart of our faith as well. With believers of all ages, we acknowledge that God has acted in this specific human life. Echoing Matthew who saw in the birth of our Lord the fulfillment of the ancient prophecy, we declare that Jesus of Nazareth is Immanuel—"God with us."

This lofty declaration, "Jesus is the Christ," is a central element in every Christian's religious vocabulary. We readily let the statement roll from our tongues. But what do we mean when we confess that God was active in Jesus? Does our confession remain intelligible two millennia after Jesus' death? And if so, how are we to understand Jesus' identity in our context? How should we answer the question "Who is Jesus?" in the contemporary world in which we live? And what difference does it make in how we live?

In this chapter we offer an answer to the question, "Who is Jesus?" In continuation with Christians throughout the ages, our understanding of Jesus' identity takes the form of three significant statements.

☞ *Jesus is fully divine.*
☞ *Jesus is fully human.*
☞ *Jesus is both divine and human.*

JESUS IS FULLY DIVINE

The Christian church was born out of the acknowledgment that Jesus is Immanuel, "God with us." His early Jewish followers believed that in Jesus they had encountered the God of the Hebrew patriarchs. As those who had known Jesus reflected on the implications of his life and ministry, they felt constrained to acknowledge that Jesus of Nazareth is both God and Savior (2 Peter 1:1). Based on their testimony, the church concluded that Jesus is divine—indeed he is *uniquely* divine.

But can we continue to affirm this classic Christian confession? Is it possible in our day to declare that a man who lived 2,000 years ago is divine? And if so, is Jesus the only person in whom we acknowledge this status?

Is Jesus Divine?

As Christians we know that it is the Holy Spirit who causes us to see the truth about Jesus. "No one can say 'Jesus is Lord,' except by the Holy Spirit" (1 Cor. 12:3). But what aspects about Jesus' earthly life does the Spirit use in bringing us to this realization? To answer this question we must review those dimensions of Jesus' life that caught the attention of the early eyewitnesses and led them to this exalted conclusion. Specifically, we look at:

☞ *Jesus' sinlessness,*
☞ *Jesus' teachings,*
☞ *Jesus' death,*
☞ *Jesus' claim,*
☞ *Jesus' resurrection.*

And we ask, Does any one of these aspects of Jesus' life lead us to understand who he is?

Jesus' sinlessness. [1] According to the New Testament, Jesus lived a sinless life. He committed no morally culpable act (Heb. 4:15), and he was free from the disposition to sin that characterizes fallen humanity (2 Cor. 5:21; Heb. 9:14; 1 John 3:5). Could this form the basis for our confession, "Jesus is Lord"?

Jesus' sinlessness stands as an attractive feature of his person. As we read the Gospel accounts of Jesus' conduct we are drawn to him, for we are led to wonder who he might be. Jesus' moral life, therefore, invites us to consider the question of his identity.

At the same time, we cannot overlook that during his earthly sojourn Jesus' sinlessness was a debatable point. The religious leaders of his day were convinced that he was a great sinner. They saw him as one who readily associated with the most impious of people. He flaunted the traditions of the Jewish community and even of Moses himself. Worst of all he was guilty of blasphemy.

In the end, therefore, Jesus' sinlessness is not immediately obvious. Only those who already know Jesus as Immanuel confess him as the sinlessness one.

Jesus' teaching. [2] We can say the same about Jesus' divine teaching. Rather than engendering universal acceptance, his words evoked a mixed reaction from his original hearers. Only when we know him as "God with us" does his teaching carry divine authority for us.

Jesus' death. Matthew reports that the Roman soldiers who saw Jesus die concluded, "Surely he was the Son of God" (Matt. 27:54). Perhaps the way Jesus died is a powerful statement about his divine identity. [3]

Yet unless Jesus' death is viewed through the eyes of faith, its significance can be easily overlooked. We could readily dismiss it as the sacrifice of a well-intended popular hero and martyr. Or we could reject it as the self-induced demise of a deluded idealist. Even when viewed in faith, Jesus' death entailed a painful experience of estrangement from God. "My God, my God, why have you forsaken me?" (Mark 15:34; Matt. 27:46), he cried in anguish.

Jesus' death derives its great significance from the truth that he is divine. Only if Jesus is Immanuel does his death become the self-sacrifice of God for sinful humankind.

Jesus' claim. All four Gospels agree that Jesus set forth a fantastic claim about his identity. Maybe we could find in his claim the clue to who he is.[4]

In his widely read book *Basic Christianity,*[5] John Stott offers a helpful summary of the portrayal of Jesus' claim as it is presented in the Gospels. First, Jesus' claim came through his self-centered teaching. Although demanding humility in others, the Master repeatedly pointed to himself: he is the bread of life, the light of the world, the resurrection and the life, the fulfillment of the Old Testament, and the one who would draw all persons to himself (John 12:32).

Second, the signs Jesus performed entailed an implicit declaration that he was engaging in a unique mission. By changing water into wine, feeding the multitudes, restoring sight to the blind, and raising the dead, our Lord asserted that he was inaugurating God's new order.

Third, by exercising functions belonging solely to God, Jesus articulated an indirect claim to deity. He forgave sins. And he claimed divine prerogatives as the one who could bestow life, teach truth, and even judge the world.

Finally, occasionally Jesus' divine claim came directly. He spoke of his unique relationship with the Father. He viewed himself as the Son who is "in the Father," knows the Father, and is one with the Father (John 10:30-38). In fact, he even appropriated to himself the divine name—"I Am" (John 8:51-59). And after his resurrection our Lord accepted worship (John 20:26-29).

What can we conclude from this apparently lofty claim?

A quick look at history suggests that making audacious personal claims is itself not unusual. Jesus is not the only person who has claimed a unique relationship with God. Other religious figures of his day made similar professions. And what about the Jim Joneses, David Koreshes, and Luc Jorets of our day—or less bizarre candidates for deity such as Sun Myung Moon? How does Jesus differ from these would-be messiahs?

Yet there remains something noteworthy about Jesus. His claim looked for, and even demanded a future vindication. Jesus asserted that his Father would one day exonerate him and his ministry.

Jesus' resurrection. According to the New Testament, God's response came swiftly and decisively: he raised the crucified Jesus from the dead. Could this be the foundation for his identity?

Before answering this question we must deal with another crucial issue. Did the resurrection truly happen? Can we continue to declare that God raised Jesus from the dead?

For "modern" people, of course, the idea of a resurrection is a historical impossibility. The dead simply do not rise.[6] Nevertheless, the New Testament authors bear consistent witness to the resurrection of Jesus as a historical fact. In making this claim, they appeal to the empty tomb and to the appearances of the resurrected Jesus. How strong is the case for Jesus' resurrection?[7]

The Gospels report that the tomb was empty on Easter. And they assert that the empty tomb is a sign that Jesus triumphed over death. We can access this appeal to the empty tomb by surveying the alternate explanations.

• Perhaps the women, being strangers in the city, went to the wrong tomb.

But the Gospels report that many other persons, including the disciples, viewed the same tomb. It seems unlikely that so many would make the same mistake about the place where Jesus' body had been laid.

• Perhaps the disciples of Jesus stole his body.

This was the theory that the guards were bribed to circulate (Matt. 28:11-15). Yet the persons who purportedly perpetrated such a hoax (the disciples) were subsequently willing to die as martyrs for their declaration that Jesus had risen. Is it likely that they would have suffered to that extent for what they knew was a lie?

• Perhaps the Jerusalem authorities took the body.

But would they not have squelched the entire Christian movement by merely producing the body when the story of Jesus' resurrection began to circulate in the city?

• Perhaps Jesus did not actually die but merely went into a swoon. Maybe the entire drama was a plot—"the passover plot"[8] —and Jesus set out to trick his disciples into *believing* that he had conquered death by feigning death on the cross.

But how likely is it that Jesus could have pulled off such a hoax? He barely survived the ordeal of the final hours of Passion week. Could he really have been in sufficient physical shape a few days later to convince his unsuspecting disciples that he had conquered death?

The New Testament accounts for the empty tomb by declaring that God raised Jesus from the dead. The alternate explanations lack plausibility.

The New Testament writers also appeal to purported appearances of the risen Lord. The resurrection must be a historical event, they argue, because many people saw Jesus alive after Easter. Does this explanation merit our acceptance? Again we must appraise the alternate theories.

• Perhaps the supposed appearances were fabrications.

But in what may be the earliest written assertion of the resurrection (1 Cor. 15:3-8), Paul appeals to living witnesses. He invites his readers to check out the story by contacting the persons who were there.

• Perhaps the appearances were hallucinations.

But the experiences of the risen Lord do not occur in the kinds of situations that are conducive to this phenomenon. There is neither a strong inward desire nor a predisposing outward setting. On the contrary, the followers of Jesus saw no hope of seeing their master again after his crushing death. And the settings of the appearances were varied in location and in time of day.

Nor were these experiences merely personal, subjective visions. Instead, they were apprehended by several persons simultaneously.

The empty tomb and the appearances of the risen Lord substantiate the claim, "He is risen from the dead."

We can draw confirming evidence from two additional sources.

First, Easter resulted in a change in the day of worship among the disciples of Jesus. These people were steeped in the strict Jewish heritage of Sabbath (Saturday) worship. Nevertheless, soon after the events of Holy Week the early believers began to gather on the first day of the week — "the Lord's day" — to celebrate the resurrection of Jesus (1 Cor. 16:1-2; Rev. 1:10).

Second, Easter also sparked the phenomenal growth of the infant church. A company of believers sprang forth among pious Jews (Acts 2:41, 47). And in a few years the message about Jesus' resurrection had become a potent force in the entire Roman world (Rom. 10:18; Col. 1:6).

Considerations such as these ought to give us confidence as we, following the early believers, boldly proclaim that God raised Jesus from the dead (Acts 2:32-36; 13:32-39; 17:18; 1 Cor. 15:14-17). Indeed, our Lord's resurrection lies at the heart of Christian faith itself (Rom. 10:9). It stands as the sign of his divine identity (Rom. 1:4), because the Resurrection is God's confirmation of Jesus' understanding of himself and his mission.

Jesus' resurrection is not only crucial to our apologetic, however. It is essential to our experience of Christ as his modern-day disciples. The Resurrection provides the link between our present experience and the historical person Jesus of Nazareth. The Resurrection guarantees that ours is nothing less than the experience of the living Lord. If God did not raise this Jesus from the dead, we could no longer claim to enjoy fellowship with the One whom Jesus called "Father" and whose kingdom he inaugurated.

> ✍ *You can state with confidence, "God raised Jesus from the dead."*

Is Jesus Uniquely Divine?

God confirmed Jesus' claim by raising him from the dead. The Resurrection offers a response to modern skeptics who reject the Christian confession that Jesus is divine. In our day, however,

Jesus' deity is often less problematic than his *unique* deity. In keeping with the pluralistic ethos of contemporary society, people are increasingly open to "gurus" who supposedly put us in touch with the supernatural and mediate experiences of the divine. What is scandalous is any suggestion that Jesus *alone* is Immanuel—"God with us."

Dare we continue to claim a unique status for Jesus in this pluralistic climate? Indeed, we must, once we understand the glorious implications of our confession of Jesus' deity. If Jesus is divine in the sense that believers of all ages claim he is, then he is uniquely divine.

Why is this so?

Jesus is the Revealer of God. First, if Jesus is divine then he is uniquely divine, because he alone reveals God to us (John 14:9-10).

The New Testament writers consistently testify that in Jesus we see God. Throughout his earthly life and ministry he showed us what God is like. His teaching informs us about God; his character shows forth the qualities of God; his death reveals the suffering of God; and his resurrection vividly declares the creative power of God.

At the heart of the picture Jesus presents is a God who is a loving heavenly Father (Luke 15:11-32). Indeed, Jesus understood his mission as the expression of God's self-giving, compassionate love.

Jesus himself was characterized by loving compassion. He saw the aimlessness of the common people who were as "sheep without a shepherd" (Matt. 9:36; Mark 6:34). He was moved by the plight of the sick (Matt. 14:14), the blind (Matt. 20:34), and the hungry (Matt. 15:32; Mark 8:2). Jesus was filled with compassion in response to the sorrow people experienced at the loss of loved ones (Luke 7:13; John 11:35).

Jesus expressed compassion by raising the dead (John 11; Luke 7:14), teaching the multitudes (Mark 6:34), and healing the sick (Matt. 4:23; 9:35; 14:14; 19:2). His godly compassion even encircled his enemies. Anticipating the final rejection he would experience from the nation he loved, Jesus wept over the city of Jerusalem (Matt. 23:37). Then, during his arrest Jesus offered his healing touch to the soldier whose ear had been injured in the scuffle (Luke 22:51). In his hour of death, Jesus prayed that his Father extend forgiving mercy to the Roman soldiers (Luke 23:34).

Jesus not only shows us the loving heart of God, his life indicates that the Triune God is love. We can understand this when we remind ourselves of the special relationship Jesus enjoyed with his Father. Jesus' sense of a special fellowship is most vividly evident in his preferred way of addressing God. He called God "Abba," an endearing name somewhat similar to "Dad."

The one who called God "Abba" is not merely a human. He is the eternal Son. This Jesus is the only begotten, beloved Son of the Father who gives back to the Father the love he receives. The Father himself confirmed this relationship at Jesus' baptism: "This is my Son, whom I love; with him I am well-pleased" (Matt. 3:17).

In his relationship to his Father, therefore, Jesus disclosed the divine love that characterizes the eternal dynamic between the Father and the Son. Just as Jesus loves and is loved by "Abba," so also the Son loves and is loved by the Father eternally. Thereby, Jesus opened a window for us to see the divine reality: God is the eternal community — the eternal love relationship — of the Father and the Son, and this community is the Holy Spirit.

Jesus' disclosure of God does not merely lead to some vague theological talk. On the contrary, the goal of Jesus' revelatory work is to introduce us to God (Matt. 11:27; Luke 10:22). He desires that the divine character become a vital reality within each of us and among us. As Paul declares, Christ — the Revealer of God — must be "formed" in us (Gal. 4:19). This is the work of the Holy Spirit (see chap. 8).

Because Jesus reveals to us the character of the God who is triune and because he forms that character in us through his Spirit, our Lord is uniquely divine.

Jesus is Lord. Second, if Jesus is divine then he is uniquely divine, because this Jesus is Lord.

The New Testament authors repeatedly use the divine title, "Lord," to speak of Jesus. And we confess with the church of all ages, "Jesus is Lord."

Through this confession we affirm a fundamental truth about the relationship between Jesus and creation: Jesus is the Lord of the universe. Consequently, he is the one before whom every person should (and will) bow in homage (Phil. 2:9-11).

"Lord of the cosmos" means that Jesus is also Lord of history. He is the embodiment of the meaning of the entire universe from beginning to end. All creation—and each human life—can find its true meaning and identity only in him and by reference to him. He is not only Lord of the universe, but he is to be Lord of our individual lives as well. The history of all creation and the histories of every person who has ever lived find their true significance only as they are connected with one brief historical life—Jesus of Nazareth.

The affirmation "Jesus is Lord" produces a great fissure that runs through humankind. This confession divides those who acknowledge Jesus' lordship from those who do not. But this confession also unites. As we will note in chapters 9 and 10, it brings together those who acknowledge his lordship into one great fellowship which transcends all human distinctions.

But this affirmation, "Jesus is Lord," is not some grand theological statement that has no bearing on personal living. On the contrary, to declare Jesus' lordship entails acknowledging Jesus as the Lord of our lives. Jesus must reign over every dimension of your existence, including every act and every thought (2 Cor. 10:5). Therefore, confessing with the church the lordship of Jesus obligates you to open yourself to the in-breaking of his lordship into your daily life.

Let's now draw our conclusions. As the revelation of God and the Lord of creation, Jesus is the standard for our understanding of who God is and what God is like. For this reason, we must measure all declarations about the divine reality by Jesus' life and teaching. As the revealer of God and the Lord of life, Jesus is also the mediator of our experience of God. The way to God comes solely through Jesus of Nazareth. Regardless of the sensitivities of the contemporary ethos, we cannot avoid affirming that Jesus is uniquely divine.

> ✍ *You can say*
>
> *with confidence,*
>
> *"Jesus is the unique Son,*
>
> *the Lord of all."*

JESUS IS FULLY HUMAN

The central confession of our faith declares that Jesus is Immanuel, "God with us." In confessing "Jesus is the Christ" we are also declaring another dimension of the reality of Jesus of Nazareth. We are saying that in this historical life we find not only full deity, but also complete humanity. Not only is he fully divine — the embodiment of God — Jesus is also fully human — the embodiment of God's intention for us.

We now explore three aspects of Jesus' humanity, three dimensions involved in the Christian confession, "Jesus is fully human":

☞ *Jesus was truly human.*
☞ *Jesus is the true human.*
☞ *Jesus is the New Human.*

Jesus Was Truly Human

The writer to the Hebrews declares, "Since the children have flesh and blood, he too shared in their humanity" (Heb. 2:14). What does this mean? In what sense did Jesus share humanness with all the children of Adam? To answer this question, we must return to Jesus' earthly life.

Jesus lived under the conditions of human existence. The Gospel writers make plainly evident that Jesus of Nazareth was truly human. That is, he lived under the conditions of earthly existence as we do.

• Living under the conditions of human existence means Jesus experienced the range of needs common to all humans.

Our Lord grew tired and thirsty (John 4:6-7). He desired companionship (Matt. 26:36-38). And he knew the importance of withdrawing from his task of ministering to the throngs of destitute people so that he might be refreshed through solitude and prayer[9] (Mark 1:35).

Jesus likewise underwent trials, faced temptations, and endured the onslaught of Satan (Matt. 4:1-11; 16:22-23; 26:36-39). But in each, he won the victory over his foe (Heb. 4:15).

This conclusion — that Jesus survived temptation unscathed —

leads us to ask the following. Were the temptations he faced real? Could Jesus have sinned? Did Jesus feel the pull of temptation as we do?

Jesus' temptations differed from ours in one important way. James declares concerning us, "But each one is tempted when, by his own evil desire, he is dragged away and enticed" (James 1:14). Because he was born without the fallenness we inherit from Adam, Jesus was not enticed by an inherited internal disposition as we are.[10]

At the same time, however, Jesus experienced genuine temptation. In fact, he bore the full weight of Satan's seductive power to a degree that surpasses our battle against evil.[11]

To understand this, think about your own experience. As Christians, we repeatedly discover that the intensity to which we sense the power of temptation corresponds to the degree to which we are resisting it. In those areas where we are especially vulnerable, we know little of the reality of temptation. We simply yield to the evil impulse without a struggle. In areas where we are growing as believers, however, we have a greater sense of temptation's power. Our knowledge of the difference between yielding without a struggle and resisting with all our might gives us a window into Jesus' battle against the devil.

Jesus knew the full fury of temptation, because he was keenly aware of the alternatives Satan offered to him. He was completely cognizant of what was at stake in the choices placed before him. And he was entirely conscious of the implications of the decisions he needed to make. In this sense, he knew in the most intense manner the human experience of undergoing trial and temptation.

• Living under the conditions of human existence also meant that Jesus was subject to the limitations we all know.

Our Lord was limited in time. His days contained only twenty-four hours. His weeks had only seven days. And his earthly sojourn lasted only thirty-three years.

Jesus was likewise limited in location. He simply could not be everywhere at once.

In addition, our Lord was limited in strength. He could not push himself beyond his capacities. And like all humans, he required the renewal brought through sleep, relaxation, and solitude.

Jesus was even limited in knowledge. He did not know the exact time of the awaited arrival of the Son of Man (Matt. 24:36).

Living under these various limitations carried an important implication for Jesus' life, just as it does for ours. To accomplish his overall mission, Jesus was constrained to make choices and to order his activities. He engaged in choosing from among the many good options that vied for his attention and time. He needed to select from among the alternatives in accordance with how they fit with the priorities of his vocation.

Need we add that Jesus did not emerge from the womb perfectly mature? Indeed, Jesus began as an infant. And during his childhood he grew physically, intellectually, spiritually, and socially (Luke 2:52). Even as an adult, Jesus continued to gain from what he experienced. "Although he was a son, he learned obedience from what he suffered" (Heb. 5:8).

> ✍ *Like Jesus, you must set priorities, choose from among many good causes that vie for your attention, and seek to do what will be most effective for the advancement of God's rule.*

In short, Jesus of Nazareth had no predisposing advantages. He traveled no shortcut to maturity, transcended none of the limiting aspects of embodied existence, was spared no difficulty in living in this fallen world. He was not Superman, an alien housed within a human body but inherently capable of superhuman feats. On the contrary, as the church has confessed throughout the ages, Jesus was fully human.

Jesus' humanness is important. Jesus' life as a human is crucial to his role in the program of God. Unless Jesus was human we are not saved from our sins (Heb. 2:14, 17).

Jesus' experience is also important for our practical, day-to-day living. Jesus can sympathize with us as we struggle with the situations of life in a fallen world. Our "high priest" is able to sympathize with our weaknesses, for he was tempted in every way as we are, yet "without sin" (Heb. 4:15). But his sympathy is not merely a passive emotion. On the contrary, because Jesus overcame Satan's onslaught, he is able to help us when we are tempted (Heb. 2:18).

In short: Jesus knows. Jesus cares. And Jesus provides us with his power—his Spirit.

Jesus Is the True Human

Our declaration "Jesus is fully human" does not merely mean he was one human being among many. Rather, we are affirming as well that Jesus is unique among humans. He is uniquely human, truly human, the true human.

Jesus claimed to be the true human. Our Lord claimed to be the true human. He proclaimed that he had come to show us how to live. He asserted that he, and not the religious leaders of his day, knew the true meaning of the Old Testament Scriptures (Matt. 5:21-48; Mark 12:24), as well as God's intention for humankind (Mark 7:9; Matt. 19:1-9). And he enjoined his hearers to follow him, to be his disciples, to take his "yoke" and to learn from him (Matt. 11:29).

By itself, Jesus' claim would have been audacious. We could view his declaration "I am the way and the truth and the life" (John 14:6) as vain and prideful. In this claim, however, just as his parallel claim to enjoy a special relation to the Father, Jesus invited a confirmation from God.

God's response came in the Resurrection. By raising Jesus from the dead, God declared that this man is indeed the true human he claimed to be.

As God's confirmation of Jesus' entire life, teaching, and death therefore, the Resurrection leads us to view Jesus as the true human. His resurrection sets forth the risen Christ as the ultimate pattern for full humanness as intended by God.

Jesus is our pattern. In confessing "Jesus is the true human" we are acknowledging that he reveals to us humanness as intended by God. In Jesus we find what God desires that we become.

This pattern is revealed in the Resurrection. The risen Lord shows us the transformed humanness we will one day share. In raising him from the dead, God transformed Jesus' earthly, bodily existence into the glorious, incorruptible state to which the early witnesses to the risen Christ gave testimony.

But this transformed humanness is precisely God's design for us: "And just as we have borne the likeness of the earthly man, so shall we bear the likeness. of the man from heaven" (1 Cor. 15:49; cf. 1 John 3:2). Therefore, by looking at the risen Christ we discover that God's purposes stand in stark contrast to our present human experience: God did not create us for estrangement but for fellowship; not for death, but for life; not for bondage, but for freedom.

God's pattern for us is also revealed in Jesus' earthly life. Jesus of Nazareth is the revelation of how we are to live. Our Lord came to teach us the pathway to greatness in God's kingdom. He declared that true greatness does not come through self-centeredness, but through servanthood, suffering, and self-denial (Mark 8:34-38; 10:35-45). And he showed us that even death can be the route to life and blessing for many (John 12:24).

For this reason, Jesus is our example. We ought to model our attitudes and conduct after him. Above all, we ought to be characterized by Christlike humility (Phil. 2:3-8), patient suffering (1 Peter 2:21-23), and love (Eph. 5:2).

Above all, Jesus indicated that the life God intends for us does not focus on the isolated individual saint. Rather, "kingdom living" is life-in-community. We are created for community.

● For Jesus, foundational to life-in-community is life in community with the Father.

The fellowship he shared with God included both communing with God in solitude and humbly acting in perfect obedience to the Father's will, even to the point of death (Phil. 2:8).

● Jesus also lived in community with others.

Our Lord was no self-sufficient recluse. Nor did he embody the Western ideal of "the self-made man." Rather, for him life included both mutuality of friendships and compassionate ministry to the needy. Jesus was both the "man for others" and the one who received the gift of friendship from others. And Jesus showed that community ought to know no boundaries; it reaches beyond friends to encompass the outcast and hurting, even one's enemies.

● For Jesus, life in community included fellowship with nature.

In his teaching Jesus appealed to God's care for plants and animals, for grass and sparrows. His spiritual life led him to embrace the wilderness and enjoy the beauty of creation. And he gave evidence to his identity by calming the sea.

In short, "Jesus is the true human" implies that he is our model. As his disciples, we are to pattern our lives after him. That is, we too are to seek to live according to the design of life-in-community Jesus revealed to us.

> ✍ *Living according to the pattern of Jesus means living in community with God, others, and creation.*

Jesus Is the New Human

Jesus is the true human, for he is our ideal, the model for human life. As the true human, Jesus is also the New Human, the New Adam, the founder of a new humanity, the fountainhead of a new order of human beings. This declaration, however, moves us beyond Jesus' life and resurrection to the reflections of Paul and other early believers.

As the founder of a new humanity, Jesus forms a stark contrast to the first Adam (see Rom. 5:12-21; 1 Cor. 15:21-22, 45-49). Adam brought disobedience, sin, and death to his descendants. Christ, in contrast, mediates obedience, grace, and righteousness leading to life (Rom. 5:19, 21; 1 Cor. 15:22).

In inaugurating a new humanity our Lord has overcome the old human hostilities and divisions (Eph. 2:14-15). Jesus has brought people from every nation into the new company, the church, which is his "body" (Col. 1:18). We participate in this new company as we are drawn together through our union with Christ (Rom. 6:3-5; 2 Cor. 5:17).

Just as the affirmations "Jesus is truly human" and "Jesus is the true human," the confession "Jesus is the New Human" carries practical importance for life in the present. It means that Jesus is "the author and perfecter of our faith" (Heb. 12:2). As our trailblazer, he goes before us and bids us to follow. As our leader, he seeks to bring us to the goal the Father sets before us. He is the fountainhead of our existence; he provides the resources for our lives.

> ✍ *Look to Jesus not only for the pattern for your life, but also for the power for living.*

Therefore, the key to living in the present does not lie with our own abilities. Instead we are dependent on the provision we derive from the risen Lord, the New Human (John 15:1-8). Jesus Christ provides these resources ultimately by sending us his Spirit, as we will view more closely in chapter 8.

We can summarize our discussion of the significance of our confession "Jesus is fully human" with a chart.

JESUS' ROLE	ITS HISTORICAL BASIS	ITS IMPLICATION
Truly human	His earthly life	He can save
The true human	Jesus' resurrection	He is our model
The New Human	Church's reflection	He is our resource

JESUS IS DIVINE AND HUMAN

As Christians we affirm that Jesus of Nazareth is fully divine. And we add that he is also fully human. This leads us to one of the most perplexing questions that theologians tackle. How is this possible? How can deity and humanity be present in one historical life? What do we mean when we affirm that Jesus is both divine and human?

How Can Jesus Be Both Divine and Human?

At first glance, our assertion, "Jesus is both divine and human," appears to be an unsolvable logical puzzle. A person who is simultaneously both divine and human seems to border on self-contradiction. But this has been the teaching of the church throughout the centuries.

To find the solution for this puzzle we need look no further than the New Testament. The early Christians were convinced that Jesus is both fully divine and fully human. And they expressed this conviction through two significant statements about him:

☞ *Jesus is the Word.*
☞ *Jesus is the Son.*

Jesus is the Word. According to the New Testament, Jesus is both divine and human because he is the Word.

John declares that Jesus is the "Word" in the prologue to his Gospel and in the introduction to his first epistle. The term John chooses *(logos;* Word) carries deep significance.[12]

According to the Greek philosophers the entire universe was ordered according to an inner law around which humans ought to orient their lives. They called this principle the "Word."

More important for our understanding of Christ is the Hebrew idea of the "Word of God." The "Word" is what reveals God's own nature. And it embodies the creative power of the God who speaks and it is so, the God who creates the world according to his wisdom (Prov. 8:22-31).

Through this term "Word," John acknowledges Jesus' creative and revealing identity. Jesus is God's creative Word: "Through him all things were made; without him nothing was made that has been made" (John 1:3; cf. v. 10). And Jesus is God's revelatory Word: "The Word became flesh and made his dwelling among us. We have seen his glory, the glory of the One and Only, who came from the Father, full of grace and truth" (John 1:14; cf. Col. 1:15-16).

The declaration, "Jesus is the Word," therefore, asserts that Jesus of Nazareth reveals the meaning of all reality—even the nature of God. That is to say, as this human being Jesus is the divine revelation of God.

Jesus is the Son. The early believers also declared that Jesus is both divine and human by acknowledging him as the Son.

In the Old Testament era, "son" denoted selection to participation in God's work. The "Son of God" was God's special agent, chosen to carry out God's mission in the world. For this reason, Israel as a people was the "son of God." And the title could designate kings or other specific persons to whom God had entrusted a special commission (Ex. 4:22; 2 Sam. 7:14; Isa. 1:2; Hosea 11:1).

The New Testament declares that Jesus is the unique Son.

God commissioned him with a unique mission, and this unique mission links Jesus directly with his Father. Jesus came to reveal God to us and thereby to make God's salvation available. And Jesus fulfilled that unique mission perfectly, for he was obedient to the Father's will to the end.

As the one who completely fulfilled a unique mission, Jesus enjoyed a unique relationship to the Father. He is the unique Son, the "One and Only," the "only begotten" (John 1:14, NASB), the divine Son of the Father. In keeping with this understanding, the author of the epistle to the Hebrews concludes, "The Son is the radiance of God's glory and the exact representation of his being, sustaining all things by his powerful word" (Heb. 1:3). And Paul adds: "For in Christ all the fullness of the Deity lives in bodily form" (Col. 2:9).

Jesus is the Son and the Word. The designations "Son" and "Word" are closely connected. Both point to Jesus' singular identity.

The designations "Word" and "Son" bring together the deity and the humanity of Jesus. As "the radiance of God's glory and the exact representation of his being" and the one through whom God made the universe, the Son is the revelation of the meaning of all reality and of God's essence. As this revelation, he is the powerful "Word of God" who sustains the universe and through whom God has spoken (Heb. 1:3).

As the Son and the Word of God, Jesus participates in the life of the Triune God. He is the Second Person of the Trinity who enjoys eternal fellowship with the Father. At the same time, Jesus shows us that true human life also entails life-in-community. God designed us to enjoy fellowship — community with God, with neighbors far and near, and with all creation. And Jesus inaugurated the new humanity, the company of those who enjoy this fellowship.

> ✍ *Do you want to know what God is like? Look to Jesus, the Son. Do you want to know what it means to be human? Look again to Jesus.*

Therefore, Jesus of Nazareth embodies true deity (what God is like) and complete humanity (what God created us to be). Jesus is indeed Immanuel, God with us.

What Does It Mean to Say That Jesus Is God Incarnate?

In speaking of Jesus' identity John declares, "The Word became flesh and lived among us" (John 1:14, NRSVB). Theologians often speak of the Word becoming flesh as the "Incarnation." Consequently, we affirm that Jesus is the incarnate one; he is the eternal Word or the Son in human form.

But what does this mean? How are we to understand "incarnation"? Some Christians picture the Incarnation as a specific historical event. This event, which perhaps occurred in the womb of Mary, was an act of the Second Person of the Trinity. And it resulted in the union of deity and humanity in the one person, Jesus. Consequently, the personal center of this life was divine, the eternal Son.

This widely held understanding seeks to preserve both the deity and the humanity of Jesus. Unfortunately, however, it runs the risk of degenerating into the myth of Superman. Often we picture Jesus as Clark Kent. Beneath his common human exterior is a regal blue uniform bearing a big "S" on it. So often we suggest that just as Superman could shed his Clark Kent disguise at any time, so also the divine Son could set aside his humanness at will. In the end, Jesus is not really human, we demur, for he is God. We reveal this tendency, for example, when we dismiss the struggles Jesus endured by saying, "Well, after all, he was God, wasn't he?"

Envisioning the Incarnation as the act of the eternal Son also readily leads us into the dangerous trap of thinking of the Word apart from Jesus. Thereby we separate what the New Testament adamantly refuses to divide, namely, the eternal Son and the historical person Jesus of Nazareth. We open the door to speaking about the Christ apart from Jesus. And we pave the way for seeing the Christ at work through other religious teachers in addition to Jesus.

The New Testament writers, in contrast, never present the Incarnation as the act of the Word at a specific point in history. For example, in his great hymn extolling the self-abasing Christ (Phil. 2:6-11), Paul carefully keeps his attention focused on the historical person of Jesus. The one who refused to clutch his divine prerogatives but was God's humble, obedient servant even to the point of death, he declares, was "Christ Jesus." Consequently, Paul does not draw the confession "Jesus is Lord" from any story of a descent of the eternal Son into our world at a specific point in time. Rather, the entire life of our Master, and especially his obedient death, provides the basis for God's exaltation of Jesus as the name above every name.

John is equally careful in speaking about the Word becoming flesh. The Evangelist avoids suggesting that the Incarnation came as an act of the eternal Word taking to himself human nature in the womb of Mary. In fact, John never pinpoints an exact historical moment (such as Jesus' conception) at which time the Incarnation occurred. Nor does he cite the virgin birth as the vehicle that facilitated the beginning of the incarnate state.

Rather than focusing on Jesus' miraculous birth, John appeals to eyewitnesses who observed our Lord's earthly life. Based on these observations, he testifies to the Incarnation: "The Word became flesh and made his dwelling among us. We have seen his glory, the glory of the One and Only, who came from the Father, full of grace and truth" (John 1:14). In Jesus, the early witnesses saw the divine glory, a glory Jesus evidenced throughout his earthly life.

Following John, then, "the Word became flesh" (the Incarnation) does not focus on *how* Jesus came into existence. Instead, it is our way of declaring the significance of the Master's earthly life: as this human being, Jesus is divine; he is God's revelation. He is the "Word" — the dynamic, revelatory word of God — in human form. In this one historical, personal life we find revealed who God is — true deity — and who we are to be — true humanity. In Jesus the Word has indeed come in the flesh.

In short, we do not celebrate the Incarnation merely at Christmas, but throughout the church year climaxing at Easter.

In What Sense Is Jesus Preexistent?

Our declarations, "Jesus is the Word" and "Jesus is the Son" lead us to yet another important consideration, namely, Jesus' preexistence.

John opens his Gospel with the bold declaration, "In the beginning was the Word . . . He was with God in the beginning" (John

1:1-2). Now if Jesus is the Word, there must be a sense in which he is eternal and hence a way in which his life overflows his earthly sojourn. In short, he must be *preexistent.*

But what does preexistence mean? Our understanding of pre-existence often arises from viewing the Incarnation as a point in time. Indeed, if we understand the Incarnation as an act that occurred at a specific moment in history (somewhere around 4–6 B.C.), our inquisitive minds naturally ask, what was the Word doing before the Incarnation?[13] And in response, we offer many fanciful conjectures about the one who would be born in Bethlehem flinging the stars into space.[14]

As with the idea of Incarnation, we must avoid the tendency to link preexistence solely with the Word and to separate it from Jesus of Nazareth. We ought not to conceive of preexistence as giving license for speculating about the activity of the Word prior to Jesus' birth. In the contemporary context of religious pluralism, such speculation leaves us vulnerable to the suggestion that the divine Word has been or is operative in other historical figures and religious leaders as well.

Whatever it may mean, "preexistence" describes Jesus of Nazareth. We confess the preexistence of *Jesus* and not that of some purported eternal being whom we can view apart from this historical human life. "Preexistence" is a declaration about the identity of Jesus of Nazareth.

But in what sense can we predicate preexistence to a historical person? At its heart, the doctrine of preexistence speaks about the uniqueness and finality of Jesus.

> ✍ To speak about Jesus' preexistence means that Jesus belongs to God's eternity.

Contrary to the opinion of many, Jesus' brief historical life is more than a blip in time. Instead he discloses the very heart of eternity. That seemingly short earthly life is nothing less than the revelation of God. As Paul writes, "God was pleased to have all his fullness dwell in him" (Col. 1:19).

By confessing Jesus' preexistence we affirm the uniqueness and finality of his earthly life. Jesus is the embodiment of truth. His teachings are true teachings, revealing the eternal truth of God. And his life shows us the true human living as God intends us to live. As a result, Jesus is the standard for measuring all religious truth and all human conduct. All other truth claims and all admonitions about the good life must be weighed by this one historical person.

• To speak about Jesus' preexistence declares that the historical life of Jesus carries significance beyond the boundaries of his brief earthly sojourn.

Jesus' life gives meaning to all history, because it embodies the meaning of all history. It clarifies events of the Old Testament, which point to him. And it is the foundation for events of the New Testament era, that is, the time between his advent and his second coming.

> ✍ Weigh all truth claims and religious teachings by the revelation of God in Jesus of Nazareth.

• To speak about Jesus' preexistence is to declare that his life is the story of history itself.

Jesus' story includes more than the thirty-three years of his earthly sojourn. All of history from beginning to end is his story, the story of the one Jesus Christ.

This is what the great confessions of the church about Jesus intend to encapsule for us.

☞ *Jesus is fully God. He has shown us the very heart of the divine life.*

☞ *Jesus is fully human. He lived a truly human existence. He lived the exemplary human existence. He inaugurated a new humanity.*

☞ *Jesus is both divine and human. He is the embodiment of the Word and the eternal Son.*

This glorious person — our Lord Jesus Christ — is Immanuel, God with us. As Immanuel, he came to bring God's salvation to sinful humankind. Therefore, we must now turn to the saving work of the one whose identity we have clarified.

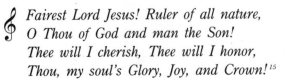

> *Fairest Lord Jesus! Ruler of all nature,*
> *O Thou of God and man the Son!*
> *Thee will I cherish, Thee will I honor,*
> *Thou, my soul's Glory, Joy, and Crown![15]*

FOR CONNECTION AND APPLICATION

1   What would be different about the Christian faith if Jesus had never been resurrected?

2   Why is our claim that Jesus is uniquely divine so "politically incorrect" today? Should we acquiesce to the contemporary mood and declare that Jesus is Lord only for Christians? What difference would this make?

3   What do we know about God because of Jesus Christ that we might not know otherwise?

4   What do we know about ourselves because of Jesus Christ that we might not know otherwise?

5   Why is it important that Jesus is not only our pattern for living but also the provider of power for living?

6   Why do many Christians prefer to see Jesus as a "Superman" who merely indwelt a human body, rather than one who was truly human?

SIX

Jesus' Mission in the Divine Program

*"For this reason I was born,
and for this I came into the world"*
(John 18:37).

Once again Charlie Brown, struggling with a bout of insomnia, was musing in bed. "Sometimes I lie awake at night," he said to no one in particular, "and I ask, 'Why am I here?' " Rolling over on his back to stare unconsciously at the ceiling, the melancholy boy added, "Then a voice answers, 'Why? Where do you want to be?' "

Why are *you* here? Where do *you* want to be in life? What are *you* seeking to accomplish? We are constantly confronted with crucial questions about our vocation and calling.

Jesus faced questions such as these as well. In fact, Satan's temptations focused on matters related to his personal identity, vocation, and calling in life. Yet throughout his ministry, our Lord revealed a profound sense of mission. He knew that his Father had entrusted him with a goal to reach, a task to accomplish. In short, he was a man with a vocation.

What did Jesus come to do? What was his calling? Throughout its history the church has spoken about these matters.

In chapter 5 we said that Jesus is our example and our resource. He came to show us how to live and to provide us with his Spirit so that we might live as we ought. Now we build on these insights.

Our chief concern in this chapter is to speak about Jesus as God's antidote for our sinful situation. We now seek to answer questions such as: In what sense did Jesus' life and death alter our relationship to God? How is it possible that the mission of a man who lived 2,000 years ago affects us today?

THE VOCATION OF JESUS OF NAZARETH

What did Jesus come to accomplish? This is no new question. During Jesus' lifetime our Lord's sense of mission challenged the greatest religious teachers of Palestine. And after his resurrection, Jesus' faithful followers diligently sought to understand the implications of what they had experienced of "the Word of life" (1 John 1:1-4).

The early Christians believed that Jesus played a unique role in God's program. He had received a special calling, a vocation from God. And he was totally obedient to that calling.

What was this vocation which Jesus' heavenly Father delegated to him? Our Lord's vocation dominates the pages of the New Testament. The apostolic writers consistently assert — in keeping with Jesus' own declarations — that our Lord came in accordance with the Old Testament. He is God's gracious fulfillment of the promises God had given to Israel through the Old Testament prophets. Hence, Jesus is God's response to the expectations and hopes of generations of righteous Hebrews from Abraham to Simeon and Anna. For this reason we rightly sing at Christmas: "The hopes and fears of all the years are met in thee tonight."[1]

Specifically, Jesus came as:

☞ *Israel's true Messiah,*
☞ *the Son of Man who proclaims God's reign,*
☞ *the Suffering Servant who dies in obedience to his Father's will.*

More important than any one of these separate roles, however, Jesus wove these diverse expectations into a profound unity of purpose. And this unity became the driving vision behind his sense of vocation.

Jesus: The Fulfillment of the Old Testament Hopes

Following the example of the New Testament writers, we read the life of Jesus in the context of the Old Testament. We claim that Jesus fulfilled the hopes and expectations embedded in the Hebrew Scriptures. Let us look at three of these:

☞ *Messiah,*

☞ *Son of Man,*

☞ *Suffering Servant.*

Jesus is the Messiah. First, we acknowledge that Jesus is the Messiah of God—"the anointed one."

Jesus' messiahship—that he is the Christ—has been central to the proclamation of the church throughout its history. In this confession we are merely echoing the early believers, who routinely spoke of Jesus as the Christ (i.e., the "anointed one" or "messiah"). In fact, this title ("Christ") became so common that it soon fused with his earthly name. "Jesus the Christ" was shortened to "Jesus Christ."

During his earthly sojourn, however, Jesus was reticent to use this title to characterize his mission. Only after the Resurrection does our Lord speak of himself as Messiah (Luke 24:26, 46).

Why? Jesus was reluctant to be connected with the title "Messiah" because he rejected the widely held anticipations surrounding Messiah's coming. Our Lord did not come to fulfill the misguided expectations of the people of his day. Instead, he desired to clarify what the Messiah would do. God's true Messiah does not come as a military hero. His goal is not to overthrow the Romans. Rather, when the Messiah comes, he will save his people—and indeed the whole world—from their *sins* (Matt. 1:21).

As the angel who announced his birth predicted, Jesus did not come as a military conqueror. He came instead as the Savior Messiah who would provide true liberation and eternal peace for sinful humankind.

Jesus is Son of Man. Our Lord also came as the Son of Man. Jesus used the designation, "the Son of Man," in several ways.[2] Most importantly, however, by speaking in this manner our Lord linked himself with a figure in one of Daniel's visions. The Old Testament saint reported seeing someone "like a son of man, coming with the clouds of heaven." This son of man came into the presence of the Ancient of Days and "was given authority, glory and sovereign power," so that "all peoples, nations and men of every language worshiped him" (Dan. 7:13-14).

On the basis of this vision, the Jews believed that the divine Son of Man would come at the end of time as the judge of humankind. He would then elevate Israel to prominence in the world.

Like Daniel, Jesus pierced the veil of our world. He spoke about the hidden realm where the Son of Man is seated "at the right hand of the Power and coming in the clouds of heaven" (Mark 14:62, NRSVB). Jesus announced a day when this Son of Man would return to judge the nations and inaugurate God's reign (Matt. 25:31-46). And he promised his disciples that they would participate in that glorious reign (Matt. 16:27-28; 19:28), for at his coming the Son of Man will acknowledge those who confess his name (Mark 8:38; Luke 9:26; 12:8).

Jesus did not merely *point to* the Son of Man, however. He declared that he *is* this Son of Man.[3]

Jesus is the Suffering Servant. Finally, our Lord came as the one sent to die.

The likelihood that he would die at the hands of his opponents came as no surprise to Jesus. As his conflict with the Jewish leaders intensified, our Lord became increasingly vocal in declaring what would mark its climax (Mark 12:1-8). Just as the prophets had suffered at the hands of God's enemies, so Jesus' opponents would put him to death. And as a prophet, he would die in Jerusalem (Luke 13:33).

Yet Jesus' attitude was not mere passive acquiescence to the inevitable. Instead, our Lord saw this event as the climax of his mission. He had come to die, and therefore he would willingly give his life (John 10:11, 18). Jesus sensed that his dying marked the highest obedience to the will of his Father (John 12:28).

For this insight that obedience to God meant suffering and death, our Lord would need to look no farther than to a specific prophecy which he undoubtedly knew well. His special mission in the program of God meant that he was to fulfill a role the prophet Isaiah had described in detail centuries earlier. He would be God's Suffering Servant (Isa. 42:1-4; 49:1-6; 50:4-11; 52:13–53:12).[4] He would glorify God by humbly obeying the Father's will, even to the point of suffering and death.

With Isaiah's prophecy in mind, Jesus willingly became his Father's obedient servant, eventually laying down his life on the cross. Thereby, he modeled his own teaching about the pathway to life. Losing our life is the means to finding life. And he commanded his disciples to follow his example (John 13:12-15).

But Jesus' obedience to the point of death does more than show us the way to true living. It makes *available* to us the divine power necessary to live in obedience to God.

Jesus drew a principle from nature to illustrate the life-giving provision of his death: "I tell you the truth, unless a kernel of wheat falls to the ground and dies, it remains only a single seed. But if it dies, it produces many seeds" (John 12:24). The meaning is clear. Jesus must give his life, in order that new life can spring forth for his followers.

During his final supper with his disciples, Jesus again illustrated the point. He offered them bread and wine. The bread symbolized his life, which he would soon give in death for them. The wine represented the New Covenant which would soon be ratified through his sacrifice on their behalf. Through his self-giving act, his disciples would be able to participate with him in God's coming reign.

Indeed, Jesus came as the Suffering Servant.

Jesus' Vision of His Mission

The church confesses that Jesus is Messiah, Son of Man, and Suffering Servant. Taken individually, however, none of these gets at the heart of Jesus' understanding of his vocation. He did not simply *choose among* the roles delineated in the Hebrew Scriptures. Rather, Jesus *drew together* these three aspects of the Old Testament expectation into a unified vision of his task.

Jesus' genius lay in his unparalleled insight that the three great expectations — the longing for a kingly Messiah who would save Israel, the anticipation of the Son of Man who would be the righteous Judge, and Isaiah's prophecy of a Suffering Servant — were to be realized in one person. And he was that person!

This vision motivated Jesus' earthly ministry, which was characterized above all by servanthood. The Master understood his task as that of suffering in obedience to his Father and on behalf of the people. He knew that he must experience rejection, even death, in fulfillment of his vocation. Only then would the promised glory follow. In short, Jesus knew that the pathway to fulfilling the task of Messiah and Son of Man required that he travel the footsteps of the Suffering Servant (Luke 24:26).

Consequently, it is as the Suffering Servant that Jesus is also the Son of Man and the Messiah.

We noted in chapter 5 that Jesus is the true human, the revelation of God's design for human living. In his vocation as the Suffering Servant Jesus shows us what that design is. Because he is the revelation of God's purpose for human life, Jesus is the righteous Judge and the standard against whom we are measured. Like him, we should live as obedient servants of our heavenly Father and minister— even suffer—for the sake of others.

> ✍ *Following Jesus means living as obedient servants of his heavenly Father and ministering—even suffering—for the sake of others.*

Similarly, he is our Messiah. Through his suffering he liberates us so that we can live in conformity with his own perfect life.

But how does his obedience to the Father's will give us life? This question takes us to what Christians have traditionally considered to be the center of Jesus' work—his death.

JESUS' DEATH ON OUR BEHALF

Jesus' entire life was molded by his profound awareness that God had sent him to die for the salvation of others. Our Lord's own teaching, therefore, led the early Christians to proclaim that Jesus is the atonement for human sin.

This is the central declaration of our faith: "Jesus died for us." But how are we to understand it? What is the significance of our Lord's death? And how does Jesus' sacrifice affect us?

Ultimately, we cannot understand the full meaning of the cross of Christ. We can only stand in silence before it, acknowledge its wonder, and submit to its power. Nevertheless, we desire to understand the depth of Christ's work on our behalf and to speak about the salvation we have experienced.

Explanations of Jesus' Death

Christians throughout the centuries have joyously accepted the New Testament message of God's provision in Christ. Christian thinkers have sought to understand this message by bringing together the various themes of that New Testament message into a single "theory" of the Atonement. Their goal has been to assist God's people in grasping the significance of Jesus' work and then in articulating the gospel of available salvation to others.

Three basic proposals have been most prominent in the church.[5] Each of them focuses on a different aspect of what Jesus has done on our behalf.

☞ *Jesus' death won the victory over evil (the dynamic view).*

☞ *Jesus' death altered God's disposition toward us (the objective view).*

☞ *Jesus' death wins our allegiance (the subjective view).*

Jesus and evil: The dynamic image. Some Christians understand Jesus' work primarily as a new power, a new "dynamic" released in the cosmos. Specifically, Jesus won the victory over the "principalities and powers" that enslave humankind.

At first, the cross appeared to be Satan's great triumph, the victory of evil and death. But viewed from the vantage point of the Resurrection, Jesus' death actually marked the defeat of all the evil powers that reign over humankind (Col. 2:15). Jesus has rescued, or ransomed, us from the prison of death and sin.

The use of dynamic imagery to explain Jesus' work dates at least to the church father Irenaeus (140–202). In fact, Irenaeus is often cited as the first proponent of what is called the "ransom theory."[6]

Humankind was in bondage through sin to the devil, Irenaeus theorized. Our bondage required that we be bought back by a ransom to which the devil would also consent. Jesus gave himself as this ransom. In so doing, he freed us from our captivity to Satan.

Irenaeus probably never intended that we understand this image literally. He did not believe that the cross involved an actual, historical transaction between God and Satan. Instead, Irenaeus was merely offering a way of picturing the meaning of Christ's victory.[7]

Other thinkers, however, were not as careful as Irenaeus. They began to speculate about the details of this glorious transaction. Some even suggested that God used trickery in gaining our release.

For example, one church father theorized that the devil was jealous over human happiness and therefore seduced Adam into sin. The power Satan exercised over his victim, however, fed his pride. Consequently, when Satan saw the goodness of Jesus, the devil wanted to destroy him. But the devil failed to see the deity that was veiled in the human Jesus. Satan, therefore, swallowed the "hook" (the Godhead) with the "bait" (Jesus' humanity).[8]

At first glance we might find the ransom theory objectionable at this point, for it seems to cast God in a bad light. This picture of the Atonement suggests that by hiding deity within humanity, God played a trick on the devil. And how could God do such a thing?

To objections such as this, some early proponents responded by claiming that God's trickery was actually intended for Satan's own good. God is like a physician who engages in a "beneficent deception," like a doctor who prescribes a placebo rather than real "medicine" to "trick" a patient into overcoming a psychosomatic illness.

With the possible exception of the Eastern Orthodox Church, contemporary believers do not generally think of the cross as Jesus' victory over Satan.[9] Yet the ransom theme emerges repeatedly in our hymnology.

There's a sweet and blessed story
Of the Christ who came from glory,
Just to rescue me from sin and misery;
He in loving kindness sought me,
And from sin and shame hath bro't me,
Hallelujah! Jesus ransomed me.[10]

And we acknowledge the victorious aspect of the cross, when we heartily sing:

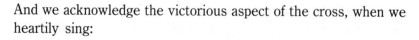
O victory in Jesus, My Savior forever,
He sought me and bought me With his redeeming blood;
He loved me ere I knew Him and all my love is due Him,
He plunged me to victory, Beneath the cleansing flood.[11]

Jesus and God: The objective image. Irenaeus' ransom theory was the reigning conception of the Atonement for the first several centuries of church history. Although it remains important among the Eastern Orthodox Church, contemporary Western Christians have been more deeply influenced by a theologian who lived nearly a millennium later. The foundation for this understanding lies in a little book, *Why God Became Man (Cur Deus Homo?)*, written by Anselm, Archbishop of Canterbury (1093–1109).

Anselm rejected the ransom theory because he believed it did not fit the feudal society which had developed in Western Europe since the days of Irenaeus.[12] According to feudal law, people in any domain must serve the sovereign over the region, even if that person had usurped the position of the rightful ruler.

The legend of Robin Hood reminds us of the situation in feudal England. While King Richard was involved in the Crusades, Prince John usurped authority in the land. To the Sheriff of Nottingham, John assigned the uncomfortable task of capturing Robin Hood whom he wanted killed as a common outlaw. Because John was the *de facto* ruler of England, the sheriff and his poor soldiers had little recourse but to serve the wicked prince in his diabolical scheme. Only when Richard returned home and reasserted his sovereignty could the hero of the story be exonerated as a loyal subject of the rightful sovereign.

In a similar way, Anselm saw in the ransom theory a debilitating fallacy. It excused humans who serve Satan. Read from the perspective of feudal society, the biblical story suggests that the devil is the *de facto* monarch over the earth. According to feudal law, as *de facto* sovereign Satan exercises legal right over humans. And we, in turn, have legitimate cause for serving him until God reasserts his sovereignty.

Anselm wanted to protect the biblical teaching that all creatures (including even the devil himself) have only one rightful allegiance — to God. To this end, Anselm envisioned our seduction by Satan as that of a mutinous slave persuading others to join in a rebellion. Consequently, Jesus' death cannot be directed to the devil, as the ransom theory suggested.

Rather than a payment to Satan, Anselm declared that the cross was directed toward God the Father. Jesus' death is an event in the history of God's dealings with *humankind*, not God's relationship with Satan.

Anselm declared that the cross effected a change in our status before God. Thus, he offered what we might call an "objective theory" of the atonement. Christ's death is an event in history which inaugurated a new historical reality.

To explain the workings of the cross, the archbishop proposed what is known as the "satisfaction theory." He based his theory on the customs of feudal society.

We are God's vassals, Anselm declared. As his vassals we are obligated to give God the honor due him as our Sovereign. But rather than doing so, we have become rebellious vassals. We refuse to acknowledge God as our King, and thereby we deny God the honor that is rightfully his.

According to Anselm, our refusal to honor our Sovereign is an outrage which demands recompense to God's honor. But we are helpless to provide the required satisfaction. We cannot recompense God's violated honor merely by pledging absolute obedience in the future. Ongoing obedience is what we rightfully owe our Sovereign.

In short, we are unable to settle our account with God by our own efforts. Satisfaction can only come through Someone who is both human and divine. He must be human, in order to recompense God for the honor we owe. But Jesus must also be divine, in order to live completely without sin. This, Anselm concluded, is the reason why "God became man."

But why did Jesus need to *die?*

According to Anselm, the satisfaction our Savior rendered could not consist in his holy life. Perfect obedience to God was also Jesus' duty as a human being. Satisfaction came through the voluntary death of the sinless one. Because Jesus' death was more than what living as God's vassal required of him, this act brought infinite honor to God. Because Jesus' death is a meritorious act, it provides forgiveness for our sin.

Anselm's theory underwent an innovative alteration during the Reformation. John Calvin, the Genevan reformer, argued that Christ did not satisfy God's *honor*, as in Anselm's view. Instead it satisfied God's *wrath* with its sentence against sin.[13]

Calvin likened our situation to a human law court. Just as a human judge must condemn a convicted felon, so also God must condemn us for our sin. Out of love, however, God sent Christ to turn aside the punishment which the Judge of the world must require of all lawbreakers. Because of its connection to human law courts, this view is known as the "penal-substitution theory."

The penal-substitution theory became the standard view among Protestants until well into the nineteenth century.[14] We use it today whenever we speak about Jesus "taking our punishment."[15] Consider a story that Christian evangelists often tell.

A young man became the proud owner of a new sports car. In his exuberance he took it out on the freeway to see how fast it could travel. Unfortunately for him he was picked up for speeding—100 miles per hour in a 55 zone. Now in the traffic court, the young man states his plea, "Guilty, your honor." He then hears the judge's sentence, "The fine required by law is $200." But the young man's wallet is empty—he faces a stiff jail term if he cannot come up with the money.

Then something marvelous happens. The judge takes off his legal robe, descends from the bench, pulls out his wallet, and places two $100 bills on the counter. The judge himself has paid the fine, and the guilty young man has been spared incarceration. But why would the judge do such a thing? The judge is none other than the young man's loving father!

This, the evangelist reminds the hearer, is what Christ has done for us. We have violated God's laws, but Jesus paid the "fine" that divine justice demands from us.

Why did the penal-substitution theory, with its focus on satisfying God's just wrath, replace Anselm's idea of payment to God's honor? The answer may lie in social changes that were occurring in Europe.

At this point in Western history, the old feudal order was giving way to the new system of national governments. The honor of the ruler was no longer the foundation for social order. The new societies that were emerging built upon the idea of civil government as lawgiver and upholder of the law. Civic duty, in turn, now meant obedience to the law of the land.

As in every era, Christians were concerned to articulate the drama of sin and salvation in this new context. To meet this challenge, Christian thinkers sought to understand the New Testament teaching about Christ's death in a way that could speak to the emerging social order. In the process they were drawn to the biblical emphasis on Jesus' willingness to suffer the punishment due us for our transgression of the divine law.

Jesus wins our allegiance: The subjective image. But what kind of a God could be pleased by the blood of an innocent person? Or what concept of justice allows an innocent person to suffer for the guilty?

Anselm's younger colleague, Abelard (1079–1142), raised the first question immediately after the archbishop proposed his satisfaction theory.[16] And since the Reformation, critics have appealed to the second query in responding to the penal-substitution theory.

Abelard believed that the idea of satisfaction harbors a false view of God. He concluded that Jesus' death cannot satisfy God's honor, because only a cruel and barbaric God would delight in the death of his sinless Son.[17]

What, then, is the significance of Jesus' selfless act? Abelard offered an alternate answer. Rather than placating *God,* Jesus' death is directed toward *us.* The goal of the cross is not to effect some great transaction in God, but to woo our hearts.

But how does God accomplish this? Abelard declared that Jesus' death is the grand exhibition of God's great love for humankind. When we see the cross, this display of divine love frees us from our fear of God's wrath and kindles in us a desire to love God.[18] This desire fulfills all that God demands and allows God to forgive our sin.

In this manner, Abelard replaced Anselm's objective understanding of Christ's death with a *subjective* approach. Through Jesus' death the loving Father seeks to draw sinful humans to himself. From the twelfth century to the present, Christians who have been repulsed by the idea of God who welcomes the suffering of the innocent Jesus have generally gravitated to variations on Abelard's "moral influence" alternative.

Despite its shortcomings, the penal-substitution theory remains the dominant explanation among believers. Yet our hymns tend to focus on the subjective dimension of Jesus' death. We rightly sing of how our Savior's death has won our hearts—how we love Him because on the cross He demonstrated His love for us.

When I survey the wondrous cross
On which the Prince of Glory died,
My richest gain I count but loss,
And pour contempt on all my pride. . . .
Love so amazing, so divine,
Demands my soul, my life, my all.[19]

Let us now summarize the most important theories of Christ's atoning work on our behalf.

THEORY	MAJOR THEME	PROPONENT
Ransom	Christ won the victory over evil	Irenaeus
Satisfaction	Christ recompenses God's honor	Anselm
Penal-substitution	Christ bore our punishment	Calvin
Moral influence	Christ displays God's love	Abelard

Jesus' Death and Us

We have reviewed how Christian thinkers have sought to assist the proclamation of the Gospel by bringing the themes of the New Testament into a unified understanding. Our survey indicates that Christians have viewed Christ's death from several angles. This observation is instructive, for it reminds us that no single understanding is the sole correct view. On the contrary, just as our human predicament has many sides, so also Jesus' death is God's multifaceted provision for human sin and failure.

Now we must return to our central question. In what sense is Jesus God's provision for the crucial needs of humanity bound in sin? How may we today view Jesus' death?

Jesus' death and our predicament. We begin by reminding ourselves that God sent Jesus to be the divine answer to our human need. Our discussion of sin in chapter 4 led us to see several central facets of the awful reality of our human fallenness. The Bible indicates that sin leaves us alienated, condemned, enslaved, and depraved.

As Christians we proclaim that Christ is God's provision for our fallen condition. As God's provision, Christ overcomes sin in its many aspects.

Let's now draw the biblical images together by filling in the middle column on the chart we introduced in chapter 4. So doing will illustrate how Jesus is God's complete provision for human sin.

HUMAN CONDITION	CHRIST'S PROVISION	SPIRIT'S APPLICATION
Alienation	**Reconciliation**	
Condemnation	**Expiation**	
Enslavement	**Redemption**	
Depravity	**Substitution**	

• Christ is God's provision for severed interpersonal relationships.

In chapter 4 we explored how sin leaves us hostile toward God. We have become God's enemies, but Jesus entered this situation to become our reconciliation (Rom. 5:10-11).

Through Jesus, we now enjoy a new relationship with God. Because of Christ, we who were God's enemies now can experience fellowship with the Father. Our Lord replaces our enmity toward God with peace (Rom. 5:1). We must keep in mind, however, that it is the Father himself who effects this restored relationship through Jesus' death. We must avoid any suggestion of a split within God—a gulf between the wrathful Father and the placating Son. On the contrary, the Father sent Jesus to be the means to reconcile us to himself. *God* was reconciling the world to himself in Christ (2 Cor. 5:18).

Jesus' reconciling work extends to human relationships as well. On the cross, he destroyed the barriers dividing human beings (Eph. 2:11-22). As a result, we can enjoy fellowship with others through our common loyalty to Jesus our Lord.

Christ's reconciling work even has cosmic implications. Because of Jesus' death, the structures of existence (mentioned in chap. 3) once again find their center in the Lord, so that their hostility toward us can give way to harmony (Col. 1:19-20). The biblical writers also envision the reconciliation of humankind with the entire creation. Because of Christ's work, one day the animals will live in harmony with each other (Isa. 65:25), and the leaves of the trees will bring healing to the nations (Rev. 22:2).

• We may also view Christ's death from the legal perspective.

In chapter 4 we spoke of how we have offended God's justice by our actions. We stand condemned before a righteous and holy God. But Christ's death turns aside God's righteous disposition against us.

This idea is closely connected to the old Hebrew sacrificial system described in the Old Testament. Each year on the Day of Atonement, the high priest entered the inner sanctum of the tabernacle or temple to offer the appropriate sacrifice for the sins of the people. This occurred at what was called the "mercy seat" (Heb. 9:5, NASB). There the blood of the animal who had been sacrificed would drip down on the floor below, symbolically covering the sins of Israel.

The author of Hebrews compares Christ's work with that of the Old Testament high priest. Jesus came in order that "he might make atonement for the sins of the people" (Heb. 2:17). Christ is the High Priest who offers an atoning sacrifice for us.

But our Lord introduces one important alteration. He is that sacrifice. The cross replaces the mercy seat. Like the blood of slain animal sacrifices, Jesus' blood shed on the cross covers our sin. Hence, Christ provides an "expiation" for us.

Yet, the question remains: How does this sacrifice effect our salvation? Paul responds by explaining that Jesus' death vindicates God's righteousness (Rom. 1:17; 3:21-26). *God* sent Christ to be the atoning sacrifice for the sins of the world (1 John 2:2; 4:10). Because Jesus' blood "blots out" our sins, his sacrifice turns aside God's anger—his set disposition toward sin—from us. God can now forgive our sins and declare us righteous. God can bring into his presence all who express faith in Jesus (Rom. 3:26). God sent Jesus to die as an atoning sacrifice. Jesus' blood covers our sin, so that God's righteous verdict of condemnation need no longer fall on us.

• There is also a cosmic dimension to Jesus' work. Our Lord died as our redemption or ransom (Eph. 1:7; Heb. 9:12; 1 Tim. 2:6).

The idea of "redemption" was understandable in the first-century world. Residents of the Roman Empire knew that when the Roman armies conquered new territories they would bring back the best and brightest of the subjugated peoples to be sold at auction as slaves. But they also knew that occasionally temple priests would outbid other merchants and then set free those whom they purchased. Through this act they "redeemed" or provided a "ransom" for the formerly enslaved persons. And as a response, the freed slaves would often serve in the temple the rest of their lives.

This is what Jesus has done for us. But what—or who—is involved in this transaction?

Jesus' death redeems us *from* something. He rescues us from our sinful living—from our "wickedness" (Titus 2:14) and the "empty way of life" handed down to us from our ancestors (1 Peter 1:18). More significantly, the cross likewise marks Jesus' victory over the principalities and powers which hold us in bondage (e.g., Col. 2:15), including the law (Gal. 3:13). But above all, he has rescued us from the sinister power of death with its connection to sin (Rom. 8:2) and from the devil, who holds the power of death (Heb. 2:14).

How is this so? As we noted in chapter 4, our offensive conduct emanates from the core of our being, because an alien power dominates our lives. Jesus' death won the victory over this alien slave master. Whether we see ourselves under slavery to the principalities and powers, to sin, to the devil, or to death, Jesus died to purchase our redemption. Because he has died, we need no longer serve any hostile power that seeks to entrap us and destroy our lives.

At the same time, Jesus' death also redeems us *for* something. Through this act, he has purchased for God a people from every nation (Rev. 5:9). As those who know Christ's costly redemption, we gladly serve in the courts of his Father.

• Jesus is God's provision for human depravity.

As we noted in our discussion of sin, we are destitute, hopelessly unable to remedy our situation or to please God. But Christ came as our substitute. In his death Jesus has accomplished for us what we are helpless to do for ourselves. He died *for us* (2 Cor. 5:21; Gal. 1:4; Eph. 5:2; Heb. 9:28).

But in what sense is this so? To understand this, we must differentiate between two important dimensions of his act. Jesus died as the substitute for our sins. And our Lord died our death.

The New Testament teaches that Jesus is the vicarious sacrifice for our sins. As we noted above, the Savior bore our iniquities — became our substitute — so that the dire effects of sin need no longer come upon us.

This act does not mean that all negative results of human failure are suddenly rendered inoperative. Indeed, each of us, we together, and even creation itself continue to suffer many of the consequences of our personal and corporate iniquity. Christ's death does not necessarily negate these. It means, rather, that we need no longer bear the *ultimate* consequences of sin.

And what are these ultimate consequences? The Bible links sin with death. Indeed, sin's awful, abiding product is death (Rom. 6:23). The good news of our faith is that Jesus tasted death for us. But in what sense? Does Jesus' death on our behalf mean that we no longer need to *die?*

Above all, Jesus' death means that we need not undergo eternal separation from God. On the cross he was forsaken by God; he bore "Godforsakenness" on our behalf so that we might enjoy eternal fellowship with God.[20]

Does this also mean we need not experience physical death? No and Yes.

No: Our Savior's death does not mean that we will never know death as a physical reality. Christians do die.

Yes: Nevertheless, even here he remains our substitute. He went through death on our behalf, in order to transform the experience for us. We may die. But because Christ has died for us, even this evil foe cannot "separate us from the love of God that is in Christ Jesus our Lord" (Rom. 8:39).

We die. But the death we die is now different. We do not suffer the hopeless death of those who have not met God through Christ. Rather, we die as those who are always surrounded by the love of the Father of our Lord Jesus Christ. Knowing that we die into God's love means that death has lost its terror.

Jesus' death and divine community. Viewing Jesus' death as God's provision for our human predicament reminds us that our Lord died in order to bring about God's purpose for creation. Indeed, the Bible declares that God's ultimate goal does not end with providing for human sin and failure. God wants to save us *from* sin so that he can bring creation *to* a higher purpose. God wants us to participate in an eternal community. God's desire is to create a redeemed humankind, dwelling within a redeemed creation, and enjoying the presence of the Triune God.

> ✍ *You can face life — and death — knowing that nothing can separate you from the love of God in Christ.*

Through his death, Jesus fulfills the central role in God's overarching program for creation. We will now look more closely at this role.

We noted earlier that Jesus embodied the divine principle of life. God created us to live in obedience to the Creator and for the sake of others. Viewed from the perspective of the Resurrection, the cross marks the climactic moment of Jesus' entire life. His death gloriously displayed what our Lord proclaimed in his teaching and modeled in his life, namely, that the fullness of life comes through the giving of one's life. Jesus' death, therefore, is the revelation of true life — life-in-community.

But Jesus did not only show us how to live. He also opened the way to life. Through his death he made it possible for us to participate in God's community. Jesus' death accomplished this in two ways.

• First, as we noted already, through this self-giving act our Lord overcame our sin, which hinders our participation in God's purpose for our existence.

Jesus' sacrifice covers the sin which evokes God's condemnatory verdict against us. As a result, the wall of guilt need no longer bar us from enjoying reconciliation with God. Further, Jesus dethroned the alien powers that reign over us. Stripped of their power, these forces need no longer bind us. They cannot stop us from returning to our heavenly Father. Nor can they separate us from God and his love (Rom. 8:38-39).

• Second, in addition to overcoming sin, our Savior opened the way to fellowship with God in another way. He bore the cost of transforming us from God's enemies to God's friends.

A cessation of hostilities never comes without costs. Think about how you may have experienced such a cost. Suppose someone dear to you has wronged you. Even though you are the wronged party, your loved one has rejected you! What will it take to overcome this awful situation and restore harmonious peace into this relationship?

Of course, your first response may be to wait for the offending person to take the first step. After all, he or she has injured you. But after some reflection, you decide to make the first move. You go to your loved one and whisper your desire that the rift be healed. And you even offer a symbolic overture — sending flowers, for example — to show your sincerity.

In each of these acts you are bearing the cost of initiating reconciliation. However, the greatest cost is the pain you experience as you take upon yourself the evil of the severed relationship. Even though you are the innocent, injured person you shoulder not only the burden of your own hurt, but also the enmity of the other. *You* take the place of the guilty person; *you* carry the shame of the offending act, so that your loved one who has turned away from you might return. And despite the pain, you do so willingly.

The cost of reconciliation includes taking the first step to end the conflict. In Christ, God took the initiative to terminate our hostility toward him and to renew the fellowship he intends for us to enjoy. By proclaiming God's offer of salvation through his life and death, our Savior took upon himself the cost incurred in seeking reconciliation.

The cost of reconciliation includes bearing the pain and hostility of the broken relationship. Our sin and failure has caused great harm to God's creation and great pain to God the Creator. In Jesus, God himself willingly bore that hurt in order to make reconciliation possible.

But how exactly did God bear that pain? We noted earlier that through his experience of Godforsakenness on the cross, Christ tasted alienation so that we might enjoy reconciliation. All the pain that has ensued from the Fall — whether pain that we inflict or pain that we experience — need no longer bar the way to true fellowship between the creature and the Creator, and by extension, true fellowship among us.

However, this does not illumine the full mystery of the dynamic of the cross. The Godforsakenness Jesus bore affected the Father as well as the Son. Just as Jesus endured the breach of community with his Father, the Father experienced the breaking of fellowship with his Son. In this manner, the cross marked the entrance of the pain of human sin into the very heart of God. The consequences of our hostility toward God interrupted the relationship between Jesus and his Father. As a result, however, we can now share in the eternal fellowship between the Father and the Son. How great is the love of our God and Savior!

Through his death our Lord took the pain of our failure into his relationship with the Father. By so doing, Jesus inaugurated a new fellowship of humans—his body, the church. As the disciples of Jesus, we experience a foretaste of the eternal community with God, each other, and creation for which we are created and which we will one day enjoy in its fullness when Jesus returns in glory. Until that great day, the risen and exalted Lord intercedes for us with the Father (Rom. 8:34; Heb. 7:25; 1 John 2:1). Yet, he also remains with us, for he is present among us through his Spirit.

> 🖎 *Because God has carried the cost of human sin, you do not need to bear either the burden of your own sin or the pain of the injuries you have received from others.*

Our reception of Christ's provision. Jesus' death opens the way to true community. But a final question remains. How do we become the recipients of his act on our behalf?

The New Testament declares that the atoning work of Jesus is an objective, completed fact (1 Peter 3:18). Our Savior died once for all. This act effected a fundamental alteration in the relationship between God and humankind, and it sealed Christ's authority over the cosmic powers. But until we personally appropriate the new status he offers, our Savior's death is of no saving effect. It is of no value unless we respond in faith to the One who purchased our salvation. Despite Jesus' sacrifice, everyone who does not believe "stands condemned already" (John 3:18).

In view of this, the New Testament also indicates that Jesus' provision is intended to move us to appropriate its benefits.

But if Jesus' death inaugurated a new state of affairs, why is our response vital? And why does God also intend that his death move us to respond?

Perhaps an analogy will help. The president of the United States has the right to pardon convicted criminals. Suppose the president announces a total amnesty for all jailed persons. Such a declaration inaugurates a new situation: all sentences are revoked. But for this new reality to affect a convict, he or she must personally respond to the offer. The convict must walk out of the jail! To be actually effective, therefore, the president's declaration must not only inaugurate a new legal reality—amnesty for all. It must be announced everywhere in such a manner that it can evoke both the appropriate response in the heart of the individual languishing in prison—belief or acceptance that the message is true—and an appropriate action—walking out of the jail into freedom.

So also in the spiritual drama. The sin that evokes God's displeasure is only one side of our wretched human situation. Not only have we offended God, we are also at enmity against him. We fear and hate the Creator who loves us.

Viewed from God's perspective, Jesus' atoning sacrifice has inaugurated a new situation. Through Christ, God is irrevocably reconciled to us. The problem, therefore, is not with him.

Unfortunately, in our sin we remain at enmity against God. We need to turn toward him, so that we might be reconciled to the God who has reconciled the world to himself (2 Cor. 5:19-20).

> *✍ Have you personally responded to the good news of reconciliation?*

For this reason, the proclamation of the gospel is crucial. As human messengers declare the good news of Christ's death for us, they become God's own voice imploring its hearers to be reconciled to God (2 Cor. 5:20).

This "imploring" is the task of the Holy Spirit, to whom we now turn in chapter 7.

FOR CONNECTION AND APPLICATION

1 What do you see as the implications for us of Jesus' teaching and example that the path to life leads through death?

2 Do you find yourself more drawn to dynamic, objective, or subjective theories of the Atonement? Why?

3 How can we best explain the meaning of Jesus' death to people today? What approach do you think would be most fruitful?

4 How should our belief that Jesus tasted death for us affect the way we live? What does it mean for the way we face death? What about our response to life-and-death ethical issues such as euthanasia?

5 What are the implications of Jesus' paying the cost of our reconciliation for our response to those who injure us?

The Holy Spirit — the Author of Life

"But the Counselor, the Holy Spirit, whom the Father will send in my name, will teach you all things and will remind you of everything I have said to you"
(John 14:26).

Recently, an installment of the comic strip "Family Circus" depicted a youngster listening intently to the pastor's sermon. Suddenly his ears caught a term he didn't understand. The youngster turned to his mother and whispered a request for an explanation: "I know the Father and the Son. But who is the Holy Spearmint?"

At one time, the Holy Spirit seemed to be the unknown, undiscussed, unmentioned person of the Trinity. Christians felt at home with talk about Jesus the Son and even about God the Father, but not the Spirit. So foreign was the Holy Spirit to many Christians that he might just as well have been the "Holy Spearmint."

All this has changed in recent years, however. In the meantime, we have witnessed the phenomenal growth of Pentecostal churches. And successive waves of the charismatic movement have lapped on our ecclesiastical shores. These developments have set off an unparalleled explosion of interest in and talk about the Holy Spirit.

This new interest has triggered a seemingly incessant production of books about the Spirit and an apparently unending onslaught of seminars and conferences focusing on the Spirit's role in our lives. Yet, we often appear as confused about the third person of the Trinity today as at any time in the past.

Our confusion moves in several directions.

● Some Christians are uncertain about the Spirit's identity. Exactly who (or what) is the Holy Spirit? Is the Spirit fully divine, or less than God? Is the Spirit fully personal or merely an impersonal force?

● Other Christians are confused about the Spirit's work. What does the Spirit do? And how and where is he at work? In short, they wonder, how can we be certain that it is the Holy Spirit who is active in, through, and around us?

In this chapter we take up these two questions. Our goal is to understand who the Spirit is and wherein the focus of the Spirit's work lies. Specifically, we view the Holy Spirit from two angles.

● First, the Spirit is the great *Completer,* the third person of the Trinity. He is God at work completing the divine program. As such, the Spirit is the personal presence of God with us.

● Second, the Spirit is the great *Addressor* who speaks in the pages of the Bible. He is God's voice confronting us through Scripture. As such, he is the personal presence of God encountering us through God's own word.

THE SPIRIT AND THE TRIUNE GOD

"I believe in the Holy Spirit." Throughout the centuries these simple words from the Apostles' Creed have capsulized the church's belief about the third person of the Trinity. As Christians we have not only placed our trust in God the Father and Jesus the Son. We have also entrusted ourselves to the Holy Spirit. Like the Father and the Son, the Spirit is worthy of our trust and adoration, because he is fully personal and fully divine.

But how do we know this? How can we affirm that the Holy Spirit is person and deity? How is it that he is worthy of the same praise that the Father and the Son deserve? In our attempt to understand this we will traverse two pathways. These two roads converge in the church's lofty confession, "I believe in the Holy Spirit."

● We begin by retracing the Spirit's footsteps through the scriptural narrative.

● Then, we raise the theological question of the Spirit's place within the Triune God.

The Holy Spirit in the Bible

Our lofty understanding of the Holy Spirit as fully personal and fully divine is a great treasure. But the people of God have not always been aware of his identity. Nor did this awareness simply fall full-blown out of heaven one day. On the contrary, the Christian teaching about the Spirit stands at the apex of a long history in which God worked with people in bringing them to understand his triune nature as well as the place of the Holy Spirit within it.

We now trace the high points in this history, noting three grand moments:

☞ *The Spirit in the Old Testament.*
☞ *The Spirit and the Christ.*
☞ *The Spirit in the church age.*

The Holy Spirit in the Old Testament era. When we look for the Holy Spirit in the Old Testament, we must keep in mind that the ancient Hebrews did not possess the fullness of divine revelation we now enjoy. Consequently, they did not know God in his triune identity—as Father, Son, and Spirit. Nor were they fully cognizant of the Holy Spirit as the third person of the Trinity.

Nevertheless, the Old Testament people had a profound awareness of God's Spirit. This grew out of the Hebrew word for "spirit" *(ruach)* which was connected to the ideas of "wind" (Gen. 8:1; Ex. 10:13) and "breath" (Ezek. 37:1-10).[1]

The ancient Hebrews were aware of the close connection between breath and life. Breathing indicated the presence of life. And the cessation of breathing meant that life had come to an end. This connection led them to use the term "spirit" to refer to the life principle in living creatures (Gen. 6:17; 7:15, 22). But they knew as well that God is the source of all creaturely life. As a result, "spirit" also referred to the divine power that creates and sustains life, that is, God's own Spirit.

The Hebrews knew as well that God's Spirit is holy. That is, he is morally upright. Because he is holy, the Spirit cannot remain with humans who sin. No wonder David cried out, "Do not cast me from your presence or take your Holy Spirit from me" (Ps. 51:11). This servant of God remembered how God's Spirit had forsaken the disobedient King Saul. Confronted with his own adultery, David feared that the divine power would now abandon him too.

But what exactly did the ancient Hebrews understand by the Spirit? Rather than seeing him through trinitarian eyes, they viewed the Spirit as God's power at work in the world. Specifically, the Spirit was God at work in two central aspects of the divine program.

• First, the Spirit was God's power active in the creation of the universe and in sustaining life on earth.

According to the Genesis creation narrative, the Spirit was active when God called the universe into existence. The Spirit of God "was hovering [or 'brooded'] over the waters" (Gen. 1:2), and then God spoke the series of creative words.

But above all, the Spirit participated in the creation of humankind. Adam became a living being when God *breathed* into Adam's nostrils — that is, when God gave to Adam God's own animating Spirit (Gen. 2:7).

The Spirit is not only God at work originating life. He is also the power that sustains life (Ps. 104:29-30; Isa. 32:15). All living creatures owe their existence to God's Spirit. But this is especially true for humans (Gen. 6:3; Job 27:3; 34:14-15). Indeed, when God recalls the Spirit, life ceases (Gen. 6:3; Ecc. 12:7).

• Second, the Spirit was God's power active in special ways in the lives of certain persons.

The Old Testament repeatedly recounts the stories of people whom God empowered in special manners. Sometimes the coming of God's Spirit merely enhanced the skills (Ex. 31:1-5; 35:31) or the leadership abilities (Jud. 3:10; 6:34) that people already possessed. But other times, the Spirit's presence resulted in superhuman feats. For example, the endowment of the Spirit allowed Samson to display extraordinary physical strength (Jud. 14:6, 19; 15:14).

The prophets were repeatedly the recipients of a special endowment of God's power through the Spirit. Sometimes they found themselves under direct divine control (1 Sam. 10:6, 10; 19:19-24). More generally, however, the presence of the Spirit resulted in the prophets sensing a compulsion to speak on behalf of God (Num. 24:2-3; 2 Chron. 15:1-2).

Whatever form it took, the Spirit's presence provided the resources necessary to complete a divinely ordained task.

After Israel settled in the Promised Land, the Spirit's endowment was increasingly connected to political and religious leaders. Above all, kings, priests and prophets were the bearers of the Spirit.

Despite the Holy Spirit's presence among them through their leaders, Israel's experience of the Spirit was ultimately unsatisfying. Throughout the Old Testament era, the Spirit's endowment always remained transient. As King Saul learned to his detriment, no one — not even the leaders of the people — could presume to possess the Spirit permanently. And the Spirit's endowment was limited primarily to special people. Not everyone in Israel enjoyed direct access to God's Spirit. Rather, the people were dependent on their leaders and others God chose to mediate his presence among them.

The unsatisfying experience led God's Old Testament people to direct their attention to the future. They eagerly anticipated a grand day when God's Spirit would dwell permanently among them — and within them all.

These hopes were fueled by the prophets who spoke of the future coming of the Anointed One (the Messiah). Not only would the fullness of the Spirit rest on him (Isa. 42:1), the Messiah would also pour out the Spirit on the people. When this glorious event occurred, all God's people — from the greatest to the least — would know God and enjoy the fullness of the Spirit (Jer. 31:34).

The Holy Spirit and the Christ. According to the New Testament, the hopes and expectations of God's Old Testament people were fulfilled in Jesus. He is the Christ, a title that means "Anointed One."

Indeed, Jesus came as the Anointed One, the one uniquely endowed by the Spirit awaited by the prophets. The New Testament writers emphasize the important role the Spirit played in Jesus' life.

The Spirit's central role dated to the beginning of Jesus' earthly sojourn, for the Spirit was responsible for our Lord's conception (Luke 1:35). His role began in earnest at the beginning of Jesus' ministry, as at his baptism the Spirit endowed our Lord for his divinely given task. And this role was equally important at the climax of Jesus' mission, for through the power of the Holy Spirit God raised Jesus from the dead (Rom. 8:11; cf. 1:4).

From conception to resurrection, therefore, the Spirit was at work in Christ's life. He guided our Lord's steps (e.g., Matt. 4:1) and empowered our Lord to carry out his ministry (Matt. 12:28).

As the one uniquely endowed by the Spirit, Jesus was also the one through whom the outpouring of the Spirit would come. As John the Baptist said, Jesus would "baptize" his followers in the Spirit (John 1:29-34).

Jesus himself promised that he would give his disciples the full measure of the Spirit, who would be a well of living water flowing from their inner being (John 4:14; 7:37-39). Following Jesus' departure his Father would send another "Counselor" to empower them for their mission (John 14:16; 16:7). The coming Helper would teach the disciples, reminding them of the Lord's instructions (John 14:25-27) and guiding them into truth (John 16:12-15). This same Spirit would testify about Jesus to the world (John 16:7-11) and assist the disciples in taking their stand as Christ's witnesses (John 15:26-27).

The Holy Spirit and the church. The glorious fulfillment of this promise occurred at Pentecost (Acts 2:1). After completing his earthly ministry, the exalted Lord poured out the Spirit on his followers on that day.

But Pentecost was no mere passing occasion. This event marked a milestone in the history of God's activity in the salvation of humankind. At Pentecost, the Spirit entered the world in a unique way. And in so doing he inaugurated a new age, the age of fulfillment (1 Peter 1:10-12).

The outpouring of the Spirit signaled the birth of the Spirit-endowed, Spirit-empowered, Spirit-led community—the church. And it commenced the age of the mission of the church. Beginning with Pentecost, the Spirit took on a new role. Throughout this age, the Spirit would focus his work on the new community, the fellowship of the followers of Christ.

In the same way, the reality of Pentecost was not limited to the disciples upon whom the Spirit fell on that day. Rather, Pentecost embraces all believers. It extends to every Christian in every nation and in every generation. We all now enjoy the presence of the Spirit, who forms us into one fellowship (1 Cor. 12:13). Through our union with Christ and his community, we participate in the fullness of the Spirit. Because we are believers, we have experienced Pentecost; we have received the endowment and the empowerment of the Spirit. In fact, if we do not "have" the Spirit we do not even belong to Christ (Rom. 8:9).

Since Pentecost, therefore, the Spirit enjoys a new identity. He is the mediator of the presence of the risen and exalted Jesus within his community. The Spirit is the teacher, leader, and empowerer of the church; he indwells the community on the Lord's behalf.

But his present role does not exhaust the Spirit's place in the life of the community of Christ. There remains a future aspect of his activity. This, in turn, suggests a further dimension of the Spirit's identity.

● The Holy Spirit is God at work bringing history to its goal. The Spirit will one day transform us into the likeness of Christ. This transformation will involve not only our inner person, but each of us in our total being, including our body. As Paul declared, through the Spirit, the God who raised Jesus will "give life" to our mortal bodies (Rom. 8:11).

This future event will likewise mark the liberation of creation from the bondage it now suffers. On that day the entire universe will participate in "the glorious freedom of the children of God" (Rom. 8:21).

In the meantime, the indwelling Spirit acts as the "down payment" guaranteeing our future salvation (2 Cor. 1:22; 5:5; Eph. 1:13-14). And he has already begun his transforming work within us (Rom. 8:10; 2 Cor. 3:18).

> ✍ *Appropriate the power of God's Spirit which is in you through your union with Christ.*

In short, the waiting is over! The Spirit is come! We live in the era of Pentecost! Therefore, rather than praying for the Spirit's arrival, our task is to "be filled constantly with the Spirit" and to "walk in the Spirit." That is, we are to appropriate the power which is ours because the Spirit promised by our Lord is now within us.

The Spirit and the Trinitarian Life

In the preceding pages, we traced the footsteps of the Spirit from the Old Testament era to the church age. But to sharpen our understanding of who the Spirit is we must return to the doctrine of the Trinity. This doctrine provides the context for us to see the Spirit's eternal identity within the Triune God.

The Spirit within the eternal God. Christian confessions of faith link the Holy Spirit with the Father and the Son as together being the one God.[2] We declare that throughout all eternity the Holy Spirit is the third person of the Trinity.

But how ought we to understand this statement? Who is the Spirit within the one God? What is his eternal identity?

To answer this question, we must invoke once again our earlier conception of the Trinity. Specifically the Holy Spirit is the Spirit of the relationship between the Father and the Son. This insight carries glorious implications.

As we noted in chapter 2, the primary movement in the eternal God is what the church fathers called "the eternal generation of the Son." Throughout all eternity the Father shares his life with the Son, and the Son draws his life from the Father. This eternal dynamic forms the identity of both the Father and the Son. The first person of the Trinity is the Father of the Son. And the second person is the Son of the Father.

The Father and the Son are not only distinguished from each other; they are also bound together. What unites the Father and the Son? In a word—"love." Throughout all eternity the Father loves the Son, and the Son reciprocates the Father's love. The bond between them is the mutual love they share. This suggests that the secondary movement in God is the eternal "spiration" or "procession" of the Spirit, as the Spirit of the relationship (i.e., love) between the Father and the Son.

But we want to say more about the reality of the Spirit. Indeed, throughout the ages Christians have affirmed that the Holy Spirit is eternal and divine. Can we continue to affirm this?

Yes, if we remember one crucial point. The love between the Father and the Son is a relationship between eternal persons. The Father loves the Son with an eternal love, and the Son reciprocates that love eternally. This means that the bond they share is likewise eternal and divine. The love that unites the Father and the Son is the Spirit, the third member of the Trinity. Therefore, like the Father and the Son, the Spirit is eternal deity.

This conclusion is confirmed by an interesting connection the Bible draws between the divine character or essence and the Holy Spirit. John writes, "God is love" (1 John 4:8), that is, "love" characterizes God's own eternal essence. According to Jesus, God's eternal essence is also "spirit" (John 4:24). With great precision, therefore, the Bible uses the same word "spirit" to speak both of God's eternal nature and of the third member of the Triune God, the Holy Spirit. In the same way, we can conclude that "love" characterizes both the eternal essence of God and the Holy Spirit.

We may readily affirm that the Spirit shares with the Father and the Son eternal deity. Perhaps more difficult for us to understand is how the Spirit can also be *personal.* Indeed, some Christians find it easier to think of the Spirit in impersonal terms. In their minds, he is more like a force — a mysterious divine force, perhaps — but nevertheless an impersonal force. They cannot see him as personal, alongside the Father and the Son.

The difficulty may become even more acute if we speak of the Spirit as "love." In our minds, love is often merely an abstract, impersonal concept. If the Spirit is the love between the Father and the Son, the Spirit must be an impersonal force, like the attraction that draws people together.

The Bible, however, teaches that the Spirit is fully person. The biblical authors refer to the Spirit as "he," not "it." Likewise, they attribute personal qualities, such as intellect, emotion, and will, to the Spirit.

How can this be? How ought we to understand this biblical language? How is it that the Spirit is personal, rather than merely impersonal?

The answer lies in the Spirit's close connection to the Father and the Son within the Triune God. The Father and the Son, of course, are persons. We may add: they are uniquely personal, the most personal of all persons. It follows from their uniqueness as persons that the relationship they share is likewise unique. Theirs is not merely some abstract, generic "love," but a unique relationship, a uniquely personal love. Consequently, we affirm that like the Father and the Son, the Holy Spirit—the one who binds them together—is uniquely personal. The Spirit is the third *person* of the Triune God.

Perhaps we can see this more clearly when we consider that our tendency to depersonalize the Spirit may be connected to our inclination to treat "love" as an abstraction. Love, however, is not something that exists "out there" as an independent idea in some realm beyond personal relationships. Rather, "love" is a description of how persons relate to each other. It is a way of characterizing a bond between persons. A person who loves someone sacrifices for the sake of the other.

This is how we use the word "love" to characterize human beings. For example, if I say "My father was a loving man," I am not speaking about some abstract quality he possessed. Rather, I mean to inform you about how he acted, how he related to people he met and knew, including how he treated me, his son. I am suggesting that in his relationships with others—whether with his wife, children, congregants in the churches he served, or neighbors—he consistently gave of himself in order to benefit them.

How much more is this the case when we talk about God! The love between the Father and the Son is no mere abstract, impersonal force located in a realm of ideas disengaged from the first and second persons of the Trinity. Nor is "it" a quality they each possess independently of the other. Rather, the love uniting them is embedded in their relationship. And because they are uniquely personal, the Spirit of their relationship is personal as well.

The biblical language about God and the Spirit confirms our conclusion in yet another way. The Holy Spirit is person, because he is the personal character of God. "God is love," the Bible affirms. We have seen how the doctrine of the Trinity forms the foundation for this statement about God's eternal character. God is love, because throughout all eternity the Father loves the Son and the Son returns the Father's love. The love that binds the Father and the Son is the essence of the one God. But our God is personal. Therefore, his essential nature—the unique love that binds Father and Son—is likewise personal. And this unique love is the Holy Spirit, the third person of the Trinity.

But why should we expend so much energy on this point? What difference does it make whether or not the Spirit is personal? It makes all the difference in the world — and beyond the world, in eternity! The personhood of the Spirit is not merely an abstract question that provides fodder for theological disputes. The church father Athanasius showed us once and for all why this is the case. He set forth the significance of this tenet of our faith in his challenge to those in his day who sought to depersonalize the Spirit. Athanasius pointed out that our eternal salvation is at stake here. Only if the Spirit is fully person, the very personal presence of God with us, does the Spirit's presence in us mean that we have fellowship with the living, personal God.

As Jesus himself indicated, the Spirit mediates our union with Christ and with his Father (John 14:16-21). If the Spirit to whom we look for this fellowship with Christ and his Father is not the personal God, then we are still alienated from God. We are lost forever.

But thanks be to God, the third person of the Trinity — the Spirit of the fellowship between the Father and the Son — has drawn us into fellowship with the Father and the Son!

♪ *O spread the tidings 'round, wherever man is found,*
Wherever human hearts and human woes abound;
Let ev'ry Christian tongue proclaim the joyful sound:
The Comforter has come![3]

The Holy Spirit — the Completer of God's work in the world. We noted in our discussion of the Triune God how each trinitarian person has a specific role within the one activity of God in the world. The Father functions as the source or originator who sends the Son and the Spirit. And the Son fulfills the Father's will in the world so that the Spirit may be sent.

The Spirit, in turn, completes the divine work, so that the grand goal of community may indeed come in its fullness. The Spirit, therefore, is the great *Completer.*

The Spirit's role as the Completer arises from his identity within the eternal Trinity. To see this, we must remind ourselves that God's program in the world is itself an outworking of the dynamic within the eternal, Triune God.

In our discussion of the doctrine of the Trinity, we suggested that the entire drama of creation and redemption flows out of the eternal relationship between the Father and the Son. God is self-giving love, namely, the love shared by the Father and the Son, who is the Holy Spirit. The loving Father willingly created the world. And the Son willingly acted on behalf of the Father to make salvation available to fallen humans. But the divine work is not yet complete. *We* must be brought to share in the salvation the Father has planned and the Son has purchased.

This is the task of the Spirit. Because he is the Spirit of the divine Father-Son relationship, the Spirit enters the world to complete the divine plan. The Spirit's goal is to bring us to share in the fellowship the Son enjoys with the Father. This work will be finished only at the end of history, when God establishes the new heaven and the new earth.

Until that great day, the Spirit brings us to experience a foretaste of the glorious future community that we will enjoy throughout eternity. As we noted earlier, the Spirit is active within us, thereby providing the guarantee that we will participate in God's future (Rom. 8:16-17; Eph. 1:13-14). And the Spirit is likewise actively renewing the natural world, thereby guaranteeing that one day God will refashion the universe into the new heaven and new earth.

Throughout the remaining chapters of our study we will be developing these great themes of our faith. In the meantime, reminding ourselves of the glorious work of the Spirit on our behalf ought to lead us to offer heartfelt praise to the Triune God.

Holy, Holy, Holy! Lord God Almighty!
All Thy works shall praise Thy name, in earth, and sky, and sea;
Holy, Holy, Holy! Merciful and Mighty!
God in Three Persons, blessed Trinity![4]

THE SPIRIT AND THE SCRIPTURES

As the third person of the Trinity sent into the world, the Spirit's mission is to complete the program of the Triune God. To this end, the Spirit is both the source of life and the power that renews life.

The Spirit will attain his ultimate goal one future day, when God establishes the glorious community for which we are created — the fellowship of the redeemed people living in a renewed world and enjoying the presence of the Triune God. En route to that day, the Spirit is at work creating and nourishing spiritual life.

Central to the work of the Spirit in this enterprise is the Bible. By means of Scripture the Spirit bears witness to Jesus Christ, guides the lives of believers, and leads the people of God. In fact, the Spirit has chosen to focus his work in the world through the Word of God inscripturated in the Bible.[5]

The Bible, therefore, is the Spirit's book. He is the inspirer and illuminator of Scripture. The Bible's purpose is instrumental to the Spirit's mission. And the Spirit, in turn, always works in accordance with the Bible. In short, there is a reciprocal relationship between the inscripturated Word and the Spirit.

But we can say more about this connection between Word and Spirit. To do so, we focus our attention on three statements that capsulize the integral relationship between the Spirit and the Scriptures.

☞ *The Spirit stands at the foundation of Scripture.*
☞ *The Spirit addresses us through Scripture.*
☞ *As the Spirit's book, the Bible is authoritative.*

The Spirit Stands at the Foundation of Scripture[6]

As Christians we are a "people of the Book." We declare that the Bible is the foundation of our faith and the source of guidance for our lives. In acknowledging Scripture in this manner, however, we are not glorifying a mere book. Rather, we are actually looking beyond the Bible to the Spirit who addresses us through its pages. We honor Scripture, because it is the vehicle through which the Spirit chooses to speak.

Two concepts clarify the foundational role the Spirit exercises toward Scripture:

☞ *inspiration,*
☞ *illumination.*

Inspiration refers to the activity of the Holy Spirit which led to the writing, compiling, and canonizing of the Bible as the Book of the church.

Viewed from one perspective, inspiration speaks of the special work of the Spirit in guiding or "superintending" the lives of prophets, apostles, and other authors and compilers so that what they came to write or collect is Scripture (Jer. 36:1-2; Ezek. 11:5; Micah 3:8; 2 Peter 1:21).[7]

Viewed from another perspective and as a result of the first, we may speak of the biblical documents themselves as "inspired."[8] They reflect what God desired to have written. Indeed, because of the Spirit's activity we can say with Paul, "All Scripture is God-breathed" (2 Tim. 3:16).

We may bring these two aspects together in a single, terse definition:

"Inspiration" is that work of the Holy Spirit in influencing the authors and compilers of Scripture to produce writings which adequately reflect what God desired to communicate to us.

Defining inspiration is relatively easy. More difficult is determining exactly *how* the Spirit worked in the production of the documents that became our Bible. Specifically, we wonder, what means did the Spirit employ in influencing the writers and compilers of Scripture? Here we can offer no simple answer. If we look at the clues found in the Bible itself, we must conclude that the Spirit used a wide range of means.

Certain texts, for example, imply that they arose through divine dictation. God himself gave human agents the very words they recorded (Ex. 19:3-6; Lev. 1:1; Num. 7:89; Num. 12:8; 1 Sam. 9:15; Isa. 6:8-9; Rev. 14:13).

Many other passages, however, suggest a more indirect means. They clearly indicate that godly people were active agents in the process of writing and compiling Scripture (Mark 12:36; Acts 1:16; 28:25; 1 Cor. 14:37). The active participation of human authors explains why we find in the Bible a wide variety of writing styles, varying accounts of the same events, and even outbursts of human emotion (2 Cor. 11:1).

Then there are those sections of the Bible that indicate they are based on eyewitness accounts or that report the encounters certain persons had with God (Ex. 24:1-11; 1 Kings 22:19; Isa. 6:1-5; 2 Cor. 12:1-4).

And still other texts suggest that the compilers drew from the wisdom of ancient cultures or from previously existing documents (eg. 1 Kings 11:41; 14:19, 29).

Can we bring together this great variety into a single theory of inspiration? Probably not. At best, we can venture only a broad statement in an attempt to summarize what the texts themselves suggest. Perhaps we must be content with only a summary, largely descriptive statement:

> By direct command, a sense of urgency, or simply a personal desire or compulsion, God's Spirit moved spiritual persons within the faith community to write or compile from dictation, experience, tradition, or wisdom those documents which reflect what God desired to have recorded in order that the divine purposes might be served.

The Spirit's work did not cease with the compilation of the canon. Rather, he has spoken through Scripture throughout the ages and continues to speak to succeeding generations through the Bible (John 14:26).

To say "the Spirit speaks through Scripture" means that he causes the Bible to "come alive" to us — dulled as we are by sin (1 Cor. 2:6-16; 2 Cor. 3:14-17; 1 John 5:7, 11). When he speaks, we gain an awareness of the significance of the biblical texts for life in the present. We may designate this ongoing activity, *illumination.*

For purposes of clarity, we readily treat inspiration and illumination as two separate tasks of the Spirit. However, we must keep in mind that they are in fact two dimensions of the Spirit's one activity in and through Scripture.

We find inspiration and illumination operating together when the Bible was being written and collected. The ancient peoples heard the Spirit's voice through the various individual books that now form our Bible. As a result, they preserved and brought together these writings as inspired Scripture. And reflection on previously collected inspired documents gave rise to subsequent books.[9] The biblical community formed the documents into one

Bible, because they found these writings to be the vehicle through which God's Spirit addressed them in their own circumstances.[10]

In a similar manner, the Spirit attunes us today to understand and apply Scripture to our present situation. We too encounter God in the pages of the Bible. And as a result of his illuminating activity, we are drawn to confess that this is the Spirit's book, the product of his inspiring, superintending activity.

One major difference separates our experience from that of Israel and the early church, however. The ancient people of God heard the Spirit's voice speaking through an as yet incomplete Bible, through a canon to which they were adding texts. The Spirit now speaks to us through the completed canon, the whole Bible. We are not writing additional books which the church will one day add to the Scriptures. Rather, the Bible is complete, and nothing we write can claim to be the chosen vehicle of the Spirit in the way that the sixty-six books of Scripture are.

The Spirit Addresses Us through Scripture

The Bible is the Spirit's book. But what exactly does the Spirit accomplish through Scripture? Simply stated, the Spirit addresses us through the message of the Bible. By speaking to us in the pages of the Bible, the Spirit seeks to nurture our spiritual life and to create in us a new identity. This occurs in several ways.

• By addressing us in Scripture, the Spirit provides spiritual sustenance.

As Christians we naturally view the Bible as the place—ultimately the only place—where we can find the message of everlasting life. Believing this, we readily look to Scripture in order to be nourished in our faith.

This natural Christian craving for the Word of God is in keeping with the role that Scripture ought to play in our lives. The old Pietists used to say, "The truth of Scripture *claims* us."[11] By that they meant that as he addresses us through Scripture, the Spirit lays hold of us in the midst of life. The Word of God provides spiritual nourishment so that we might grow in Christlikeness and in service as disciples of our Lord. Indeed, as Peter suggests, what milk is to the newborn child, Scripture is to the believer (1 Peter 2:2).

The ultimate goal of the Bible, therefore, is what we may call "spiritual formation." As Christians our chief desire ought to be that we be *formed* spiritually through the Bible, in order to please God in every aspect of our lives.

With this goal in view, we must diligently apply ourselves to the reading of Scripture. Using the best tools we have, we ought to direct our efforts toward the task of discovering the meaning of the biblical text. But we do not apply ourselves to Bible study merely to gain knowledge about the text itself. Rather, our intent is to allow the Spirit to address us through Scripture, so that we might be instructed as to what we should believe and how we should live. Through the words of Scripture, the Spirit desires to encourage us and to empower us to love God and others as we should. And through the Bible he also seeks to sustain us and renew us in the battle against the enemy.

> ✍ *Drink deeply at the well of the Spirit by feeding hungrily on the "bread of life."*

As we read and study, therefore, we patiently listen for God's voice. We anticipate that the Spirit will address us through the text.

> *Break thou the bread of life, Dear Lord to me,*
> *As thou didst break the loaves Beside the sea;*
> *Beyond the sacred page I seek thee Lord,*
> *My spirit pants for thee, O living Word.* [12]

• By addressing us through the Bible, the Spirit calls us into a new identity.

Throughout the centuries, Christians have acknowledged the Bible as the foundational document of the Christian community. But why? The answer lies in what the Spirit accomplishes through Scripture. The Bible provides the foundation of our faith, in that through its pages the Spirit directs us toward the new identity that is ours by faith in Christ. Indeed, as he speaks through the Bible, the Spirit creates in us this new identity. [13]

To understand this dynamic — to discern *how* the Spirit bestows on us a new identity through the pages of Scripture — we must remind ourselves of how we form our personal identity.

Each of us is confronted with the question of the meaning of our lives. We ask the foundational personal questions: Who am I? Why am I here? How can I make sense out of my life? As we find answers to these questions, we gain a sense of identity. Indeed, personal identity is the product of the process of bringing all our life into a meaningful whole. But for this to happen we must discover a framework by means of which we are able to see that the diverse and divergent aspects of our lives somehow fit together.[14]

There are several possible sources for such an identity-giving framework. Your identity may arise from a sense of vocation, a sense that you have a great task to accomplish during the short span that you are alive. Or you may derive this framework from the belief that you are a participant in something that is larger than your life.

Christians discover in the Bible the "interpretive framework" by means of which our lives come together—make sense—as a unified whole. This interpretive framework is linked with the biblical narrative, the story of God at work in the world bringing creation to a glorious future goal.

The Spirit addresses us through this narrative. Through it, he invites us to see our lives in the light of God's work. He summons us to link our personal stories with God's story and the story of God's people. Through the "old, old story," the Holy Spirit calls us into God's new community. And the Spirit leads us to view our personal lives from the perspective of this ancient Gospel narrative. As we look at all of life from this vantage point, our lives begin to make sense. And we begin to see a unity within the variegated experiences that form the ingredients of our existence.

We must take this a step farther. How exactly does the Bible provide a special interpretive framework for our lives? Succinctly stated, the Spirit speaking through the Bible leads us to reorient our lives on the basis of the biblical story of God's past actions and in accordance with the scriptural vision of God's future.[15]

● Our identity arises from the story of God's past activity.

Through the biblical narrative the Spirit transposes us back to the events that lie at the foundation of Christ's community and form the basis of our participation in that community. At the heart of this story is the Gospel narrative—the recounting of the passion and resurrection of Jesus and the subsequent sending of the Spirit at Pentecost.

But the Spirit's goal is not merely that we might gain knowledge of these events as facts of ancient history. Rather, he seeks to draw us *into* the story. He wants us to see our lives—to organize the seemingly disorganized, pointless events of our existence—in the light of what God has done for us in Christ. Through the recounting of the narrative, the Spirit draws our present into Christ's past. The Bible calls this "union with Christ," for through the Spirit, Jesus' death and resurrection become real in our spiritual experience. In this manner, the Gospel narrative of Jesus' life becomes the structure—the interpretive framework—by means of which we now understand our own lives.

From this point on, we speak of our lives by appeal to words related to "before" and "after." We divide our journey into the "old life" and the "new life." We talk about the former days when we were "lost," "strangers," "at enmity with God." But then we quickly add that through Christ we are now "saved," "reconciled," and "members of God's family" or "God's new community." And we cite specific incidents in our lives that illustrate what we mean. We talk about the futility of our former way of living. We narrate the events surrounding our encounter with God in Christ. And we add examples of how our lives are different now.

● In creating a new identity in us, however, the Spirit does not merely draw from the past. Speaking through the biblical story, he also leads us to orient our lives according to a vision of the future.

The biblical authors declare that God has a glorious goal for us, which includes the entire universe. They present a vision of a new creation in which we—created for community—will live in harmony with each other, with all creation, and above all with God (Rom. 8:18-21; Isa. 65:17-25; Rev. 21:1-5).

Addressing us through this biblical vision, the Spirit draws us to view our lives in the light of God's future. He brings us to orient our goals and aspirations so that they fit with God's goals.

And he assists us in discovering a personal purpose for living, a vocation that links us as participants in God's program for the world.

The Bible not only provides the interpretive framework from which Christians derive their identity. The Spirit addressing us in Scripture actually fosters growth in us in living out that identity. Through Scripture the Spirit leads us to discover what it means to live in accordance with God's story. He teaches us what Christians ought to believe and how they ought to act. And the Spirit moves us to appropriate the power he has made available to us. By linking our lives to God's future, the Spirit admonishes us to open ourselves and our present to the power of God's future, which is already at work in our world.

> ✍ Orient your life according to Christ's past and God's future.

As the Spirit's Book, the Bible Is Our Authority

Through the Scriptures, the Holy Spirit addresses us. For this reason, we honor the Bible as our authority. But what does "honoring the Bible" mean? And to what extent is Scripture authoritative for us?

For many Christians the authority of the Bible is connected to its veracity or truthfulness. Indeed, as believers we acknowledge that the Bible is *true* and therefore authoritative. Two pairs of theological words underline this belief. They come together in this affirmation:

Because the Bible is given through *verbal, plenary* inspiration it is *infallible* and *inerrant.*

The words "verbal" and "plenary" summarize what we believe about the *extent* of biblical veracity. Because the Bible in its entirety is the Spirit's book, it is true in its entirety.

"Plenary inspiration" means that the Holy Spirit's involvement in the writing and compiling of Scripture extends to the entire Bible. All that is found within Scripture is the product of the Spirit's activity (2 Tim. 3:16). We need not pick and choose where we think the Spirit will speak. Instead, we must be open to his address everywhere in the Bible.

"Verbal inspiration" declares that the Spirit's involvement extends to the very words of Scripture. To understand the importance of the Spirit's "superintending" of the choice of words, let's remind ourselves of the dynamics of communication.

When we talk face-to-face with others we have many vehicles through which to communicate. In addition to the actual words we say, we "speak" through such tools as gestures, body language, and tone of voice. But when we communicate through written documents, we are dependent on the *words themselves* to convey our meaning.

Think of what this means for God's decision to communicate with us through words — that is, the Word of God inscripturated in the Bible. To say, "The Spirit inspired the Bible," means to affirm that he played a role in word selection and word order.

As we have already seen, it would be a mistake to assume that the Spirit *dictated* every word of Scripture. Nevertheless, we believe that his activity insured that the words of the text are able to convey God's intended message to us.

Because the Bible is the Spirit's book, we can trust it. Or stated theologically, we believe Scripture is *infallible* and *inerrant*.

"The Bible is infallible" means that these writings are "not liable to deceive." Because the Spirit moved in the lives of the authors and compilers of Scripture, we can believe them. They do not intend to lead us astray.

"The Bible is inerrant" means that the Bible accurately presents what God desires to teach us. The central goal of Scripture, of course, is to convey theological and ethical truth. But it also touches on other areas of human knowledge. When it does so, the information it provides is accurate to the extent that is necessary to serve the purposes of its author.

To say the Bible is infallible and inerrant is to declare that Scripture is totally trustworthy. Consequently, we must approach the text humbly and expectedly, open to being taught by the Spirit.

Declarations about the Scriptures such as these are helpful reminders of the foundational role the Bible ought to play in our lives. We read Scripture expecting to find out what we should believe and how we should live.

But we must remember that in the end we are speaking about the Holy Spirit who addresses us through Scripture. In offering our lofty affirmations about the Bible, we are affirming our faith in the Spirit who announces his revelatory message through the pages of Scripture.[16]

Thus, the Bible is trustworthy and authoritative because it is the vehicle of the Spirit. The Bible's infallibility and inerrancy derive from the veracity of the Spirit who speaks truly through it. And the Bible's authority is nothing else but the authority of the Spirit who illumines its divinely inspired, revelatory message.

Biblical authority and you. The Bible is authoritative because it is the Spirit's book. But if it is to serve as our authority, it must become our *ultimate* authority. And its authority must reach into every dimension of our lives.

Why is this so? Why can't we merely compartmentalize the Bible into some "religious corner" of our lives?

The all-encompassing authority of Scripture arises from the all-encompassing nature of religious commitment. Try as we will, we cannot successfully marginalize theological convictions to the fringes of life. Such commitments eventually work their way out of the closet and begin to color other areas as well.

Placing ourselves under the teaching of the Bible commits us to view the world through eyes informed by Scripture. We strive to make our foundational commitments square with the Bible. We desire to be informed and motivated by convictions derived from Scripture and the biblical community.

And like all religious convictions, a biblically informed outlook will not remain in the closet or cellar of our being. Indeed, biblical convictions demand that they permeate our attitudes and actions in every facet of life.

In short, if we acknowledge the Bible as our authority, we are committing ourselves to the task of living out in every area of life what the Spirit is saying through the Scriptures. We are committing ourselves to the goal of becoming obedient disciples of our Lord. As Christians, we desire to connect belief with life. For this to happen, we must open ourselves to the Spirit to bathe our hearts with Scripture until our lives reflect the very mind, character, and vision of Jesus.

> *May the mind of Christ, my Savior*
> *Live in me from day to day,*
> *By His love and pow'r controlling*
> *All I do and say.* [17]

Indeed, this is exactly what our Lord demands. He admonished his disciples to put into practice his teachings (Matt. 7:24-27). As James reminds us, the Christian life means being "doers" and not only "hearers" of the word (James 1:22-25).

Contrary to what many Christians assume, being a "doer" of the word is not some grievous burden. On the contrary, it is the greatest privilege a human can ever experience. As we place ourselves under the tutoring of the Spirit who speaks through the Scriptures we discover the divine design for human life. We find in the Bible the only sure foundation upon which to build a life that is not only meaningful now, but also will count for eternity.

Knowing this, we can sing heartily:

> *How firm a foundation, ye saints of the Lord,*
> *Is laid for your faith in His excellent Word!* [18]

FOR CONNECTION AND APPLICATION

1 Why do you think there is so much confusion about the Holy Spirit? What aspect of this dimension of Christian belief is most confusing to you? To people you know? To the church in general?

2 Christians differ with each other concerning our relationship to Pentecost. Do we need to experience a personal "Pentecost" or is the Spirit's fullness ours at conversion? What is your view? And what are the implications of each position for how we live as believers?

3 Do you think whether the Spirit is personal or merely impersonal makes a significant difference? What pronoun should we use to refer to the Spirit?

4 Recount a specific situation in which you sensed the Spirit speaking through Scripture. How does this occur? What is the role of "exegesis" (i.e., detailed study of the biblical text itself) in this process?

5 What aspects of Christ's past and God's future do you find most meaningful in providing orientation to your life?

6 How important are popular words such as "infallibility" and "inerrancy" in explaining the authority of the Bible?

7 A bumper sticker read, "The Bible has ALL the answers." Do you agree? Explain your response.

EIGHT

The Holy Spirit and Our Salvation

"Very truly, I tell you, no one can enter the kingdom of God without being born of water and Spirit. What is born of the flesh is flesh, and what is born of the Spirit is Spirit"
(John 3:5-6, NRSVB).

One day Lucy was leaning against Schroeder's piano and musing. "I have examined my life and found it to be without flaw," she confidently declared. Lucy then articulated her bold plan. "Therefore, I'm going to hold a ceremony and present myself with a medal. I will then give a very moving acceptance speech. After that I'll greet myself in the receiving line." Schroeder remained too caught up in his rendition of Beethoven to pay attention to the girl. Lucy caught his attention, however, when she explained smugly, "When you're perfect, you have to do everything yourself."

If we are honest with ourselves, we must admit the exact opposite of what Lucy claimed. We are neither "without flaw" nor so perfect that we have to "do everything" ourselves. On the contrary, we are so hopelessly impaired that ultimately we can do *nothing* ourselves.

Yet, at the same time, as Christians we know that we are God's children. God has reached down to us in our failure and inability. God has brought us into fellowship — community — with himself, doing for us what we are unable to do for ourselves.

Contemplating God's action on our behalf leads us to extol grace. Rather than joining Lucy in planning our own individual self-congratulation parties, we are drawn instead to sing with John Newton:

♫ *Amazing grace! how sweet the sound,*
That saved a wretch like me!
I once was lost, but now am found,
Was blind, but now I see.[1]

In chapter 7 we spoke of the Holy Spirit as the Completer. He is the third person of the Trinity. The central task of the Holy Spirit in the economy of the Triune God is to finish the divine program in the world.

For us, no aspect of the Spirit's activity is more crucial than that of completing in us the great work of salvation. The Holy Spirit applies Christ's provision to our personal lives, thereby bringing us to enjoy the community for which we were created. As a consequence of the Spirit's work, we experience fellowship with God, one another, and all creation.

Yet the Spirit does not complete this work all at once. Instead, the Spirit's activity in effecting our salvation is a process. And salvation remains incomplete until that process reaches its goal, until that great day when the Spirit has fully transformed us into our ideal and model—the Lord Jesus Christ.

We may therefore offer the following definition.

Salvation is the Spirit at work in bringing us into full conformity with the likeness of Jesus Christ.

In this chapter we explore in greater detail the Spirit's role in our salvation. Specifically, we view the Spirit's saving activity as three moments. These are capsulized in the old dictum:

☞ *I have been saved.*
☞ *I am being saved.*
☞ *And one glorious day I will be saved.*

This saying speaks of salvation as encompassing:

☞ *conversion,*
☞ *sanctification,*
☞ *glorification.*

Although we will look at these one by one, we must devote most of our discussion to conversion, the beginning point in our spiritual journey.

THE SPIRIT AT WORK IN OUR CONVERSION

At the foundation of our Christian experience is a transforming encounter with God. We call this encounter "conversion." Hence, our experience of salvation begins with conversion.
Consider this terse definition:

> Conversion is that life-changing encounter with the Triune God which inaugurates a radical break with our old, fallen existence and a new life in fellowship with God, other believers, and eventually with all creation.

To define conversion seems simple enough. But when we seek to understand the ins and outs of the experience, our questions begin. How does conversion work? What transforming experience actually inaugurates the Christian walk? And what occurs in the wonderful encounter which lies at the basis of our faith?
Christian thinkers have struggled with these questions throughout the centuries. Despite their efforts, conversion ultimately remains a mystery. Exactly how the "great transaction" transpires—how God brings us into community with himself—lies beyond our comprehension. Nevertheless, we can say *something* about this mystery. To do so, we will look at the single dynamic of conversion from three vantage points.

☞   Our personal response to the gospel.
☞   The Spirit's gracious work in our lives.
☞   Our incorporation into the faith community.

CONVERSION OCCURS AS WE PERSONALLY RESPOND TO THE GOSPEL

At the heart of Jesus' message was a call to respond to his proclamation of God's reign: "After John was put in prison, Jesus went into Galilee, proclaiming the good news of God. 'The time has come,' he said. 'The kingdom of God is near. Repent and believe the good news!' " (Mark 1:14-15)
"Repent and believe the good news"—this command capsulizes conversion. This grand transformation occurs as we repent of sin and exercise faith in God through Christ. To understand

conversion, therefore, we must look more closely at these two ingredients of our personal response to the gospel.

Repentance. Simply stated, "repentance" is a radical turning within the human heart (Luke 1:16-17; 2 Cor. 3:16-17). This "turning" involves our entire being.[2]

• Repentance begins with an *intellectual* change.

It involves a change of mind, an altered opinion about ourselves, about how we have been living, and about what we have done. What we once thought was OK, we now see as it really is—failure, sin. Whereas we once thought ourselves to be basically good—oh, perhaps not perfect like Lucy, but decent persons nevertheless—we now know that we are "spiritually poor" (cf. Matt. 5:3).

• Repentance entails an *emotional* change as well.

When we change our opinion about ourselves—who we have become and what we have done—we come to regret our previous course of action. Whereas formerly we were basically satisfied with our lives, we now sense deep displeasure, even sorrow. Like Paul, we now hate what we find ourselves doing (Rom. 7:15).

• And repentance also involves a *volitional* change, an altered will.

A changed opinion and heartfelt, sorrowful regret naturally lead us to desire to alter who we are and what we do. No longer do we want to live as we did in the past. Instead we resolve to reform our lives. We realize with Paul, "what I do is not the good I want to do" (Rom. 7:19; cf. Matt. 5:6).

To get a handle on the radical nature of repentance, think of an area of your life that you once felt quite proud about, but now even the thought of it brings you shame.

Let's say it was your driving habits. Perhaps when you first learned to drive you consistently drove faster than the posted speed limits, ran yellow lights, and weaved in and out of traffic. All the while you smugly thought that these actions brought you a step ahead of others on the road.

Just today, however, your speeding through a "pink" light nearly resulted in a fatal traffic accident with a car already starting through the intersection. Suddenly you realize how dangerously you have been driving. You are no longer smug about pushing the limits. Instead, you feel sorry about your attitude and actions behind the wheel. You vow to never again exceed the speed limit. You promise to always stop when a traffic light turns yellow. And you commit to being a safe, courteous driver.

That is repentance.

Radical repentance is indispensable for conversion. Unless we recognize our failure and need, we will not cry out to God to save us.

By itself, however, repentance is not sufficient for salvation. We simply cannot make amends for the past. Nor are we able to radically alter the future. Despite our reflection, regret, and resolve, sin continues to hold us fast in its grasp.

Think again of our example. What is the outworking of your change of heart over your driving habits? Try as you will, your ensuing good behavior can never erase the scare you put into the other driver. And had you caused an accident, twenty years of subsequent safe driving could never erase the blemish on your record.

Further, your crisis-produced repentance is rarely the end of the story. How long does your resolve to be a model driver last? Perhaps you toe the mark for a time—a day, a week, even a month. But before you know it, the old habits have once again raised their ugly heads. Once more you find yourself exceeding the speed limit, sneaking through "pink" lights, and dashing around traffic. Your momentary repentance has not freed you from the long tentacles of past driving habits.

To repentance, therefore, must be added faith.

Faith. Faith ranks high among the list of "humankind's most misunderstood concepts." Some see it as tantamount to intellectual suicide: faith is believing what is impossible and nonsensical.

At one point in Lewis Carroll's story *Through the Looking Glass* Alice (of *Alice in Wonderland* fame) was discussing these matters with the White Queen.

"Now I'll give you something to believe," said the Queen. "I'm a hundred and one, five months and a day."

"I can't believe that," Alice replied.

"Can't you?" the Queen declared in a pitying tone. "Try again;

draw a long breath, and shut your eyes."

Alice laughed. "There is no use trying," she said, "one *can't* believe impossible things."

At this point the Queen uttered the clincher: "I dare say you haven't had much practice. When I was your age, I always did it for half an hour a day. Why sometimes I've believed as many as six impossible things before breakfast."[3]

Others see faith as a leap beyond the givenness of reality, a blind dash beyond what is presently real.

One episode of "Star Trek: The Next Generation" ("Rightful Heir") illustrates this. Worf's spiritual quest led to a crisis when the man who claimed to be the long-awaited Klingon messiah turned out to be a fraud. In a discussion with Worf, Data muses about his own experience of crisis that ensued when his creators told him he was just a machine. But, Data reports, he "chose to believe" that he had the potential to be more than "a collection of circuits and subprocesses." How did he come to this decision? Worf wonders. Data replies, "I made a leap of faith."

Genuine Christian faith is neither the acceptance of nonsense nor a leap into the impossible. On the contrary, saving faith encompasses three components, which form a natural progression.[4]

● Faith begins with knowledge *(notitia).*

We first learn about God's promises contained in the gospel, including the historical narrative of Jesus' death and resurrection *for us.* Indeed, faith begins with the hearing of the gospel message, as Paul indicated (Rom. 10:12-17).

● Knowledge leads to assent *(assensus).*

We acknowledge intellectually the truth of the gospel message. We accept the gospel message as true. Knowing and giving assent are evident in the repeated New Testament use of phrases such as "believe that" or "have faith that." "Believing that" is an intellectual act. The declaration "I believe that" is always followed by a statement which capsulizes what I hold to be true.

Consider three statements:

"I believe that snow is white."

"I believe that Abraham Lincoln was President of the United States during the Civil War."

"I believe that Jesus died for my sins."

Although these declarations are quite different from each other, each entails a personal acknowledging that certain statements are true representations of specific aspects of reality.

Saving faith involves personal assent to the truth of certain statements which comprise the heart of the gospel. These include:

> "I believe that Jesus is 'the holy one of God' " (John 6:69; 8:24; 20:30-31).
>
> "I believe that Jesus died, was buried, rose again, and appeared to witnesses, all in accordance with the Old Testament" (1 Cor. 15:1-8).
>
> "I believe that 'Jesus is Lord' and that 'God raised him from the dead' " (Rom. 10:8-9).

Faith doesn't end with knowing and giving assent, however.

• Rather, faith comes to completion in trust (fiducia).

Trust means that we personally appropriate the truth of the gospel for ourselves. It involves personal commitment. Faith means committing yourself through Christ to the God who in Christ has acted on our behalf. We see trust or commitment in the New Testament talk about "believing in" (literally, "believing into"). Repeatedly we are instructed to "believe in Jesus" (John 3:16). This means, "entrust yourself to Christ for salvation."

Faith is at work each day in both the large and the small aspects of life. For example, after an eventful day, you go to a friend's house to relax. Your eyes focus on a particularly inviting easy chair in the living room. Suppose you do some preliminary research, inquiring from the manufacturer about the chair's weight-bearing capabilities. Their report asserts that the chair is capable of carrying 700 pounds without collapsing. This information carries the promise that the chair will indeed be a relaxing location in which you can safely recline. You not only hear the report, you also accept it. "I believe that this chair can safely hold my weight," you conclude silently.

Yet, you are still one step away from enjoying what the chair has to offer. Knowledge and assent must lead to commitment. You must commit yourself to the chair; you must entrust your well-being to the chair for good or ill. You must sit in the chair.

This is faith. Saving faith moves beyond hearing and acknowledging the message about the God who has acted in Jesus. It also includes entrusting ourselves to Jesus as Savior and committing our lives to him as Lord.

Decades ago a famous tightrope walker sparked a sensation. He set up a high wire across the Niagara Falls. A crowd quickly gathered to watch the man risk his life by walking back and forth on the thin wire above the falls. They were awestruck as they saw him push a wheelbarrow across the wire. The tightrope artist then turned to the crowd. "Do you believe that I could push a person in the wheelbarrow across the high wire over the falls?" he asked. The people cheered enthusiastically. Then he added, "Who will step into the wheelbarrow?"

Conversion as repentance-faith. In our discussion, we have separated repentance and faith. We have viewed them as two distinct responses to the gospel.

For some believers this is indeed the case. They may have come to Christ through a lengthy process in which repentance preceded faith. But ultimately, the two are inseparable. Together they comprise the one personal response that God requires of us. Genuine repentance presupposes and includes faith. And vital faith carries repentance within it.

Viewed from the perspective of the believer, conversion — "coming to Christ" — is marked by repentant faith or faith-filled repentance. But what does it involve for our actual lives? What are its implications for the way we live?

Obviously, genuine conversion entails a great personal turning point. It marks a break with the old way of living and an entrance into an entirely new life. This change leads to a grand reorientation of our entire life.

● Crucial is the direction of this change.

Above all, conversion consists in a redirection of our lives *toward God.* Whereas we had previously been turned away from God as we served sin, Satan, and self, we now turn to the one who in Christ has loved us and has made salvation available. And we now want above all to please God in all we do.

This turn toward God leads to a turning *toward others* (Mark 12:28-34; 1 John 4:20). We leave behind the old self-centered way of living. And we dedicate ourselves to follow the example of

Jesus, who was "the man for others." We forsake the old impulse to treat others as means to *our* goals. Instead, we begin to see them as persons whom God loves and for whom Christ died. We desire to minister to people in their need, knowing that in so doing we are actually serving Christ (Matt. 25:40).

Implicit in conversion is a turning *toward creation* as well. We once saw the world as existing primarily for our benefit. But now we desire to imitate God in all areas of life. This includes sharing his concern for creation. We now seek to be the good stewards that God intended (Gen. 2:15). And as we do so, we begin to show forth God's own character to creation.

> ✍ *True conversion involves a turning toward God, others, and creation, and in this manner it is a turning even toward yourself.*

Conversion also means a turn *toward yourself.* It leads to an understanding of your own true self as God designed you. Repentant faith is a commitment of ourselves to live out in our lives God's goal for human existence—that is, his design for our own personal lives. When we find God—or perhaps better stated, when God finds us—we also find our own true self.

Conversion Requires the Spirit's Gracious Work in Our Lives

Conversion occurs as we respond to the gospel with repentance and faith. But how is this possible? How can we turn away from Satan, self, and sin? How can we turn toward God, others, creation, and our true self?

The answer to this question comes as no surprise—the Holy Spirit. Conversion occurs through the Spirit's gracious work in our lives. In fact, without the activity of God's Spirit, conversion cannot occur.

In chapter 4 we saw why this is so. We are totally depraved. This means that sin has spread to every aspect of our existence, leaving no nook or cranny of our being untouched and no innate capability unaffected. We are devoid of the spiritual power necessary to effect our salvation. Depravity means that all our attempts to earn salvation are ultimately fruitless (Rom. 3:20; Gal. 2:16, 21). If we are to be saved, the initiative must come from God.

The good news is: God has indeed acted on our behalf. As we explored in chapter 6, Christ has made provision for our salvation. Since Christ's ascension, the Holy Spirit has been active in the world completing God's saving work. The Spirit takes Christ's provision and makes it real in our lives. In so doing, God's Spirit authors new, spiritual life in us (John 3:5-8).

The Spirit's role in conversion. The Holy Spirit, therefore, is God at work in the conversion of sinful human beings. The Bible suggests four specific roles that the Spirit fulfills in the conversion process.

• The Spirit convicts us of sin.

You cannot accept God's gracious forgiveness unless you realize that you need to be forgiven. You cannot be converted unless you realize that the direction of your life is wrong. You cannot turn from sin to God unless you are aware that you are at enmity with him. You cannot sense regret and sorrow for your failures and acts of unrighteousness unless you are conscious that they are displeasing to God. You cannot cast yourself on the merciful God revealed in Christ unless you sense that you need divine mercy. In short, you cannot be saved unless you realize you are a sinner.

How does the realization of sin arise? Ultimately, the answer is: through the work of the Holy Spirit.

There may be many factors which lead us to an awareness of sin. For some, the consciousness of sin may be sparked when they begin to "reap" what they have "sown," when wayward living results in some awful tragedy. This may come in the form of a financial collapse following shady business practices, rebellious children produced through years of parental neglect, a deadly illness sparked by unhealthy habits or licentious living, or a legal trial triggered by the transgression of some civil statute.

Others gain an awareness of sin simply when seemingly minor offenses against their upbringing lead to a guilty conscience.

Many Christians testify that they were awakened to personal sinfulness through Sunday Schools that taught the biblical truth about our lost existence.

Regardless of the circumstances, however, conviction of sin is always the Spirit's work. Regardless of how we come to acknowledge our sin, the Spirit is the one who brings us to see its awful reality.

Our Lord himself assigned this task to the Holy Spirit: "When he comes, he will convict the world of guilt in regard to sin and righteousness and judgment" (John 16:8). When the Spirit is at work, we become conscious of our own sinful status in the light of God's standard of righteousness. And we become aware of a coming day of judgment.

We must add one "footnote" to this great theological truth. Knowing that conviction is the Spirit's task takes an enormous load off our shoulders as we proclaim the gospel. We do not need to *prove* to others that they are sinners. We do not need to focus our attention on how bad they are. The Spirit will do that without our help. Our role is to announce the good news that God has acted in Christ to save sinful human beings. As we elevate the beauty of Christ in this manner, the Spirit will engage in his work of convincing the hearers of their need.

● The Spirit *calls* us to respond.

Awareness of sin can be a dangerous thing. Deep sorrow may drag us down. We may fall into despondency, hopelessness, and despair. Sorrow may even evoke in us thoughts of suicide, just as Judas' remorse led him to take his life.

The Spirit's intent in conviction, however, is not to cause our death, but to foster eternal life. He desires that we not only see our sin, but that we also turn to God for forgiveness and healing. Therefore, in addition to convicting us of sin, the Spirit issues a call to sinners to respond positively to God's gracious offer of salvation. He calls us to repent and have faith in the God who through Christ can save us.

The Spirit summons us to share in the salvation God offers. But how does he call us to repentance and faith? Jesus suggested an answer in the parable of the wedding banquet (Matt. 22:1-14). In the story, the king's servants announce his invitation throughout the land. Through the words of his servants, the king himself calls the guests to the banquet. So also in the spiritual realm. As human messengers announce the good news, the Spirit calls the hearers to respond.

This means that the Spirit chooses to energize human words. Indeed, this is exactly what the Bible asserts. Through Isaiah, for example, God compared the potency of his word with the life-giving force of water: "As the rain and the snow come down from heaven, and do not return to it without watering the earth and making it bud and flourish, so that it yields seed for the sower and bread for the eater, so is my word that goes out from my mouth: It will not return to me empty, but will accomplish what I desire and achieve the purpose for which I sent it" (Isa. 55:10-11).

That is why the Bible extols gospel messengers: "How beautiful are the feet of those who bring good news" (Isa. 52:7; Rom. 10:15). The voice of the messenger is the voice of God. As Paul said concerning himself and his associates: "We are therefore Christ's ambassadors, as though God were making his appeal through us. We implore you on Christ's behalf: Be reconciled to God" (2 Cor. 5:20).

Through the proclamation of the gospel, the Holy Spirit issues God's gracious call. He summons the hearers to share in God's salvation. As we answer this summons, we discover that we are the uniquely called of God. We are those whom God "called . . . out of darkness into his wonderful light" (1 Peter 2:9; cf. Rom. 9:24; 2 Tim. 1:9).

• The Spirit *illumines* us to accept the Word.

But how can we respond to the gospel when we cannot understand it? How can we accept the message when it seems so inconceivable? Or to echo Paul's words, how can we entrust ourselves to Christ when the god of this age has blinded our minds so that we cannot see "the light of the gospel of the glory of Christ?" (2 Cor. 4:4)

These questions remind us that sin poses an intellectual barrier to conversion. Our fallen human minds, coming under the spell of Satan as they do, may simply dismiss the gospel as so much gibberish. We may reject the good news as pure nonsense. How, then, can we believe the gospel if our minds tell us it is simply not true. How can we come to Christ, if we are incapable of seeing the truth of the message about his work on our behalf?

Again the Bible offers a straightforward answer to this problem—the Holy Spirit. The Spirit opens our minds so that we can perceive the truth of the gospel (1 Cor. 2:10). When we hear the gospel, something happens. Either we walk away shaking our heads in disbelief. Or our curiosity is sparked so that we want to learn more.

If we do not immediately dismiss the message, but rather are attracted to it, the Spirit is at work. If we come to see its sublime intellectual beauty, and if its truth begins to claim our lives, then the Spirit has been enlightening us. You see, the Spirit's role is to shed light in our minds so that we can understand and accept the divine truth proclaimed in the gospel. Only when he is at work in us do we come to be so grasped by the truth of the good news that we respond to the proclaimed message with repentance and faith.

No wonder Paul exclaims, "For God, who said, 'Let light shine out of darkness,' made his light shine in our hearts to give us the light of the knowledge of the glory of God in the face of Christ" (2 Cor. 4:6).

● The Spirit *enables* us to respond to the good news.

Our difficulty is not merely intellectual, however. Not only are our minds blinded to its truth, our wills *cannot* turn toward God. As we noted in chapter 4, depravity means that our individual wills are in bondage. We lack the power necessary to overcome sin's control and freely respond to the Spirit's call. To embrace the salvation our loving Father offers, we must be enabled by a power greater than the debilitating hold sin has over us.

What possible power could achieve this? The biblical answer is clear: the Holy Spirit, who is the power of God completing God's purposes in the world. The Spirit enables us to respond to the gospel. He provides the spiritual power that makes repentance and faith possible.

Paul spoke of this dynamic. In his first epistle to the Corinthian believers he reminded them about the manner in which he had proclaimed the gospel in their city: "I came to you in weakness and fear, and with much trembling. My message and my preaching were not with wise and persuasive words." And why this approach? So that his announcing the Gospel might not be a grand demonstration of human ability, but "a demonstration of the Spirit's power." As a consequence, the faith of these believers did not rest on human wisdom, but on divine power (1 Cor. 2:4-5).

Whereas illumination overcomes the blindness of our fallen mind, the Spirit directs his enabling power toward our misdirected *will*. The Spirit woos the will, in order that we both desire and are made able to respond to the good news with repentance and faith. He gives us the fortitude to say "No" to sin and "Yes" to the gospel summons.

As with other aspects of his role, the focal point of the Spirit's enabling action is the announcement of the good news (Rom. 10:17). As human messengers proclaim the gospel, the Spirit is at work strengthening the hearer to respond. Because the Spirit chooses to act through human proclamation, the good news is God's powerful Word. Energized by the Spirit, the gospel indeed becomes "the power of God for the salvation of everyone who believes" (Rom. 1:16).

The results of the Spirit's work in conversion. The Spirit is at work in the proclamation of the gospel—convicting, calling, illumining, and enabling. The goal of his activity is our repentance and faith.

> ✍ As you proclaim the gospel, trust the Spirit to engage in his work.

But this does not exhaust the Spirit's work in conversion. As the divine Completer, the Holy Spirit applies to our lives—makes real in us—Christ's provision for human sin. In so doing, the Spirit becomes God's solution to our human predicament. He completes God's work in rescuing us from sin, so that we may participate in the eternal fellowship for which we were created. At conversion, he "takes up residence" in our lives. He makes our lives his "home." The Spirit's presence within us overcomes sin and places us in fellowship with God, others, and all creation.

We may capsulize the implications of his work with four grand theological terms: regeneration, justification, liberation, and empowerment.

• The Spirit effects regeneration.

As we noted in chapter 4, because of sin we are alienated from God our Father. Designed to be his friends, we have made ourselves enemies of the Creator. And as a result, we are alienated from each other, from creation, and from ourselves. In chapter 6 we spoke of how Jesus Christ entered this situation to provide reconciliation. In him, God opened the way to bring our hostility to an end.

At conversion, the Spirit applies this provision to our lives. He regenerates us (Titus 3:5) or causes us to become "born anew" or "born again" (John 3:1-16). That is, the Spirit authors new, spiritual life in us through his presence within us.

Just as physical birth endows us with a special relationship to our physical parents, so also our spiritual birth means that we have a special relationship with God. We are sons or daughters of God (John 1:12-13). Through the Spirit we become God's spiritual offspring. And this means that we enjoy fellowship — community — with God.

The Spirit's role in effecting this fellowship is the outworking of his identity within the eternal Trinity. As we noted in chapter 7, he is the Spirit of the relationship between the Father and the Son. Consequently, when the Spirit indwells us, the very community of the Triune God is present within us. In regenerating us, the Spirit brings us to participate in the eternal relationship the Son enjoys with the Father, for this relationship is who the Spirit, in fact, is.

> Through the Spirit you participate in the glorious relationship of love the Son enjoys with the Father.

We do not enjoy this new relationship with God in isolation, however. Rather, the Spirit causes us to be born into a new *family*. We are therefore participants in a new people, a reconciled people, a people among whom the old hostilities have been erased (Eph. 2:14-18).

• The Spirit effects *justification.*

Our sin carries a second awful result. We stand condemned before the holy God. In love, however, God sent Christ as the provision for our sin. Through his death, Jesus covered our sin so that God's just sentence of condemnation need not fall on us.[5]

At conversion, the Holy Spirit applies Christ's provision to our lives. His presence in us effects a new standing before God. We are justified — declared righteous — in God's sight.[6]

Our unrighteousness formerly barred the way to community with God. The Spirit, however, strips off our "filthy rags" of sin and replaces them with the "coat" of Christ's righteousness.[7]

Clothed in the righteousness of the eternal Son we now enjoy fellowship—community—with the Father.

Community with God naturally leads to community with others. Knowing that we are justified in God's presence, we now seek to act righteously toward each other and toward all creation, just as Jesus taught (Matt. 18:21-35). Because we know we are all sinners saved by God's amazing grace, we give careful attention to the special bond of unity and peace that the Spirit produces among us (Eph. 4:3).

● The Spirit effects *liberation*.

Sin overwhelms us as an alien power. Enslaved to sin, we lack the freedom to live as we ought. Rather than obeying God, we willingly and necessarily find ourselves ruled by an evil taskmaster—sin (John 8:34). Our bondage to sin places us under the grip of death (Rom. 6:23). We are spiritually dead now. One day we will die physically. And in all eternity we will be separated from fellowship with God.

Into this situation God sent Christ. Jesus won the victory over the forces of evil. By conquering sin, death, and Satan, he provided redemption for us; he effected the release of those who were in bondage.

At conversion, the Spirit applies Christ's redeeming work to our lives. His presence, as the presence of Christ within us, liberates us. He replaces our former bondage with a new freedom (John 8:36; 2 Cor. 3:17). One day the Spirit will cause us to experience full liberation from the power of sin and death (Rom. 8:11). Even now, however, through his indwelling presence we can be victorious over the control of sin (Rom. 6:14). The Spirit gives us the ability to reject sin and choose God's will.

We must be careful not to confuse this freedom with the everyday experience of acting as disinterested decision-makers. Standing before our closet in the morning trying to decide which color shirt or dress to wear, we view ourselves as choosing among the options unencumbered by any overpowering inclination to decide in one direction or the other. In the face of *moral* decisions, however, we are never neutral. Instead, we face these choices already predisposed. And unfortunately we are predisposed toward evil.

The Spirit's presence liberates us. He overcomes our predisposition toward evil, so that we can choose the good. Therefore, the freedom he offers us is the ability to live in accordance with our destiny. Thereby, he liberates us for community, for participation in the freedom the Son enjoys with the Father.

Living in freedom, however, does not mean living without restraint. On the contrary, the Spirit liberates us *for* discipleship (John 8:31-32). We are liberated from bondage to sin in order to be "slaves to righteousness" (Rom. 6:18) or "slaves to God" (v. 22). And discipleship links us with all Christ's disciples. We are liberated for life in community. Our freedom, therefore, includes the freedom to "be for others" (cf. Gal. 5:13), even to renounce our own freedom for the sake of others (1 Cor. 9:19; 10:23-24).

• The Spirit effects *empowerment.*

Human sin is radical. It touches every dimension of life, leaving us depraved. Because of sin, we are powerless to serve God and others in the way he intends. Into this hopeless situation Jesus came as our substitute. He accomplished for us what we cannot do for ourselves.

At conversion, the Holy Spirit applies Christ's provision to our lives, endowing us with divine power—his own empowering presence. The Spirit within us is the power we need for a lifetime of service to God (Acts 1:8).

As the Spirit of the Triune God, he gives us the power to live according to the pattern that characterizes the Son's response to the Father. This pattern includes serving one another and together showing forth to all creation God's own character as we live as the mage of the Triune God. Indeed, only as we demonstrate through our actions that the Spirit of love is among us can we truly show to the world that we are a people in fellowship with God.

Let's now draw this grand sweep of the Spirit's work into the chart we started in chapter 4 and augmented in chapter 6:

HUMAN CONDITION	CHRIST'S PROVISION	SPIRIT'S APPLICATION
Alienation	Reconciliation	**Regeneration**
Condemnation	Expiation	**Justification**
Enslavement	Redemption	**Liberation**
Depravity	Substitution	**Empowerment**

Conversion Involves Our Incorporation into the Faith Community

There remains yet one more perspective from which we must view the dynamic of conversion. Conversion is no mere transaction between God and a single individual. Nor are we converted in isolation. We do not experience a saving encounter with God totally on our own. Rather, conversion always involves the faith community, the church of Jesus Christ. Christ's community plays a significant role in the process of coming to faith. And our life-changing encounter with God involves our incorporation into the community of Christ.

We must look more closely at this aspect of the conversion dynamic, focusing on a question. What role does the community play? What is the connection between the Spirit-empowered personal response to the gospel and the community of believers?

The community is the agent of gospel proclamation. Faith requires hearing the gospel message. Hearing the message requires a proclaimer. But a proclaimer requires a sending body (Rom. 10:14-15). This is precisely the role of the church. Ultimately, Christ's community is the agent of the gospel proclamation.

We can readily understand this relationship between the believing community and personal conversion when we think of the announcement of the gospel to unbelievers. Whether the context be "foreign" or "home" missions, a church commissions certain persons to preach. And through their efforts others come to faith.

The role of the community in our conversion is not limited to this obvious aspect, however. When we respond to God's saving action in Christ, we do so not only because a member of a church told us the good news. Viewing the process from a wider perspective, we are confronted with the gospel because the community of Christ's faithful disciples has remembered, preserved, and guarded the story of God's activity. And through its representative this believing community that spans the ages has now announced that story to us. Even if we come to faith simply by reading the Bible, the community is still at work, for the Scriptures contain the one church of Christ announcing the gospel.

Nor is the actual verbal announcement the only manner in

which the church proclaims the gospel to us. On the contrary, the good news forms the heart of Christian worship, as the community recounts in word, symbol, and practice the story of Jesus and its significance for us.

The good news finds expression in the nurturing life of the community as well. Indeed, the church offers a powerful articulation of the message of Christ by being a genuine fellowship of love and care (John 13:35). Through the life of the community, those who have not yet come to faith repeatedly encounter the gospel message in spoken, enacted, and lived proclamation.

The community incorporates us into its life. Conversion does not occur in isolation, because we can come to God only as we are the recipients of the church's proclamation of the gospel. There is another sense in which conversion doesn't occur in isolation: Repentant faith marks not only our turning from sin to God; we also turn toward a new community in which we participate.

But in what sense are we now part of a new community? Our initial answer might be to think merely of formal membership in a local congregation. Or we might speak about our belonging to some nebulous "invisible church" of all believers of all time. While each of these ideas has its place, we have a deeper sense in mind when we speak of incorporation into the church.

To see this we must speak about the role in our lives of the social groups in which we participate.

In the previous chapter we introduced the contemporary idea of an "interpretive framework." Contemporary thinkers have shown how we draw from our social groups the foundational categories—the framework—through which we view, experience, and speak about ourselves and the world.[8]

Conversion involves our acceptance of the interpretive framework of the Christian community, which views the world through God's action in Jesus Christ. In conversion, we look to the categories of the gospel story. And through these categories, we reorient our understanding of ourselves and the world.

Perhaps we can see this connection more clearly by reflecting again on the role of an interpretive framework in the process of identity formation. As we noted in chapter 7, our sense of personal identity is dependent on our ability to find a set of categories that brings the diverse aspects of our lives into a meaningful unity. This set of categories leads us to "tell our story," to draw together the crucial events of our lives into a single autobiography or "narrative."[9]

But our personal stories are never isolated units. They are touched by the stories of other persons and ultimately the story of a larger people of which we are a part.[10] In fact, it is from this larger story that we draw our ideas of value and ultimate meaning.

In conversion, we reinterpret our personal story in the light of the story of the Christian community and the categories it exemplifies. Following the biblical narrative, we speak of "old" and "new," "being lost" but "having been found," "sin" and "grace."[11] Reinterpreting our story in this manner entails accepting the story of the Christian community as our own. We now are part of *this* people; we are incorporated into *this* community.

Conversion entails our incorporation into the community of Christ in another way as well. We gain from this people a new set of values.

The gospel story not only embraces a framework for viewing the world, it also embodies a way of living in the world. The believing community seeks to live in accordance with the values of the gospel narrative. In conversion we accept the ideals of the gospel. We claim its values as our own, and we commit ourselves to embodying in our beliefs, attitudes, and actions the meanings and values that characterized Jesus' own life. In short, we desire to connect Christian beliefs with life.

This commitment marks us as Christ's disciples. That is, it entails incorporation into the community of discipleship. And as we participate in the life of the fellowship of disciples, its values increasingly give shape to our own life.

This leads us to another way in which conversion and incorporation are connected. Repentant faith marks a grand change of loyalty. We lay aside all the old allegiances and pledge our fidelity to the God revealed in Jesus Christ.

Allegiances, however, are never purely individual. We never believe anything all alone. Instead, personal loyalties always link us with those other persons who share them with us and by extension with communities that have preserved and propagated them.

As we renounce the former loyalties through conversion, we also renounce the former community of allegiance. And as we pledge allegiance to Christ, we are incorporated into a new community—into the fellowship of those who have pledged their loyalty to their common Lord. With all of his disciples we confess faith in Jesus. Through conversion, we become one in confession and loyalty with a new community, the followers of Christ.

In one sense, incorporation into the community of Christ seems to occur automatically. It is an unavoidable aspect of conversion. We simply *are* members of each other, participants in the one fellowship of disciples. Yet, Christ has left us with certain specific acts by means of which his community formalizes or makes public the incorporation of a new believer. In chapter 10, we will look more closely at this aspect of our more formal incorporation. Here we need only mention baptism, which serves as the sign of the new identity in Christ which is ours in conversion.

> ✍ *Conversion means that you have become a participant in a community that spans the ages and transverses the globe.*

Like conversion itself, baptism never occurs in total isolation. Indeed we do not baptize ourselves. Rather than merely an act of the individual, baptism is an ordinance or sacrament of the church. By means of this act (which may be coupled with formal local church membership), the church—through its representatives—symbolically incorporates us into its life. And through baptism, we in turn declare that we belong to a new community, that we are a part of the people who name Jesus as Lord.

THE SPIRIT AT WORK IN OUR SANCTIFICATION

Just as physical birth is not the *goal* but only the beginning of physical life, so also the new birth—conversion—is only the beginning of our spiritual journey.

This means, by the way, that our outreach efforts are not merely directed toward "winning" the lost. Our responsibility has not ceased when they are baptized and join the church. Rather, our goal is *disciple-making* (Matt. 28:19-20).

This means, as well, that we ought not to view personal salvation merely as conversion. Instead, salvation is an all-encompassing process. Viewed from our perspective, this process begins with conversion, continues throughout life, and comes to completion only at our Lord's return.

We now turn our attention to the "throughout life" aspect of salvation, which we call *sanctification.*

"Sanctification" is an important concept in the Bible. Although it is broad in scope, its meaning is always closely related to *holiness.* To be sanctified means to be set apart or separated. And the act of sanctification marks an object or a person with a new status before God (2 Thes. 2:13).[12]

Important to our discussion, however, is a narrower meaning of the word. Sanctification is connected to the quest for holiness.

> Sanctification is the ongoing process whereby the Holy Spirit makes us holy by setting us apart, transforming us into the likeness of Christ and leading us into service to God.

To explore sanctification, we raise four questions about this quest.

Why Be Holy?

We may ask, why be holy? Why should I worry about holiness? After all, I am saved. In the end I'll make it to heaven. So why concern myself with the matter?

The Bible offers a straightforward, terse answer to this question: Be holy because God is holy (1 Peter 1:15). And the Holy Spirit is at work in our lives seeking to do just that — to make us holy after the pattern of God.

The Scriptures place this summary response in the context of God's program for creation. God is calling out a people to be his own. That is, God wants to establish a people who will reflect the divine character — love — for all creation to see. That is why God chose Israel in the Old Testament. And that is why the Holy Spirit is now calling out a worldwide fellowship in the present age.

This means that holiness begins with our frame of mind. In view of God's glorious purpose, we are to see ourselves as God's own possession. We belong to the God who has chosen us. And we exist in order to honor God and to serve God's own purposes (Eph. 1:11-12).

What Does It Mean to Be Holy?

When we read the New Testament we quickly come across an apparent contradiction. We are already declared to be holy—"a holy nation" (1 Peter 2:9). At the same time, we are told that we are not yet holy. We are admonished to become holy or to be holy in all we do (1 Peter 1:15). Which is it?

We can find our way through this apparent contradiction by realizing that sanctification has two dimensions. We may call these "positional sanctification" and "conditional sanctification."

• Positional sanctification speaks of our "position" before God as those who are "in Christ."

Because of Christ's work on our behalf, God has pronounced us "holy" or "set apart" as his own possession. We belong to God. Positional sanctification, therefore, is an unalterable reality. Solely because of the grace the Father extended to us in Christ, which the Holy Spirit applies to our lives, we stand before God as holy people. This status is not affected by the day-to-day gyrations of our personal feelings, attitudes, or conduct.

Our fixed status before God is crucial. Because it sets our relationship with God on solid footing, it is the fountainhead out of which our life as Christians emerges.

• Conditional sanctification is another matter. It is connected to our present spiritual condition or level of spirituality.

Conditional sanctification refers to the process in which the Holy Spirit seeks to transform our life or the way we are actually living. It speaks about the Spirit's attempt to bring our character and conduct into conformity with our position in Christ.

Rather than fixed and unalterable, therefore, the condition of our sanctification is subjective, experiential, and consequently variable, transient, and changing. But if our lives are on track, we should note genuine, observable progress. We should be discovering that we are moving beyond our previous immaturity. We should discover that we are becoming mature, growing into increasing conformity with God's standard, which is Christ (Eph. 4:15).

What Is Our Role in Becoming Holy?

Positional sanctification—our holy status before God—is ours solely because of God's gracious fiat. Viewed from this perspective, we can do nothing to become holy. We can only receive the gift of holiness by faith.

What about conditional sanctification? Here, too, we must acknowledge that holiness is God's work. It is the fruit of the Holy Spirit at work in our lives (Gal. 5:22-23). We gain the victory only because the Spirit provides the necessary power for living godly lives (1 Cor. 10:13; Rom. 8:12-14). We grow only because the Spirit is changing us to become more like Christ (2 Cor. 3:18).

Yet, the Bible clearly points out that we have a role in the process. While the Spirit is the agent of our sanctification, he works through our cooperation. We must diligently apply ourselves to the task of being brought into conformity with Jesus Christ (Heb. 12:14; 2 Peter 1:5-11). Even as exemplary a Christian as Paul testified to the necessity of diligence: "Not that I have attained all this, or have already been made perfect, but I press on to take hold of that for which Christ Jesus took hold of me" (Phil. 3:12-14; cf. 2 Cor. 3:18; Eph. 4:14).

> ✍ *Our resources for holiness include Bible study, prayer, other believers' support, and the Holy Spirit.*

Of course, diligence includes making use of God's provision in order to combat sin, Satan, and self (Eph. 6:10-18; 2 Peter 1:3). But to diligence in overcoming sin (which we may call "negative holiness"), we must add another dimension. We must set ourselves to grow in Christlikeness (positive holiness). In this process our resources are many. They include Bible study, prayer, the support of other Christians, and the strengthening the Holy Spirit offers us.

Will We Ever Become Holy?

The goal of the Holy Spirit is to make us like Christ in character and conduct. He desires that we attain "the whole measure of the fullness of Christ" (Eph. 4:13).

When we look at our own lives—at the short distance we have traversed compared to how far we have yet to go—we wonder, will this ever happen? Will we someday attain the goal of our efforts?

One text of Scripture seems to hold out hope that we might indeed become perfect—like Lucy—in this life:[13] "No one who lives in him keeps on sinning. No one who continues to sin has either seen him or known him. . . . No one who is born of God will continue to sin, because God's seed remains in him; he cannot go on sinning, because he has been born of God" (1 John 3:6, 9; cf. Luke 1:69-75; Titus 2:11-14; 1 John 4:17).

At closer inspection, however, we discover that these verses may not provide the strong assurance that they at first appear to offer. Earlier in the same epistle, John asserts the exact opposite point. Sin, he declares, is continuously with us: "If we claim to be without sin, we deceive ourselves and the truth is not in us" (1 John 1:8). Although the apostle *desires* that we live perfect lives, he anticipates that we will in fact continue to fall: "My dear children, I write this to you so that you will not sin. But if anybody does sin, we have one who speaks to the Father in our defense—Jesus Christ the Righteous One" (1 John 2:1).

It seems, then, that John did not teach that Christians can attain perfection in this lifetime. Rather, our goal will be realized only when Christ returns (1 John 3:2).

How, then, are we to understand John's declaration that the believer does not sin? (1 John 3:6, 9) To find an answer, we must look at the Greek language in which John wrote. In Greek, present tense verbs (those which in English talk about action in the present) regularly designate continuous action. The apostle's point is that believers do not continuously or habitually sin. We will continue to commit specific acts which displease God, but we seek to keep such sinning from becoming habitual. We work diligently, so that no sin will ever gain mastery over us—so that no sin will gain the force of habit in our lives.

So long as we live on this earth we never move beyond the need to exercise diligence in cooperating with the Holy Spirit. We never outgrow the need for further growth in holiness. We never leave the process of sanctification behind. So long as we live on this earth, we long for the goal of our salvation, which the Bible calls our final "glorification."

The Spirit at Work in Our Glorification

"I have been saved" — conversion. "I am being saved" — sanctification. There remains yet a third verb tense: "I *will be* saved." Indeed, at each moment in life our salvation remains incomplete. We await the goal of the Spirit's work in our conversion and sanctification. We call this goal *glorification*. Glorification is the work of the Spirit in bringing our salvation to its final completion — perfect conformity to Christ.

We unpack this hope by responding to two questions.

What Does Glorification Involve?

In speaking about our future glorification, John declared, "But we know that when he appears, we will be like him, for we shall see him as he is" (1 John 3:2). What does this entail?

Simply stated, glorification — perfect conformity to Christ — encompasses our entire existence. We will be like Christ in every way, short of becoming divine ourselves.

• Glorification will include the transformation of our character.

We will be like Christ, for we will come to mirror perfectly the fruit of the Spirit (Gal. 5:22-23), which Jesus himself exemplified. When this happens, both positional and conditional sanctification will merge. No longer will we be holy solely by God's gracious declaration. Now we will also be righteous in our character and conduct.

For this to happen, of course, the Spirit must root out our fallen sinful nature. Because we will no longer be susceptible to temptation and sin, we will be totally free to obey God perfectly.

• Glorification will include the renewal of our physical bodies.

Through the resurrection, the Spirit will transform our bodies so that they will be like the glorious body of our risen Lord (Rom. 8:11). No longer will our bodies be subject to decay, sickness, disease, or death (Rev. 21:4). They will be made perfect, in accordance with the pattern of the glorified body of Christ (1 Cor. 15:20, 23).

• Glorification will bring us into the fullness of community.

We have spoken of glorification as the culmination of our personal salvation. But as we will see in chapter 12, it is actually an experience that we will share together. The doorway to glorification is the resurrection of all believers at the end of the age. We will share in this event only insofar as we are united with Christ, only as we are participants in the one body of Christ. Indeed, all who are united with him will share together in the resurrection. And all who are his will be conformed together into his likeness. Likewise, the resurrection does not usher us into a life of isolation. Instead, it brings us to enjoy an eternal fellowship with God, the people of God, and the new creation.

In short, conformity to Christ means sharing with him in the fellowship he enjoys, that perfect eternal community for which we were created and toward which even now God is directing his saving activity. What a glorious thought! How we long for that day! How we cry out with the church in the Book of Revelation, "Amen. Come, Lord Jesus" (Rev. 22:20).

How Can We Be Certain That We Will Be Glorified?

The New Testament writers had no doubts about our future glorification. So certain was Paul, for example, that he spoke of it as if it were a past event: "those he justified, he also glorified" (Rom. 8:29-30).

The Bible gives us two irrefutable reasons why we can share Paul's certainty.

• Our full salvation is being kept for us.

We know that we will be glorified because God is keeping our inheritance—full salvation—for us until that great day (1 Peter 1:3-5). And *where* is this great treasure? In heaven with God, which is the only location where it is completely secure. As Jesus said, in heaven our treasure is secure both from corruption and from robbers (Matt. 6:19-21).

But how do we know this? How do we know there is a treasure—salvation—awaiting us in heaven? To answer the question we need look no farther than the Holy Spirit. God has given us the Holy Spirit. And this Spirit is God's pledge guaranteeing our final salvation (2 Cor. 5:5; Eph. 1:13; 4:30). The Spirit who is now present within us will accomplish the final transformation of God's people at Jesus' return (Rom. 8:11, 13-17).

• We are being kept for our full salvation.

We know that we will be glorified because God is keeping us unto that great day. But how do we know this? Here again, we do well to look to the Holy Spirit. The Spirit is God at work facilitating the divine project every step of the way. And we can trust God's Spirit to complete his work. As Paul confidently declared, "He who began a good work in you will carry it on to completion until the day of Christ Jesus" (Phil. 1:6).

This divine project includes God's defense of his own. Like an army sent to defend an envoy traversing hostile territory, God has garrisoned divine power—the Holy Spirit—around our lives. The Spirit's presence guarantees that though we will travel through a hostile world, we will arrive safely in our eternal home. Therefore, Peter speaks of us as those "who through faith are shielded by God's power until the coming of the salvation that is ready to be revealed in the last time" (1 Peter 1:5).

Knowing this, we are indeed led to sing with John Newton: "Amazing grace!"

 When we've been there ten thousand years,
Bright shining as the sun,
We've no less days to sing God's praise
Than when we first begun. [14]

FOR CONNECTION AND APPLICATION

1 Which is more difficult for people today, repentance or faith? Why?

2 Do we ever "move beyond" conversion in our spiritual walk? In what sense, yes; in what sense, no?

3 Describe the interplay of personal response, the Spirit's activity, and the involvement of the church community in your conversion.

4 Why is it important to see ourselves as members of a new community, rather than merely as individual believers?

5 Do you agree with the distinction between positional and conditional sanctification? Why is this differentiation important?

6 Why is the vision of our future glorification important for Christian living in the present?

The "Pioneer Community"

"But you are a chosen people, a royal priesthood, a holy nation, a people belonging to God, that you may declare the praises of him who called you out of darkness into his wonderful light"
(1 Peter 2:9).

Pastor Will B. Dunn, leading character in the comic strip "Kudzu," was reading from the pulpit Bible during the worship service one Sunday. "Now, according to the Scriptures, brothers and sisters," he begins, " 'Ye are the light of the world.' " Then in a burst of uncontrolled honesty, he adds off-the-cuff, "But in the case of this congregation, we're definitely talking dim-bulbs."

Unfortunately the pastor's seemingly humorous remark is all too often true. But why? Why does the church appear to be made up of nothing but "dim-bulbs." Why are we not radiant lights who shine forth in a dark world? And more importantly, what can we do to reform the church so that we become the vibrant fellowship of believers that our Lord intends?

If we would become the community our Lord desires us to be, we must gain a clear understanding of what the church is. Only as we remind ourselves what we can be by the grace of God will we begin to draw upon the great Power within our fellowship — the Holy Spirit whom Christ has given to his people.

With this goal in view, we now look at the biblical view of the church. Specifically, we explore what God intends for us within the divine program. To this end, we raise two crucial questions:

☞ *What is the church?*

☞ *What is the church's mission?*

THE CHURCH'S IDENTITY

What is the church? Consider the language we use. We often talk about the church as if it were simply a building. "My church is on the corner of First and Main," we say. Sometimes we equate "church" with the worship service. "Are you going to church next Sunday?" we ask. Or, "What are you going to do after church today?" And occasionally we speak of the church as an organization we join. "I have decided to move my membership to First Church," we announce. Or, "Are you church members?" we ask people we meet.

Is this what the church is? Is the church a great structure of bricks, wood, and mortar? Is "the church" a building in which worship services are held on Sundays? Or is the church the Sunday services themselves? Is "church" an event we can attend? Then again, is the church rather a giant organization? Is it a society or a club in which each of us may choose to hold membership as we see fit?

No! None of these popular uses of the term gets at what the church actually is. To understand the church we must ask the question, "What is the church?" from the viewpoint of the Bible. When we do so, we receive a startling response. Viewed from the biblical perspective, the church is "people." But not just any people. The church is a special people, a people whom the Spirit is forming together into a community. And the purpose of this people is to live, as we continue to emphasize, in fellowship with God, each other, and creation, thereby pointing in the direction that the Lord is taking all history.

In short, the church is the "pioneer community." It is that people who are seeking to point toward the future God has in store for creation. Under the guidance of the Spirit, this people desires to live out in the present the glorious community for which God created us.

To say that the church is the pioneer community succinctly means that it is:

☞ *a relational people,*
☞ *a future-oriented people,*
☞ *a fellowshipping people.*

The Church Is a Relational People

The church of Jesus Christ is not a club we join. We are not members of a giant organization. Rather, we are a special people. We are a people in relationship with the God who saves us through Christ and a people in relationship to each other who together share in God's salvation. This focus on people-in-relationship is evident in the ways in which the early Christians spoke about their fellowship.

The ekklesia. Even the Greek word translated "church" highlights this people orientation. Today we tend to regard the word as part of the "language of Zion," one of those special terms we use when we want to speak about matters of faith. Yet the early believers did not coin the term. Instead, "church" *(ekklesia)* was a common word in the first-century Roman world. Arising from the verb "to call" *(kaleo)* plus the preposition "out of" *(ek)*, *ekklesia* simply means "assembly." More specifically, an *ekklesia* was a gathering of the citizens of a given community who had been called together to tend to city affairs (assembly, Acts 19:32, 39, 41).[1]

The early Christians found in this term a helpful way of expressing their own sense of identity. They were a people called together as well. They were the "called out" ones. They had been called out of the world by the proclamation of the gospel for the purpose of belonging to God through Christ.[2]

Their choice of *ekklesia* to designate who they were indicates that the New Testament believers viewed the church as neither an edifice nor an organization. They were a people — a people brought together by the Holy Spirit — a people bound to each other through Christ — hence, a people-in-relationship.

God's nation, Christ's body, the Spirit's temple. Not only did they designate themselves as the *ekklesia*, the early Christians described themselves through a variety of metaphors. Three of these are especially important.[3]

• The New Testament speaks of the church as *God's nation* and a holy *priesthood* belonging to God (1 Peter 2:9).

"Nation" highlights the new status we share. Just as God had chosen ancient Israel, so now the Spirit has called out the church to belong to God. But this status is no longer based on birthright within a specific ethnic group. Now the Spirit calls together people from the entire world. Consequently, the church is an international fellowship comprising persons "from every tribe and language and people and nation" (Rev. 5:9).

"Priesthood," in turn, informs us about our function. Just as priests played a special role in the life of ancient Israel, so also we have a significant task to fulfill in God's program. Yet, we dare not overlook one crucial difference. Whereas in Israel only a few were selected from among the people to act as priests, in the church *all* the people of God belong to the priestly order. And the ministry of the priesthood is shared by *all.*[4]

Later we will describe how we are to function as priests.

• The New Testament writers also speak of the church as *Christ's body* (1 Cor. 12:27; Eph. 1:22-23; Col. 1:18).[5]

Like the human body, the church is a unity made up of diversity (1 Cor. 12:1-31). Not all members have the same task to fulfill. But all have the same goal; all are to be concerned for the others and to use their gifts in service to the whole. Together we are to carry on Christ's own ministry and be his physical presence on earth.

We will look more closely at this task later.

• The New Testament describes the church as the *Spirit's temple* (Eph. 2:19-22; 1 Peter 2:5) as well.

In ancient Israel the temple served as God's earthly dwelling place (2 Chron. 6:1-2). Now, however, the focus of the Spirit's presence is no longer a special building, but a special people. Because we are the temple of the Spirit, we must live holy lives (1 Cor. 6:19-20).

The church, then, is a people-in-relationship. But we have not yet answered the practical question: Exactly where is the church? In what form do we find this people-in-relationship?

The church as congregation. The New Testament writers provide a definitive answer to this question. Repeatedly they use the designation "church" to refer to a local congregation of believers. Using the New Testament as a guide leads us to conclude that whatever else it may be, "church" is the visible fellowship of

Christ's disciples in a specific location.[6] Consequently, each congregation is the church of Jesus Christ.

"Church" emerges whenever the Holy Spirit brings believers in any location to join together under Christ to be a people-in-relationship. It emerges whenever a group of Christ's disciples pledge themselves to be a "called-out" people. "Church" exists whenever believers join together with the purpose of walking with one another as God's people, under Christ's authority, and by the empowerment of the Spirit.

While focusing on the "local" nature of the church, we must not forget that each congregation is a visible expression of a larger people. This people transcends any one location

> ✍ *The congregation of believers in which you participate is the church of Jesus Christ.*

and any one time. Indeed, we participate in one body composed of all believers of all ages (Heb. 12:22-23). And we are part of the one worldwide fellowship of believers.

The Church Is a Future-Oriented People

The church is not an end in itself. God does not call us out of the world to become a cozy little clique or a "holy huddle." Rather, the church exists to serve a larger intention. The Spirit forms us into a people through whom he can bring about the completion of God's work in the world. This suggests that we must be a future-oriented people. Our task is directed toward a grand goal which will come in its fullness only at the end of the age.

To understand this, we must introduce the biblical drama of God at work establishing his *kingdom* or *reign*. Indeed, the church initially emerged in the context of Jesus' announcement, "The kingdom of God is near" (Mark 1:15).

God's reign. The biblical drama begins with the declaration that as Creator, God is the sovereign ruler of the universe. God alone possesses the right to rule over all creation. And in this sense the entire universe is God's kingdom.

What is true in principle *(de jure)*, however, is not yet fully true in fact *(de facto)*. On the contrary, humans have rejected the kingship of the Creator and have erected an enclave of rebellion in which another — Satan — appears to reign.

Into this situation, Jesus came. Through his ministry, death, and resurrection he demonstrated God's claim to rulership. As a result, God has installed Jesus as the Lord of the universe. Even now, some people acknowledge his lordship and thereby enter God's kingdom.

The biblical drama does not end in the past, however. Its grand sweep moves to the future. At Christ's appearing, what is God's prerogative by right (de jure) will also be universally true in fact (de facto). On that great day all persons will acknowledge Jesus' lordship (Phil. 2:10-11). The principles of God's kingdom will hold sway throughout the new human society. And the entire universe will become the realm of God's rule.

Ultimately, therefore, God's kingdom is a gracious gift God will bestow on us one glorious future day. Nevertheless, kingdom power is already at work in our world, for it breaks into the present from the future. As a result, we can experience the divine reign in a partial, yet real sense prior to the great "day of the Lord."

What is the link between the kingdom and the church?

God's reign and the church. The church father Augustine was one of the first theologians to wrestle with the question of the relationship between God's reign and the church.[7] His position — or perhaps a misunderstanding of it — led theologians in the Middle Ages to link the divine kingdom to the church. The church *is* the kingdom, they concluded.

In the late 1800s certain thinkers devised a diametrically opposite response to the question. Their proposal, which we may call "classic dispensationalism," introduced a rigid distinction between the church and the kingdom. The kingdom is a future, 1,000-year rule of Messiah over the earth.[8] The millennial kingdom will mark the completion of God's program with Israel. This program began in the Old Testament, but was interrupted when Israel rejected Christ on Palm Sunday. The church, in turn, is merely a "parenthesis" in God's "Israel-program." In this sense, the older dispensationalists claimed that the church is unrelated to the divine reign.

The biblical drama will not let us follow either of these propos-als. We ought neither to equate the kingdom with the church nor to drive too radical a wedge between the two. Rather, we must understand the church in the context of the kingdom.

The Bible plainly indicates that God's kingdom is "bigger" than the church. "Kingdom" refers to God's domain in all of its aspects. When viewed from the perspective of the future, God's domain includes not only the church of Jesus Christ, but the entire created universe as well as the heavenly court.

The church, in contrast, arises from God's saving action in history. It was inaugurated by Christ, whom the Father sent to earth to bring God's will — God's goals and purposes — to pass. Since Pentecost, the Holy Spirit draws people to respond to the gospel proclamation. And as we respond in repentance and faith, he brings us to participate in the church, which is the company of those who acknowledge Christ's lordship.

The church, therefore, is the *product* of the kingdom.[9] It comes into being through the obedient response to the announcement of the divine reign.

In addition to being the product of the gospel message, the church derives its *purpose* from God's activity in the world. The Holy Spirit calls the community of faith into being, in order that we might proclaim the gospel and live in the world as the compa-ny of those who acknowledge in the present the coming reign of God. In this sense, the church is the "eschatological company," a people of the future. We are the body of those who bear testimo-ny by word and deed to the divine reign, which will one day come in its fullness.

The church and the future. This connection between the church and the kingdom has far-reaching implications for our under-standing of the church. It means that we must be a future-ori-ented people.

We have repeatedly noted that the goal of God's work in histo-ry still lies in the future. God is establishing an eternal communi-ty. This has great implications for us. It means that this future reality, and not the past or even the present, defines who we are.

In chapter 8 we applied this principle to our personal lives. Our personal identity, we said, lies in the future. Each of us is a glorious, resurrected saint participating in God's eternal community.

In the same way, our *corporate* identity lies in the future. What the church is, is determined by what the church is destined to become. And the church is destined to be nothing less than a new humanity, the glorious company of God's redeemed people who inhabit the renewed creation and enjoy the presence of the Triune God.

In the meantime, the Spirit calls us out of the world so that we might be an "eschatological people," a company who "pioneer" in the present what the future will be like. Our task is to live according to the principles that characterize God's future goal for creation. Our purpose is to be a foretaste of the glorious eternity that God will one day graciously give us in its fullness. Our goal is to connect Christian belief with Christian living.

In short, the church is a *sign* of the kingdom. We are to point the way toward the future.

The Church Is a Fellowshipping People

The church is a people-in-relationship and the sign of God's kingdom. In fact, it is as a people-in-relationship that we become a sign of the future. This leads us to yet a third perspective, one which is implicitly present in the other two: the church is a fellowshipping people, a *community.*

As a people-in-relationship we are a fellowshipping people. We noted that the early believers saw themselves as a special people, a group united together because they had been called out of the world by the gospel to belong to God. The New Testament writers referred to the church as a nation, a body, a temple. And although this people transcends spatial and temporal boundaries, it is chiefly manifested in a visible congregation of believers who band together to be the local expression of the church. This means that the church is a "community fellowship."

The church is more than a loosely related group of people. We share a fundamental vertical commitment—loyalty to Christ—which shapes our very lives. But our common allegiance to Jesus, in turn, forms a bond between us that is greater than all other human bonds.[10] Jesus himself spoke of this in his radical call to discipleship: "Anyone who loves his father or mother more than me is not worthy of me; anyone who loves his son or daughter more than me is not worthy of me" (Matt. 10:37).

This felt bond adds a horizontal commitment to the vertical. Our common allegiance to Jesus draws us together. Because of our loyalty to him, we are committed to each other. We desire to "walk" together as one discipleship band, to be a people in relationship with one another. We who name Jesus as Lord, therefore, become one body—a fellowshipping people, a community.

How does this happen? The answer is: through the Holy Spirit. Although Christ *institutes* the church, the Spirit *constitutes* it.[11] The Holy Spirit is the one who transforms us from a collection of individuals into a fellowshipping people. In conversion, he draws us out of our isolation and alienation. In so doing, he knits us together as one people. Indeed, there arises among us a oneness which is nothing less than the unity of the Spirit himself (Eph. 4:3). In this manner, the Spirit brings us together to be the contemporary expression of the one church of Jesus Christ.

As a future-oriented people we are a fellowshipping people. In speaking about God's work in salvation, we repeatedly emphasize the individual: God saves individual sinners. Correct as it is, this focus all too often settles for a truncated understanding of salvation. And this results in an inadequate view of the church.

God's purpose is the salvation of individuals. But God saves us *together,* not in isolation. And he saves us *for* community, not *out of* it.

The Bible teaches that we are alienated from God, of course. But this estrangement also taints our relationships with one another, with creation, and even with ourselves. Consequently, the divine program leads not only to peace with God in isolation; it extends as well to the healing of all relationships—to one another, to creation, and in this manner to ourselves (that is, to our true identity). And God's concern does not end with the redeemed person as an individual, rather God desires a reconciled humankind (Eph. 2:14-19) living on the renewed creation and enjoying God's own presence (Rev. 21:1-5).

To effect the transformation of estrangement into community, the Father sent the Son and poured out the Holy Spirit. In this new community the old distinctions of ethnic origin, social status, and gender are no longer significant (Gal. 3:28-29). The church, therefore, is far more than a collection of saved individuals who band together for the task of winning the lost. Rather, we are a fellowshipping people, the community of salvation.

But we have not yet mentioned the most foundational consideration. Our understanding of the church as a fellowshipping people arises from the Triune God.

As God's image we are a fellowshipping people. In chapter 3 we declared that God intends to bring his highest creation—humankind—to reflect the eternal divine nature. That is, God desires that we be the image of God.

In chapter 2 we provided the foundation for understanding what that divine image must be. We declared that God is characterized by "love." Throughout eternity God is the social Trinity—Father, Son, and Holy Spirit—the community of love. More specifically, the dynamic of the Trinity is the love shared between the Father and the Son, namely, the Holy Spirit.

God's purpose is to establish a reconciled creation in which humans reflect the very character of the Creator. Even more awesome, the Triune God desires that we be brought together into a fellowship of reconciliation. This fellowship not only reflects God's own eternal essence; it actually participates in God's nature, which is love (2 Peter 1:4).

Where is this to happen? According to the New Testament, beginning with Pentecost the focal point of the reconciled society in history is the church of Jesus Christ. As a people set apart for God's special use, we are to show what God is like. We are to reflect God's own character as we become a genuine fellowshipping people, a loving community.[12]

How does this happen? The clue lies in the role of the Holy Spirit as the Completer of the program of the Triune God. We are a fellowshipping people insofar as we share in the communion of the Spirit.

To understand this, we must review the grand sweep of God's eternal purpose as it relates to his own triune nature. The Father sent the Son in order to realize God's eternal design to draw humankind and creation to participate in the divine life. As we noted in chapter 8, through conversion the Spirit causes us to become the children of God. But this filial status is exactly the relationship the Son enjoys with the Father.

At conversion, therefore, the Spirit—who is the Spirit of the relationship between the Father and the Son—makes us the brothers and sisters of Christ. Thereby he brings us to share in the love the Son enjoys with the Father. Through the Spirit, we participate in the love that lies at the very heart of the Triune God.

Participation in the dynamic of trinitarian love, however, is not ours merely as individuals in isolation. Rather, it is a privilege we share with all other believers. The Spirit's activity within us makes us *co-participants* in the relationship enjoyed between the Father and the Son. In mediating this relationship to us, the Spirit draws us together into one people. Only in our Spirit-produced corporateness do we truly reflect to all creation the grand dynamic that lies at the heart of the Triune God. As we share together in the Holy Spirit, therefore, we participate in relationship with the living God and become the community of Christ our Lord.

Consequently, the community of love which the church is called to be is no ordinary reality. The fellowship we share with each other is not merely that of a common experience or narrative, as important as these are. Our fellowship is nothing less than our common participation in the divine communion between the Father and the Son, mediated by the Holy Spirit.[13]

We are one people, therefore, because we are the company of those whom the Spirit has already brought to share in the love between the Father and the Son. We truly are the community of love, a people bound together by the love present among us through God's Spirit. As this people, we are called to reflect in the present the eternal dynamic of the Triune God—that community which we will enjoy in the great fellowship on the renewed earth.

> ✍ *The church of which you are a part is no "ordinary" community. It is to be a people who participate in a divine communion.*

This is who we are. This is our identity: we are the pioneer

community of God, the people who by the Spirit within us participate together in the fellowship of the Triune God. Our identity, in
turn, forms the foundation for our ministry in the world.

THE CHURCH'S TASK

As the church we are a pioneer community. But what does the
church do? What is our divine calling? What task has Christ given
us to complete? What is our *ministry* as Christ's disciples? To
answer this question we must first ask another. What is the
fundamental *purpose* of the church's existence? Only after answering this can we then explore the church's *mandate*.

Our Purpose — to Glorify God

Why did Christ institute the church? And for what end does the
Spirit continue to constitute the church today? Our answer to
this question can only be: "for God's glory." The church exists
ultimately for the sake of the glory of the Triune God.

The biblical authors repeatedly suggest that God's glory is the
fundamental purpose of all creation (Ps. 19:1). As God's special
creation and the recipients of God's special concern, however,
humans are to offer special praise to their Creator (Ps. 147:1).

Unfortunately, in our sin we fail to praise God as we should.
Therefore, God is at work in bringing us to participate with all
creation in glorifying him. To this end the Father sent the Son.
Our Lord purchased us *from* sin *for* the sake of God's glory (Eph.
1:5-6, 11-14). And he has poured out the Spirit in our hearts so
that we might live for God. Throughout all eternity, therefore, we
will stand as "trophies" of God's grace (Eph. 2:6-7). Consequently, the purpose of the church is to bring glory to God.

This conclusion carries far-reaching significance for our corporate life. It means that the ultimate motivation for all planning,
goals, and actions must center solely on our desire to bring glory
to God. We must direct all that we say and do toward this ultimate purpose, that God be glorified through us.

At this point we must clarify what we mean in the context of a
possible objection. Talk about glorifying God can too readily be
interpreted as implying that God is a cosmic egotist. We know

that the biblical ideal is humility. Paul commands us to "do nothing out of selfish ambition or vain conceit, but in humility consider others better than yourselves" (Phil. 2:3). In this Jesus Christ himself is our model (vv. 5-8). How different appears the attitude of a God who directs all the divine activities toward his own exaltation, demanding that all creation glorify God alone!

To understand how God's glory is, indeed, the final goal of all his actions we must remind ourselves of who this God is. The God we are speaking about is not a solitary subject who is so enamoured with his own surpassing greatness that he relishes the acclamations of his creatures. That God is more akin to Aristotle's Unmoved Mover, who as the only reality worthy of his own contemplation sets himself to be cognizant only of himself.[14]

Rather, the One whom we glorify is the Triune God—Father, Son, and Holy Spirit—the God who desires that we reflect the divine character, which is love. As we live in fellowship, we bring honor to the one who is the divine community of love. But true community requires that its participants relate to each other with humble servanthood motivated by love. For this reason, the Bible elevates humility, exemplified by Jesus' humble obedience to the will of his Father, as our ideal.

We are to be a community bound together by the love present among us through the power of God's Spirit. This divine love is exemplified by humble service to each other and to the world. Indeed, as we exist in love, we are the image of God—that is, we reflect what God is like. Thereby, we bring glory to him, for we exemplify the love that lies at the heart of the dynamic of the Triune God, which Christ himself has revealed to us.

Our Mandate — Worship, Edification, and Outreach

We are to be the community of God's people who bring glory to God. The Bible links the glorification of God with love-motivated obedience to an entrusted vocation. Jesus glorified his Father by completing his work on earth (John 17:4). Our Lord's obedient fulfillment of his vocation expresses the eternal love of the Son for the Father.

So also our obedient acceptance of the vocation God has given us brings glory to Christ and through him to the Father. Indeed, in his great prayer, our Lord rejoiced in the glory he had received through his disciples (John 17:10). Earlier, he told his friends that their fruitfulness brings glory to the Father: "This is to my Father's glory, that you bear much fruit, showing yourselves to be my disciples" (John 15:8).

The church glorifies God, therefore, as it is obedient to its Lord; that is, as it fulfills its divinely given mandate. Specifically, in our common life we are to be a true community of faith, manifesting the community bond in:

☞   *corporate worship,*
☞   *mutual edification,*
☞   *outreach to the world.*

Worship. Jesus entrusted a joyous responsibility to his followers. We are to "worship the Father in spirit and in truth" (John 4:23). As Christ's church we are to be a worshiping community, offering to God the glory due his name (1 Cor. 14:26; Heb. 10:25). For this reason we speak of the church as "gathered to worship."

• The Bible informs us as to the focus of our worship.

Worship means attributing worth to the one who is worthy.[15] Therefore, only the Triune God can be the focus of true worship. We praise this God for who he is and for what he does.[16]

We worship God for who he *is.* As we praise God for being the Holy One (1 Chron. 16:29; Pss. 29:2; 96:8), we consciously join with the angelic hosts who continually proclaim, "Holy, holy, holy is the Lord God Almighty, who was, and is, and is to come" (Rev. 4:6-8; cf. Isa. 6:3). As we worship God the Creator we join the twenty-four elders in declaring, "You are worthy, our Lord and God, to receive glory and honor and power, for you created all things, and by your will they were created and have their being" (Rev. 4:11).

We also worship God because of what he *does.* Indeed, God's saving acts display the divine character.

The focal point of God's saving work is Jesus. We gather to commemorate the foundational events of our spiritual existence, at the center of which is the action of God in Christ delivering us from the bondage of sin. To this end, we praise the crucified and risen Lord (Rev. 5:9), as well as the Father who "so loved the world that he gave his one and only Son" (John 3:16).

• The biblical writings also speak about the means of worship. We may offer praise to God through such vehicles as music, declaration, prayer, and symbolic acts.

Perhaps no activity is more central to biblical worship than music (Ex. 15:1-18; Matt. 26:30; 1 Cor. 14:26; Eph. 5:19). This is not surprising, for music offers us a medium through which to give expression to all dimensions of our being. Song can incorporate the intellectual aspects of life, expressing in lyrics and in the structure of the music the composer's conception of the world. But music also captures feelings, emotions, and moods, thereby giving expression to what cannot be said through words alone. In expressing our Christian consciousness through music we offer to God our emotions in addition to our creeds, our feelings, as well as our beliefs. Through music we offer God our joy as redeemed people (Pss. 92:1, 4; 95:1), we share in the sorrow and pain Christ bore on our behalf, and we anticipate the glory of the great day when our Lord will return. As we respond in this manner, God delights in us (Ps. 149:1-4).[17]

Although music is important, center stage is reserved for *declaration*. We come together to speak and to listen.

Worship includes verbalizing our praise to God, offering "the fruit of lips that confess his name" (Heb. 13:15). We not only tell each other about the greatness and goodness of God, we also extol God for who he is and what he has done (1 Chron. 16:9, 23; Pss. 95:1; 96:1-3; 1 Peter 2:9).

Worship entails as well the proclamation of God's word. This may take the form of prophetic utterances (1 Cor. 14:1-5, 26-32). But more importantly, proclamation centers on the reading and explication of the Bible (Neh. 8:1-9; 1 Tim. 4:13), such as in the sermon. As the church gathers to hear the sermon, they are celebrating the divine provision of instruction in the present as the Spirit speaks through the Scriptures.

One specific aspect of declaration is a third element of corporate worship, *prayer*. In prayer the community focuses its address directly to God.

Corporate prayer moves among four aspects (which follow the acrostic ACTS). We honor God for who he is and extol God for his perfect character *(adoration)*. We acknowledge our human failure and express agreement with God concerning it, namely, that it is displeasing in his sight *(confession)*. As we receive God's gracious forgiveness (1 John 1:9), we are moved to express gratitude to God for all that God has done and is doing *(thanksgiving)*. Finally, we petition God concerning human need *(supplication)*.

A final vehicle for corporate worship is *symbolic act.*

The central symbols in the life of the church are the ordinances, or sacraments, which represent the gospel. Because we will discuss baptism and the Lord's Supper in chapter 10, we need only mention them here.

Although often overlooked, many other symbolic acts enhance our worship. Consider, for example, the friendly handshake through which we extend to others the welcome and acceptance we have received from God. In this way, the act becomes a way of indirect praise to God for the divine goodness. Similarly, joining hands in a circle (especially following the Lord's Supper) as a symbol of our oneness in Christ can bear silent praise to the Spirit who fosters Christian unity.

Consider as well how many congregations collect the financial gifts of the worshipers. Passing offering baskets through the congregation and then having the ushers bring the collected money to the front symbolizes our offering of gifts to God in one community act. And the giving of money itself can be symbolic. The gift can be an expression of our gratitude to God for his goodness to us as a people. The monetary gift ought also represent our entire selves, symbolizing that in this act we are offering to God all that we have and are.

> ✍ *Respond to God's grace by engaging in the kind of worship that encompasses the various dimensions of your being and person.*

Mutual edification. After Jesus washed the feet of the Twelve in the Upper Room, our Lord mandated that we follow his example (John 13:12-17); he entrusted to us the responsibility of mutual edification. Christ calls us to build each other up, so that we might all become spiritually mature (Eph. 4:11-13). Mutual edification is crucial to us all. The Christian life is not merely an individual struggle for perfection. Rather, in an important sense it is a community project.

If we would become a people who edify each other, we must take seriously our calling to be a fellowship of mutuality. Mutuality arises from the sense that we share a fundamental oneness with each other as those who are bound together by common values and a common mission. Mutuality grows as we seek to live in harmony with each other (Rom. 12:16). Mutuality blossoms as we come to sense sympathy, compassion, and empathy for each other — as we learn to "rejoice with those who rejoice" and "mourn with those who mourn" (Rom. 12:15).

Christ calls us to build each other up in several ways. We are to minister to each other's material and spiritual needs. We are to share the burdens of those who are facing difficulties (Gal. 6:1-2), encourage and admonish each other (Heb. 10:24-25), and nurture those who are new or weak in the faith (Rom. 14:1, 19).

Mutual edification also occurs as we become accountable to each other. True accountability does not entail blind obedience to a group or to dictatorial leaders. Rather, it involves taking seriously the simple truth that we are one body — an interrelated, interdependent community of faith. What each of us does and how each of us lives affects the entire fellowship. Any willful, blatant sin casts a shadow over our common testimony to the gospel (1 Peter 2:12). Conversely, as each of us grows spiritually, we all benefit (Eph. 1:18). Accountability also means that we are open to learning from another, knowing that each of us can be an instrument of the Spirit's work in fostering maturity in us.

Mutual edification occurs through many activities. Obvious examples are the preaching and teaching that occur within church life. Churches regularly provide structures designed to foster mutual nurture — inquirers' classes, small caring circles, and larger fellowship groups. Even involve-

> ✍ *How you live as a believer affects all of us; how I live, in turn, affects you.*

ment in the other two aspects of the church's mandate — worship and outreach — serve its edification ministry. Such common activity can be a means of solidifying the bonds that tie us to each other and to fostering growth within our lives.

But above all prayer is a central means of mutual edification. We carry out our edification mandate as we become a praying people, practicing the art and privilege of intercession (James 5:16).[18] We intercede for each other because together we are a "priesthood."[19] Each of us functions in the church as a priest.

The Old Testament provides the context for understanding this. In Israel, priests offered sacrifices to God and interceded before God on behalf of the people. As a kingdom of priests purchased by Christ (Rev. 5:10), we now share the privilege of praying for each other.

In the Upper Room Jesus provided a model for our intercession. "My prayer is not that you take them out of the world," he said, "but that you protect them from the evil one. They are not of the world, even as I am not of it. Sanctify them by the truth; your word is truth" (John 17:15-17). Following Jesus' example, we do not petition God that our friends experience a life of ease—that they be spared all the trials of life. Rather, the focus of our intercession is that God protect them from the evil one as they live in the midst of the world and that they be sanctified— built up—by the truth which is God's word.

Finally, we engage in edification as we act as a "community of memory and hope."[20] We continually remind each other of our common story. This story focuses on God's past action in Christ for our salvation, but includes as well the stories of the great people who have left to us a lasting legacy of faith (Heb. 11). Our common story also involves our future. One day Christ will return in glory. Until then, he promises to be with us through his Spirit.

The grand biblical drama provides a transcendent vantage point for life in the present. This story allows us to connect our personal lives with something bigger, namely, God's own work in history. As we remind each other of this connection, we engage in the ministry of edification. We follow the example of Paul, who drew from our future participation in Christ's resurrection an exhortation to steadfast action in the present (1 Cor. 15:58).

Outreach. No true community of faith fails to set its sights outward—toward the world in which it is called to live. Indeed, our vision drives us beyond the boundaries of our fellowship. We long to see the whole human family reconciled to God, one another, and creation. As we direct our energies toward those who yet stand outside, we become obedient to the outreach mandate Christ entrusted to us, and we bring glory to the Triune God. This outreach mandate encompasses two interdependent activities—evangelism and service:

• Outreach is evangelism.

Evangelism, of course, entails *proclamation*. Jesus himself declared, "And this gospel of the kingdom will be preached in the whole world as a testimony to all nations, and then the end will come" (Matt. 24:14; cf. Rom. 10:14). Following Jesus' own example, we announce to people everywhere that God has intervened in history to bring about our salvation (Mark 1:15). We announce that God is acting toward the fulfillment of his purpose for creation, namely, the establishment of the new community of reconciliation. Evangelism, therefore, includes telling "the old, old story of Jesus and his love."

Evangelism is also *presence*. Evangelism occurs not only as we proclaim the good news. It also happens as the Holy Spirit fashions us into a community of faith in the world. Our very presence in the world testifies that God has acted, is acting, and will act.

We are a sign to the world in various ways. For example, as we offer in the midst of the fallenness of the present the praise that one day will reverberate throughout the universe, we remind the world that God has not forsaken creation to the forces of evil.

We are a sign likewise when we live as a community in the world. By being a true community of believers, we indicate what God intends for all humankind, namely, the establishment of the new community. Therefore, as we are a community in the world we implicitly call others to join us, to be reconciled and participate in God's community. Indeed, the gospel must be embodied—credibly demonstrated through our life together—if others are to see and acknowledge its truth. For this reason, truly being the presence of the community of Christ in the world is central to our evangelistic mission. And a vibrant fellowship of believers is one of our greatest apologetics for the truth of the gospel.

In the evangelism task, prayer is crucial. Our prayer focuses on intercession for individuals who have not as yet acknowledged Jesus as Savior and Lord. But it also encompasses the world. We intercede for political leaders, invoking on their deliberations the Spirit of wisdom in the cause of the kind of peace that is condu-

cive to the spread of the gospel (1 Tim. 2:1-3).[21] And we petition
God that the church may accomplish the task of proclaiming the
good news to the entire world, in accordance with Jesus' declaration (Matt. 24:14). Such supplication includes prayers for specific
proclaimers. We ask that their words be energized, so that the
message will spread and that they be protected from their enemies (2 Thes. 3:1-2).[22]

- Outreach is also service.

Our mission is not limited to the expansion of the church's
boundaries. Rather, it includes sacrificial ministry to people in
need.

We engage in service because it is a natural extension of Jesus'
own ministry. Our Lord placed his task of proclamation in the
context of service: "The Spirit of the Lord is on me, because he
has anointed me to preach good news to the poor. He has sent
me to proclaim freedom for the prisoners and recovery of sight
for the blind, to release the oppressed, to proclaim the year of the
Lord's favor" (Luke 4:18-19). True to his word, Jesus engaged in
service to people in need. The sick, the outcasts, the demon-
possessed, the sinful, and the sinned-against found in him a
friend and healer. Then, prior to his death he promised the disciples that they would carry on his work, doing even greater things
than they had observed in his ministry (John 14:12). As Christ's
body—his presence in the world—we now seek to accomplish
those "greater works" under the direction of his own Spirit.

We serve likewise because service is inherent in the gospel
itself. The biblical gospel is explicitly social. It focuses on reconciliation with God, of course. But the Bible teaches that reconciliation must also be a social reality. We are in right standing with God
only as we are likewise being brought into right relationship with
others. Consequently, the gospel demands that reconciliation with
God be embodied in social relationships, as well as in earthly social
institutions such as family, business, and government.[23]

As the community of those who have responded to the gospel,
we are concerned about compassion, justice, righteousness, and,
above all, love. Hence, we naturally seek to be instruments of the
Holy Spirit in advancing the lordship of Christ in all facets of
human life.

Following Jesus' example leads us to a ministry of service that focuses on meeting the needs of the less fortunate. Like the Good Samaritan, we bind up the wounds of the injured and outcast of the world. Service to the world also demands that we become the advocates of the wounded by attempting to change those structures that wound people. And as those who acknowledge Christ's lordship, we desire that society reflect to an increasing extent the principles that characterize the reign of God.

Prayer is indispensable to our service as the people of God in the world. The attempt to minister to the wounded and the quest for social justice are spiritual activities for which prayer is a powerful spiritual resource.

In the midst of the evil present in contemporary society, we petition God in accordance with the prayer of our Lord, "your kingdom come, your will be done on earth as it is in heaven" (Matt. 6:10). Through prayer bathed in the Scriptures, God's Spirit brings us to sharpen our focus. In prayer, we view specific aspects of the current world order in the light of the biblical vision of the future new order allowing us to perceive the shortcomings of our world in the backdrop of God's purposes. And the Spirit illumines our minds to see what the will of God might mean for the situations we now face.

Prayer, however, is more than an envisioning of our world in the light of God's future; it also provides resources for battle. Our attempt to minister to human needs pits us against structures which lie beyond our ability to affect. If we are to be victorious, we require the resources of God for which prayer is crucial (Eph. 6:12, 18). By means of prayer, we are strengthened for service and renewed in faith.

> ✍ *Your mandate as a participant in the community of Christ is to proclaim, support, and serve.*

Above all, however, through prayer we tap the power of God, which alone is able "to demolish strongholds" (2 Cor. 10:4). Our petition becomes the cry for God to act in the present needy situation. We know that ultimately only God's power is sufficient to overcome the "spiritual forces of evil." Therefore, prayer lays hold of and releases God's willingness and power to act in accordance with the divine will on behalf of the creation, which God loves.[24]

This, then, is the church. We are a people—a community. Together we seek to glorify God as we obey Christ through fulfilling our mandate of worship, mutual edification, and outreach. In the light of this mandate we admonish each other: "O Zion, haste, thy mission high fulfilling. . . ."[25]

Our participation in the church is enhanced through certain practices of commitment which our Lord himself ordained. These symbolize and strengthen us for the task of being his people in the world. And the New Testament provides guidelines as to how we should organize ourselves for the completion of our mandate. To these we now turn our attention.

FOR CONNECTION AND APPLICATION

1   What misconceptions of the church do you hear from people today? Why is it important that we have a correct, biblical understanding of the church?

2   What difference would viewing the church from the vantage point of the future make in our life together as Christians?

3   Why is the style of worship music so controversial in many churches today?

4   We sometimes hear remarks like "I can worship God just as well in the woods (or on the golf course)." Do you agree? What are the implications of such sentiments for the local church body?

5   What are the benefits of participating in an "accountability group"? What are the potential pitfalls? How can these dangers be minimized?

6   What role ought prayer to play in the life of the church?

7   If "the biblical gospel is explicitly social," what implications does this have for a societal problem such as race relations?

8   Which of the three aspects of our mandate — worship, edification, or outreach — is the most important? Elaborate why.

Participating in the "Pioneer Community"

*"All authority in heaven and on earth has been given to me.
Therefore go and make disciples of all nations, baptizing them
in the name of the Father and of the Son and of the Holy Spirit,
and teaching them to obey everything I have commanded you"*
(Matt. 28:19-20).

Two pastors were sitting in a packed stadium watching a college football game. Suddenly one turned to his colleague. "I hate football," he remarked candidly. Then in response to his friend's astonished, inquisitive expression, he added, "But I love to be where people are excited about *something.*"

Why does it seem that the only aspect of contemporary life that excites people is entertainment? Why does a sporting event seem to generate more excitement—even among Christians!—than church? And what can we do to rekindle a heightened enthusiasm about being in the community of faith?

In chapter 9 we pointed to the importance of cultivating a renewed understanding of the nature and task of the church as the "pioneer community." Now we take the discussion a step farther. In this chapter we direct our attention to our participation in that community. Specifically, we explore three themes:

☞ *membership in the community,*
☞ *community acts of commitment,*
☞ *organization for community life.*

MEMBERSHIP IN THE COMMUNITY

As Christians, we belong to God's pioneer community. This statement, however, raises the question as to the form participation in the church ought to take. And discussions of this issue invariably lead to the matter of church membership. Does the focus of participation in Christ's community lie in our being a member of a specific congregation?

Many Christians assume that the answer is yes. They automatically connect belonging to the fellowship of Christ with being listed on the roll of a local church. Of course, an unequivocal affirmation of this viewpoint poses a danger. We dare not equate having our name on a membership list with actual participation in God's eschatological community. We are not "saved" by church membership. Our eternal destiny is not secured by joining a local congregation.

Nevertheless, the connection Christians often assume between church membership and belonging to Christ does harbor an important truth. We are surely not misguided if we realize that ultimately we only participate in Christ's body as we become part of a local fellowship. As we have noted repeatedly in this volume, coming to Christ entails belonging to a people.

But what about membership as it is practiced by many organized churches today? What does the formal act of joining a congregation have to do with participation in the pioneer community? In short, we must explore the

☞ *why?*
☞ *who?*
☞ *and what?*

of church membership.

Why Membership?

No doubt we have all at one time or another asked about the "why?" of church membership. Why should we concern ourselves with this topic? Why bother with some mere formality? Isn't simply becoming a Christian sufficient? What additional value — if any — does the act of joining a church offer?

Christians who reject church membership often appeal to the practices of the early church. "Why don't we merely return to the simple pattern of the New Testament?" they lament. Lying behind this suggestion is an assumption that the early believers had a more informal approach to church membership than we do today. In contrast to our elaborate structures, the argument goes, the biblical authors never speak of "formal" church membership.

This contemporary quest for the restoration of the first-century church suggests that our search for an answer to the "why?" of church membership must begin with the early believers.

Church membership in the first century. At first glance, the elaborate, codified statements of formal membership requirements often used by churches today seem quite foreign to the New Testament. In the Book of Acts, for example, Luke merely speaks of persons being "added to their number" (Acts 2:41, 47). Although reporting that "the number of disciples in Jerusalem increased rapidly" (Acts 6:7), Luke presents no elaborate record-keeping system. Indeed, the membership processes we often take for granted came later, perhaps arising out of the baptismal practices the persecuted church developed in the late second century.[1]

At the same time, we ought to avoid oversimplifying the practices of the early church. The New Testament indicates that the first-century believers did have a more formal understanding of church membership than our pictures often allow, for letters of commendation, similar to contemporary transfer letters, were carried from one locale to another (1 Cor. 16:3; 2 Cor. 3:1; 3 John 5-9).

Although membership procedures may have been less formalized in the New Testament than today, the early believers held inclusion in the church in high esteem. Rather than living as "lone-ranger" Christians, they saw themselves as persons who had been personally incorporated into a larger community (Acts 8:14-17; 18:24-27; Rom. 15:26-27). In fact, the idea of a self-sufficient, isolated Christian was inconceivable to Christ's first-century disciples. In their understanding, the individual believer and the community were intertwined (1 Cor. 12:12-27).

This heightened sense of belonging together meant that exclusion from the Lord's congregation was a serious matter. Through excommunication, a congregation severed their bond with the wayward member (Matt. 18:17; 1 Cor. 5:13). But the ramifications of this act were immense. It entailed more than a breach of human fellowship. Excommunication signified expulsion from

Christ himself. Such removal from the sphere of the Lord's presence and protection made a person once again vulnerable to Satan's attack (1 Cor. 5:5).

The first century and our situation. Like other communities, the community of Christ is—and always has been—a "bounded set." It is a social group with certain boundaries. Consequently, the question of who is "in" and who is not is important. Some form of church membership is inevitable.

Who Is a Member?

But what determines inclusion in the church? Exactly what marks a person as a member of the pioneer community? That is, who is "in" and who is not?

Nearly all Christian traditions in some way connect participation in the pioneer community with an initiation act called "baptism." Because this rite is a sign of entrance into the community of Christ, it marks or symbolizes initiation into the institutional church as well. While most uphold a connection between baptism and membership, Christians are divided on its implications.

The "pure membership" position. Some believe that church membership should be reserved for those who are able to make a conscious declaration of faith. This "believer's baptist" view excludes infants and very young children, of course. Such persons simply have not yet reached the stage in life in which they can testify to a personal conversion experience through baptism. Because infants are not proper candidates for baptism, they cannot be members of the baptized community.

Believer's baptists claim that their position is the logical outworking of the principle of "regenerate church membership," or the "pure church ideal," articulated by the radical Puritans in the late 1500s. If the church is a people—a covenant community, the company of the redeemed—only those who give evidence of regeneration (or election) can be included in the church. And this declaration is made in baptism.

What may appear to be a rigid membership requirement, therefore, is not motivated by a spirit of legalism. Believer's baptists simply want to insure that, as far as possible, church membership is reserved for those who are truly Christ's disciples.

The "mixed membership" position. Other Christians believe that the church encompasses more than the regenerate. Their goal is not a "pure church" of the "elect." Rather, the church is always a "mixed company." It includes others as well.

Who are these "others"? Some traditions include all persons within a geographical area (such as a parish, a diocese, or even a nation) among those who belong to the church. Others limit church membership to persons who profess Christ plus their children.[2] In either case, churches which see themselves as a mixed company generally practice infant baptism. That is, they are "paedobaptists."

The implications of the two positions. By extending to infants the privilege of baptism, which is the sign of entrance into the church, paedobaptists readily suggest that persons can in some sense be church members from infancy. Yet for full participation in church life, paedobaptist traditions generally require an additional rite, such as confirmation. This event—rather than baptism—marks the entrance into conscious discipleship.

The paedobaptist view is a reminder that children—especially the offspring of church members—have a special claim on the watchcare and nurture of the community.[3] (Believer's baptist churches often acknowledge this point through "baby dedication" services.) Nevertheless, as all traditions indicate but believer's baptists emphasize, we ought not "number" children "with the believers" until they give public expression to their faith and embark on the path of conscious discipleship.

What Are We Doing When We Become Members?

So far we have viewed church membership in isolation. This may be helpful for discussion purposes. But in fact, membership cannot be separated from the larger whole of which it is a part.

In chapter 8 we spoke of incorporation into the church as the climax of the conversion experience. Joining a local expression of Christ's church is the final initiatory step into the Christian life. It is the completion of our initial response to the call of the gospel. This response involves personal repentance and faith in Christ as Savior and Lord; it is publicly expressed in water baptism, and it culminates in church membership.

Placing membership in this context—as connected to a person's embarking on the road of discipleship—steers us away from the danger of reducing the act of becoming a church member to the level of joining a club. Church membership involves sealing a "covenant" (a mutual agreement) with like-minded, "like-committed" persons in a specific location to walk together as Jesus' disciples.

Above all, initiation into the church is the incorporation into a community. It means participation in a body of people who share a story, a vision, and a mandate. The process of initiation into the church of Christ, therefore, comes about through the combination of inward personal faith, baptism as the outward expression of faith, and membership in a local congregation. Faith marks our acceptance of the story of Jesus for us. Baptism symbolizes our transfer of loyalties, as we publicly affirm that Jesus is our Lord. And church membership marks the public meshing of our personal story with the story of God's people, as well as that of a specific, local embodiment of that people.

COMMUNITY ACTS OF COMMITMENT

We are a special people. Our *raison d'etre* is to glorify God by walking together as a community and thereby reflecting the character of the Triune God, who is love.

> ✍ *Take your membership in the church seriously.*

All communities engage in certain symbolic acts that represent their life together.[4] As Christians, two practices are especially significant—baptism and the Lord's Supper. Through them we symbolically confirm our participation in the grace God offers us through Christ and in the fellowship of God's people. Hence, for us these two practices become community "acts of commitment."

What Acts of Commitment "Do"

Throughout the church age, Christians have participated in these acts. Yet there remains much confusion and disagreement as to what baptism and the Lord's Supper "do." Exactly how do these rites become acts of commitment?

Sacraments or ordinances? A clue to the answer lies in the words we use to designate these practices. However, even the proper designation has been a source of contention among believers.

Many Christians refer to baptism and the Lord's Supper as "sacraments." "Sacrament" (Lat.: *sacramentum*) was a common word in the ancient world. Upon enlisting in the army, every Roman soldier would swear an oath *(sacramentum)* of fidelity and obedience to one's commander. (Or the persons who were party to a legal dispute would deposit bond money *[sacramentum]* in a temple pending the settlement).[5] From this designation comes a widely known definition:

> A sacrament is an outward, visible sign of an inward, invisible grace.[6]

Other Christians, however, prefer not to speak of baptism and the Lord's Supper as sacraments, because they fear the term still carries vestiges of the magical understanding that prevailed in the Middle Ages. These believers substitute the word "ordinance." This designation is derived from the verb "to ordain," yielding the following alternate definition:

> An "ordinance" is an act which Christ ordained and, therefore, which we practice as a sign of our obedience to him.

Calling baptism and the Lord's Supper "ordinances," reminds us that we practice these acts because Christ has given them to the church as a means for us to declare our loyalty to him. Yet, Christ commanded their observance because baptism and the Lord's Supper are beneficial to us.[7] As sacraments, they provide a vivid means for affirming our fidelity to Jesus as Lord. Through these acts we confess our faith, and we do so in a special manner.

Baptism and the Lord's supper are "visual sermons," the Word of God symbolically proclaimed, for they present a picture of

God's grace given in Christ.[8] As we participate in them, we announce the gospel and bear testimony to our obedient response to the good news. We declare that we have received God's grace in Christ, and we affirm (through baptism) or reaffirm (by the Lord's Supper) our commitment to God. As we affirm our faith in this vivid, symbolic manner, the Holy Spirit brings us to participate in the reality the acts symbolize.

Our past and God's future. But we have not yet provided the complete answer to our question. To do so, we must see how participation in baptism and the Lord's Supper involves us in the biblical drama of salvation. These acts put us in touch with the past and the future.

Baptism and the Lord's Supper transport us into the past. Through these symbols we reenact the gospel story, including our death and resurrection with Jesus. Thereby the Spirit vividly reminds us of our union with Christ. And he confirms in us our identity as new persons.

These acts transport us into the future as well. Through baptism and the Lord's Supper we celebrate that great day when the risen and exalted Lord will return in glory. His presence will mark the consummation of the gospel story. It will mean the transformation of his followers (together with all creation) into his likeness.

The acts of commitment are a powerful means of sustaining this vision in us. They provide a symbolic reminder that our true identity lies in God's future: we *are* what we *will be*. And as we tell the story of God's saving action in history from past to future, the Spirit empowers us for living in the here and now.

Baptism: The Seal of Our Identity

Baptism is the act of commitment which initiates a person into Christ's community. It occurs as a representative of the church applies water to a new believer in the name of the Triune God as a symbol of the new identity God bestows on us through our union with Christ.

Actually, "baptize" is not an English word. Our term is a transliteration of a Greek verb *(baptizō)* which refers to washing with, or plunging into (literally, surrounding with) water.

Christians baptize new believers in obedience to Jesus' command (Matt. 28:19) and in keeping with his own example (Matt. 3:13). But why is this important? Why should we be baptized?

> ✍ *Your baptism and your participation in the Lord's Supper are reminders that you are whom you will be.*

Baptism initiates us into a new life. To answer why we should be baptized, we must remind ourselves of what we said earlier: baptism is an act of initiation.

We have already noted that both baptism and the Lord's Supper proclaim the gospel. They are visual sermons. These acts speak about Christ's death and resurrection, and they assert that he died and rose again for us. In addition, baptism and the Lord's Supper symbolize our response to that message.

More specifically, in baptism we give symbolic expression to the meshing of our personal story with the narrative of Jesus and hence with the story of the faith community. Baptism initiates us into a new life.

• Baptism initiates us into a new life, because it symbolizes our spiritual union with Christ.

Baptism reminds us that we participate in Good Friday and Resurrection Sunday. Indeed, by faith we have died with Christ to the old, sinful life so that we might be raised with him to new life (Rom. 6:3-8).

Baptism declares that Christ's death has brought us forgiveness of sins (Acts 2:38; 1 Peter 3:21). Just as our body becomes clean through physical washing, so also our participation in Jesus' death, symbolized by baptism, cleanses us from sin. This cleansing occurs, because our participation in Christ's resurrection means that we have received the Holy Spirit (1 Cor. 12:13), who causes us to be born anew. The Spirit within us, in turn, acts as the pledge and power of our future resurrection (Rom. 8:11; 2 Cor. 1:22; 5:5; Eph. 1:13-14).

• Baptism initiates us into a new life, because it marks a transfer of loyalties.

Through baptism we publicly declare that we are relinquishing all former allegiances in favor of our new allegiance to Christ as Lord. Whatever commanded our loyalties in the past must now give way to our highest and central loyalty, namely, Jesus.

• Baptism initiates us into a new life, because it seals a new agreement — our covenant with God.[9]

Through this act, we publicly pledge ourselves to God (1 Peter 3:21). We announce our intention to tread the pathway of discipleship.

This initiation into new life is at the same time an initiation into a new community. Baptism does not place us into an isolated realm of personal piety. Rather, it brings us into a new community, the fellowship of God's people. Because our baptism symbolizes union with Christ, we now belong to the fellowship of those who have died to sin and are raised to new life. Because this act marks a transfer of loyalties, we now are a part of the fellowship of those who — like we — confess that Jesus is Lord. And because baptism seals an agreement with God, it places us among God's people. We belong to those who seek to live for God's glory.

Hence, we are baptized "into one body," Christ's church (1 Cor. 12:13). No longer do we define our lives in accordance with the categories of the old community. Rather, we have passed from sin and condemnation into fellowship with God and, therefore, with each other. And as those who have been baptized, we now share the same story, the one story of the people of God. We have become a part of that community which is defined and ruled by the story of Christ, especially his life, death, and resurrection.[10]

Baptism promises us a new future. Why be baptized? Because baptism initiates us into a new community. But our response goes farther. This act doesn't only view our "present" from the perspective of the past. It also moves to the future. Indeed, baptism is oriented — and orients us — toward the future.

Jesus' story, which we commemorate in baptism, did not end with Good Friday and Resurrection Sunday. On the contrary, he ascended into heaven, where he is seated "at the right hand of God" (Rom. 8:34; cf. Eph. 1:20; Heb. 1:3). And one day he will return to earth in glory.

In the same way, baptism is not the end of our narrative.

Indeed, this act places our incorporation into the new community in the context of the final goal of God's saving activity. As we will see in chapter 12, this goal is glorification — our complete transformation which will occur at the Lord's return (Rom. 8:11; 1 Cor. 15:51-57). Baptism points beyond our present to God's eternal community. And it symbolizes our hope of participating in that fellowship. The presence of the Spirit, whose coming into our life is symbolized by baptism, is God's pledge that we will enjoy full salvation at Christ's appearing (2 Cor. 1:22; 5:5; Eph. 1:14).

Viewed in this light, baptism carries immense ethical demands. This act declares that we are to live in accordance with the new identity God has freely bestowed on us. It challenges us to allow the Spirit to transform us into the community of those who belong to God — which we are. And it admonishes us to live in accordance with the grand vision of who we *will be.*

Baptism affects our lives. Why be baptized? We can offer yet a third response: because of the effect God intends this act to have on our lives.

We have described baptism as a "visual sermon." This symbolic act speaks about the death and resurrection of Christ on behalf of sinners, as well as his future return in glory. Just as the Spirit's voice can be heard through a spoken sermon, so also the Holy Spirit issues a call through this visual proclamation.

But who does the Spirit address? For whom can baptism become a visual sermon? Who may be affected by this act? Consider three "audiences."

• An obvious recipient is the one being baptized.

For this person baptism ought to be "a day to remember." From this day forward, the memory of our baptismal experience should act as a powerful motivation for godly living. Our baptism should continually remind us of the commitment we made to Christ and of the importance of living according to the confession we made that day. But our baptism should continually remind us as well of the Holy Spirit whose presence in us was sealed on that day.

> 📖 *Whenever you witness a baptism, reaffirm your own baptismal pledge.*

His baptism seemed to have worked just such an effect on Martin Luther. Whenever Satan would buffet him with doubts, the great Reformer would grab the devil by the collar, take him back through time, and throw him down in front of the baptismal font. He would then say, "You see, Satan, Martin Luther is baptized."

• Baptism ought to have a powerful effect on the baptizing community as well.

By sponsoring this act, we are reaffirming our commitment to fulfilling the mandate our Lord gave us. This mandate includes mutual edification. Everyone who enters the baptismal water is a reminder that the new birth is but the beginning of the spiritual journey. By witnessing his or her baptism, we are accepting the task of nurturing this new believer, as well as all those God has entrusted to our care.

Our mandate also includes outreach. The baptismal candidate reminds us of the many in the world who have not yet responded to the gospel. Through this act, therefore, the Spirit calls us to pledge ourselves anew to the yet incomplete disciple-making task our Lord has given us. Hence, baptism becomes a visual sermon, admonishing us to be vigilant in proclaiming the good news to all people.

• The audience also encompasses all who witness the act.

Through baptism the Spirit addresses everyone present who has not yet come to faith. This visual sermon depicts the good news of the death and resurrection of Jesus for the sins of the world. And the baptism of a new believer announces the necessity of personal conversion. Consequently, through this act the Spirit challenges those who watch to make the same confession now being affirmed by the participant and the community.

The Lord's Supper: Reaffirming Our Identity

Baptism initiates us into Christ's church and seals our identity as God's people. Therefore, it can only occur once. But our Lord has ordained a second act of commitment which we are to practice repeatedly. Our participation in this act marks an ongoing reaffirmation of what we initially declared in baptism.

This second act of commitment is known by various names.

"Communion" emphasizes the fellowship with Christ and one another that this act produces. "Eucharist," arising from the Greek word meaning "to give thanks" *(eucharisto)*,[11] suggests that the act is a thankful celebration of what God has done and will do. "Mass"[12] hearkens back to the medieval focus on the act as an offering to God. Following the Reformers we will designate it "the Lord's Supper" (1 Cor. 11:20). This term anchors our practice in the table fellowship Jesus shared with his followers, especially the last meal with the Twelve in the Upper Room.[13]

Regardless of the name we choose, the Lord's Supper confronts us with the same question we raised concerning baptism: "Why?" Why should we repeatedly participate in this act of commitment? In response, we will venture three answers, before tying the discussion together.

Through the Lord's Supper we celebrate the past. The designation "the Lord's Supper" immediately indicates one reason why we should participate in this act of commitment. Through it, we celebrate the past. We commemorate what God has done for our salvation.

The Lord's Supper commemorates the past because it is a memorial meal. When we gather around the table, we reenact the Last Supper, including our Lord's command "Do this in remembrance of me" (1 Cor. 11:24).

As we commemorate that meal, we symbolically enter into the story of our Lord. We sit with the disciples in the Upper Room, as it were, and recall Jesus' teaching about the pathway to life. We call to mind the fellowship he shared with publicans and sinners, which signaled the inauguration of the new community. But above all, we remember his sacrificial death to which that meal pointed.

As we remember our Master in this way, the Spirit rekindles our devotion to our Lord. He leads us to renew our commitment to discipleship. And he strengthens us that we might live as Christ's followers.

The Lord's Supper leads us to remember Christ, thereby becoming a visual sermon. As we eat and drink, we proclaim in a symbolic manner "the Lord's death" (1 Cor. 11:26). We declare how Jesus sacrificed his life. The broken bread speaks of the giving of his body, and the poured wine refers to the shedding of his blood.

This act declares not only the *fact* of Jesus' death, however. We also proclaim its *meaning* — why Jesus died. The poured wine refers to Jesus' giving of his life for sin in order to seal a new covenant between God and his people (Heb. 9:22; Mark 14:24; Matt. 26:28). By our eating and drinking, we personalize Jesus' death: he suffered for us — *for me* (John 6:54).

The Lord's Supper is also an enactment of our participation in Christ (1 Cor. 10:16). This is vividly portrayed through the in-gesting of bread and wine, for this act represents faith. Just as we must take food to ourselves to sustain physical life, so also we must receive Christ's work on our behalf for spiritual vitality.

The Lord's Supper celebrates the future. Designating this act as "the Lord's Supper" offers a second reason why we should participate in it. As we gather around the table we anticipate the future. We celebrate what God will one day do.

When he ordained the memorial meal, our Lord lifted our eyes from the past to the future: "I tell you, I will not drink of this fruit of the vine from now on until that day when I drink it anew with you in my Father's kingdom" (Matt. 26:29). This promise is our Lord's invitation to see his sacrificial death within the grand sweep of the biblical drama. His story does not end in the past. Rather it moves to the future, to the climax of God's program at the end of history.

We participate in the Lord's Supper conscious of the promise Jesus gave to his disciples. The Lord's Supper, therefore, is a reminder that there is more to come. It is a celebration of the story of Jesus from cross to crown.

But the "more to come" isn't limited to his original disciples. It also includes *us.* Through his resurrection the risen Jesus has gone before us into God's future. In the supper, he comes to us through the Holy Spirit and announces the promise to us as well. *We* will one day eat and drink "anew" with him in the kingdom. *We* will enjoy eternal fellowship with our Lord.

Christ's promise, which he speaks in the meal, directs our attention to the future. We celebrate the eternal life which God has provided through Christ's death and resurrection.

The Lord's Supper celebrates the present. But Jesus' promise doesn't only speak about the future. It doesn't only create in us a grand hope about a far distant day. It isn't merely "pie in the sky by and by."

As we noted in chapter 8, our Lord has given us his Spirit. Because the Holy Spirit is with us, the fellowship Jesus purchased on the cross and promises for all eternity is already ours. For this reason, we celebrate the biblical drama knowing that what it points to affects us right now and right here. The Lord's Supper, in short, becomes our celebration of the experience of community in the present.

Exactly what do we celebrate? — above all, fellowship with Christ. This includes *Christ's* fellowship *with us,* of course. By his grace, our Lord chooses to commune with us in the here and now. His presence is symbolized in the Lord's Supper. We eat and drink conscious that he meets us at the table. But it includes as well *our* fellowship *with him.* As a symbol of community with our Lord, participation in the supper signifies our reaffirmation of our faith. Through our presence at the Lord's Table we publicly confess our loyalty to Christ. We reaffirm the pledge or covenant we made at our baptism.

Through the Lord's Supper we also celebrate our present community with each other within Christ's body. The one loaf symbolizes the oneness of the fellowship we share (1 Cor. 10:17). And our eating and drinking *together* reminds us that the foundation of our unity rests with our common communion with Christ.

Connecting the Lord's Supper with Christian living. The presence of Christ through the Holy Spirit lifts our observance of the Lord's Supper beyond being merely a solemn memorial of our crucified Savior. It is also a joyous celebration of our risen and returning Lord who is present among us.

Participation at the Lord's table is *our* act. We reaffirm our faith, reenvision our hope, and declare anew our love for our Lord. As we do so, we cannot but thank God for the great salvation which is ours by divine grace.

At the same time, the Lord's Supper is *God's* act. Through our participation, the Holy Spirit powerfully reminds us of our identity as persons in Christ, of our covenant with God and one another, and of our participation in the community of God. By reminding us of Jesus' sacrifice, the Spirit admonishes us to follow Christ's example.

By reminding us of the good news of forgiveness in Christ, the Holy Spirit refreshes us in the midst of our failure and sin. By reminding us of Christ's power available each day, the Spirit encourages us to appropriate the divine resources. And by reminding us of Jesus' soon return, the Spirit motivates us to hopeful, watchful service until that great day.

> ✍ *Come to the Lord's Table to reaffirm your faith and to receive God's strengthening grace.*

Finally, our celebration carries sobering ethical implications. Participation in the supper is a vivid reminder that we can serve no other gods (1 Cor. 10:18-22). No other loyalty dare usurp the place of Christ. And as we eat from the one loaf which symbolizes that we belong to each other, the Spirit admonishes us to be concerned for the welfare of one another.

♫ *In remembrance of me, eat this bread.*
In remembrance of me, drink this wine.
In remembrance of me, pray for the time when God's own will is done.
In remembrance of me, heal the sick.
In remembrance of me, feed the poor.
In remembrance of me, open the door and let your brother in, let him in.
Take, eat, and be comforted.
Drink, and remember, too, that this is my body and precious blood, shed for you, shed for you.
In remembrance of me, search for truth.
In remembrance of me, always love.
Do this in remembrance of me....[14]

ORGANIZING FOR COMMUNITY LIFE

Every human social group organizes itself in some manner. Groups devise acts of commitment which integrate new members into the group and provide opportunities for members to reaffirm their loyalty to the shared vision. And they devise certain structures designed to facilitate the group in carrying out its purposes.

As the community of Christ, our purpose is to bring glory to the Triune God by fulfilling the mandate our Lord entrusted to us. How can we best accomplish this? What structures facilitate us in carrying out our task?

Of course, we could simply turn ourselves loose to engage in the Lord's work as each of us sees fit. This approach would fit well with the "rugged frontier" spirit of independence and the entrepreneurial spirit of individual initiative. But it would not embody the biblical ideal of the church as a community. Nor would it ultimately prove successful in assisting us in accomplishing our mandate.

The completion of our corporate task requires that we all pull together. And for this to happen, we must organize ourselves in a manner that best channels our efforts toward the fulfillment of our common calling. To this end, we now give consideration to the two central questions about community organization.

☞ *Who should decide issues of community life?*
☞ *Who should lead in community life?*

Who Should Decide?

The fulfillment of our mandate requires that we develop certain structures. The goal of these structures is not to squelch, but to release all of us to live out our calling within the context of the fellowship of believers. At the heart of all such structures is the question of the decision-making process we will follow. Specifically, who is in charge? Who should decide?

Decision-making in community life. The idea of church decision-making immediately draws our attention to the local church. It raises some questions. How can we best facilitate the working together of individuals within the congregation? Who should decide matters of congregational concern?

Our basic answers lie already within the word we have repeat-

edly used to speak of the church. We are a *community*. Therefore, our corporate life, including its decision-making structures,
must reflect and facilitate community life.

But we are no ordinary community; we are the community of
Christ. Therefore, we look to the Bible—and especially Jesus'
narrative—for insight as to how we are to live as his community.
For this reason, we must ask, what characterized community
decision-making in the first-century church?

At the heart of the New Testament teaching about community
life is a principle which we may call "the priesthood of all believers." The biblical authors declare unequivocally that all believers
are priests (1 Peter 2:5; Rev. 1:6; 5:10; 20:6). Rather than de-
pending on a human mediatory hierarchy (Matt. 23:8-12; Mark
10:42-44; 1 Tim. 2:5), we all have the privilege and responsibility
to engage in priestly functions. Through Christ each of us may
approach God (Heb. 4:15-16; 10:19-20). Each is to offer spiritual
sacrifices to God (Rom. 12:1; Heb. 13:15; 1 Peter 2:5). And each
is to intercede for others (1 Tim. 2:1-2; 2 Thes. 3:1; James 5:16).

Our life together should give concrete expression to this principle. Specifically, the priesthood of all believers means that all
should participate in the fulfillment of the church's mandate[15] by
using their spiritual gifts for the benefit of the whole (1 Cor. 12:7;
1 Peter 4:10-11). In addition, because the church's mandate is a
common responsibility, diligent discernment of Christ's will for
the church should be a matter for the concern of all, not merely a
select few.

We see this principle operative in the early church. Crucial
decisions pertaining to ministry—such as the choosing of Judas'
replacement (Acts 1:23-26), the se-
lection of the first deacons (Acts 6:3-
6), and the commissioning of Paul and
Barnabas (Acts 13:3)—were made by
an entire congregation. Even the Jerusalem Council did not involve
merely a select few, but the entire
congregation (15:22). And the early

> 📖 *Take seriously your
> privilege and responsi-
> bility as part of the
> priesthood.*

writers addressed their epistles to entire churches, thereby rein-
forcing the importance of the people as a whole in the life and
decision-making of the local congregations.[16]

This does not deny the crucial role of leaders, however. Our life together is best facilitated when leaders equip the whole people for their task (Eph. 4:11-13). By teaching and through personal example, leaders ought to assist each church member in becoming an active, informed, conscientious participant, who shoulders the responsibilities of membership and seeks the Spirit's leading.

Structures of community life. Facilitating the ministry of each believer within the context of the congregation does not exhaust our discussion. We must also inquire about the working together of the local congregations within the life of the whole people of God. Who decides matters of importance to the church as a whole?

In answering this question we must remind ourselves that just as no Christian exists independently of others, so also no fellowship of Christians is an entity solely to itself. Rather, each is the local embodiment of something bigger, namely, the church of Jesus Christ. Churches acknowledge this principle by constructing lines of connection among themselves. But what form should this take?

The New Testament sets forth two foundational principles that ought to guide us in this matter. In our church life, we must carefully maintain a balance between a focus on the local congregation and an acknowledgment of the relationship among all churches. Hence, we must give place to both independency and interdependency, to both the autonomy of the local congregation and the associational principle.

• In the New Testament era, individual congregations took the initiative in living out the Lord's mandate.

The church in Antioch, for example, commissioned Paul and Barnabas into missionary service (Acts 13:1-4) and later received their report (Acts 14:27). Paul admonished the Corinthian congregation to take charge of its own internal problems. Its members were to address the schism within their ranks (1 Cor. 1:10). They were to assume jurisdiction for the observance of the Lord's Supper (1 Cor. 11:33-34). And reminiscent of Jesus' own instructions (Matt. 18:15-17), they were to maintain membership purity (1 Cor. 5:4-5; 12-13).

This is independency or congregational autonomy at work.

Autonomy means that each congregation possesses what we may call "church powers." This includes the "power of membership." Each assembly may welcome new members, commend to sister congregations members who relocate, and exercise discipline — even excommunication — toward wayward members. This includes as well the "power of mandate." The Lord has charged each group of believers to fulfill within its own context the mandate of worship, edification, and outreach. To this end, each congregation retains the "power of organization" — the prerogative to select its own officers (Acts 6:1-5) and to set apart or commission leaders for the entire church, within the context of the advice of sister congregations (Acts 13:1-4; 1 Tim. 4:14).

● Yet, congregational autonomy was not the only principle that operated in the New Testament churches. It was balanced by a profound sense of interdependency.

In addition to reminding the Corinthians of his own authority, Paul appealed to what was practiced in all churches as carrying a certain authority (1 Cor. 11:16; 14:33). And he desired that the Gentile congregations provide a practical demonstration of their unity with the mother church by taking up a collection for the Jerusalem saints (1 Cor. 16:1-4; 2 Cor. 8–9).

This reveals the associational principle.

The principle of association is operative when congregations express their participation in, and responsibility to the larger whole by means of a wider framework — whether regional, national, or international. Such associations facilitate congregations in the task of seeking the Lord's will for his people. Associations likewise promote a wider experience of fellowship. And through associations congregations are able to combine resources in order to engage in the task they all share, but cannot complete alone.

Who Should Lead?

We have already mentioned that believer priesthood does not eliminate the importance of leaders in the church. On the contrary, leaders play a crucial role in guiding the people of God. But who are these leaders? And how should they lead God's people?

Again we look to the early church for assistance in answering this question.

Supervisors and assistants. The New Testament suggests that congregational life was facilitated by the leadership of persons serving in two basic types of offices — "bishops" and "deacons" (Phil. 1:1).

Bishops (Gk.: *episcopos)* or elders (Gk.: *presbyteros),* as they were also called[17] (Acts 20:17; 1 Tim. 5:17-19; Titus 1:5; James 5:14; 1 Peter 5:1ff), engage in oversight or administration[18] (see Acts 20:28; 1 Tim. 3:1-2; Titus 1:7). They are to "shepherd" or guide the people of God (Acts 20:28; 1 Peter 5:2). And they are to coordinate congregational ministry (1 Tim. 3:5; 5:17), providing administrative leadership. Their spiritual oversight also involves preaching, teaching, admonishing, and guarding against heresy (Titus 1:9).

A second group of officers — deacons or helpers (Gk.: *diakonos)* — work alongside the supervisors. They can take responsibility for some of the administrative and pastoral tasks. And they should engage in the ministry of the church in its various facets.[19]

Pastors. The New Testament speaks about other leaders as well, persons whose ministry is often connected to, but not always limited to a single congregation. The most prominent of these in the first century were apostles, prophets, evangelists, and pastors and teachers. Of these, pastors remain the most significant for structured church life today.

The New Testament assigns a variety of functions to pastors. They engage in administrative oversight, congregational leadership, and "shepherding." These are augmented by such activities as leading worship, teaching, preaching, and evangelism. By ministering in these various ways, pastors serve as visionaries among the people. Fundamentally, Christ intends that the pastoral office facilitate the spiritual growth of the community so that all can engage in the common task (Eph. 4:12). To this end, pastors keep before the people the vision of community life embodied in the biblical narrative.

Because of the responsibility pastors shoulder and the crucial role they play, no one should seek this office whom the Holy

Spirit has not called to it. As Timothy's experience indicates, the Spirit's act of choosing pastoral leaders involves two aspects—a personal sense of call and the confirmation by the church (1 Tim. 1:18; 4:14; cf. Acts 13:2-3).

We refer to the public confirmation of a personal call as "ordination." Consider this definition:

> Ordination is that act whereby the church sets apart persons whom the sovereign Spirit has selected and endowed for the fulfillment of special leadership tasks in service to the people of God.

Hence, ordination is a confirmation that the Spirit has called, gifted, and empowered a person for pastoral ministry (1 Tim. 4:14; 2 Tim. 1:6-7). Ordination also marks a public commissioning of someone whom the Spirit has called (Acts 13:3; cf. Num. 27:18-23).

Servant leaders. Regardless of the names we use to designate church offices, one theme lies at the foundation of the New Testament understanding of leadership: leaders are servants.

Positions of church leadership do not entail license to promote selfish, or even personal, goals. Instead, leadership exists for the sake of the people. The goal of leadership is to empower the whole people of God to discern and to discharge the Lord's will (Eph. 4:11-13). Therefore, rather than seeking to dominate the people, leaders are to enter into office with all humility and with the intent of seeking the good of those under their watchcare (1 Peter 5:1-3). Leaders ought to realize that they have not been set over the people, but stand with them as together the whole church seeks to be obedient to its Lord.[20] To this end, leaders are to be "examples to the flock" (1 Peter 5:3) "in speech, in life, in love, in faith, and in purity" (1 Tim. 4:12).

Jesus provided the foundation for this understanding of leadership when he instructed his disciples as to how they should relate to each other. He repeatedly contrasted the attitudes of authoritarianism characteristic of the Gentiles and the Pharisees with the spirit of mutuality he desired for his followers (Mark 10:42-43). Rather than looking for special status, Christ's disciples are to remember that he is their sole master and they are all sisters and brothers (Matt. 23:8). Our Lord not only declared that those who would lead his people must be humble servants (Mark 10:42-43), he also illustrated this teaching with his own example of humble service on our behalf (2 Cor. 8:9; Phil. 2:6-8).

As the community of Christ, our goal is to embody and advance the program of God until our Lord returns. Hence, the church exists for the sake of eternity. Knowing this and sensing that God himself has called us to participate in the divine work in history ought to motivate us to enthusiastic action. To this biblical vision of the future we now turn our attention in chapter 11.

FOR CONNECTION AND APPLICATION

1 We often hear remarks like, "I'm a Christian, but I don't need the church." Why do people find this attitude appealing? Do you agree with it?

2 What are the strengths and weaknesses of the "pure membership" and the "mixed membership" approaches to church life?

3 Is a person who has "prayed to receive Christ," but who is reticent to be baptized a Christian? What counsel would you give to such an individual?

4 How would you respond to a person who was baptized as an infant but now wants to express his or her recent profession of faith through believer's baptism?

5 What effect should your baptism or confirmation have on the way you live?

6 Paul told the Corinthians that they couldn't eat at the Lord's Table and at the table of demons (1 Cor. 10:21). How would you paraphrase the apostle's admonition in our contemporary context?

7 Are the several ways in which churches structure and organize themselves equally valid? Why or why not?

ELEVEN

The Climax of
Our Story

*"The seventh angel sounded his trumpet, and there were
loud voices in heaven, which said: 'The kingdom of the
world has become the kingdom of our Lord and of his Christ,
and he will reign for ever and ever'"*
(Rev. 11:15).

In April 1981, a successful Arizona surgeon, James McCullough,
terminated his medical practice. His wife sold her Nevada bou-
tique. And they got rid of their Porsche.

Why? Together with the other members of the Lighthouse
Gospel Tract Foundation, the McCulloughs were preparing for
the "rapture"—for the arrival of Jesus to snatch them away to
heaven. The group's leader, Bill Maupin, had calculated that this
event would occur soon—on June 28. And he had assured them
that their readiness would be rewarded: they would be among the
faithful few who would escape the ensuing tribulation and the
rule of the Antichrist. Later they would return to earth with
Christ, who would set up his millennial kingdom on May 14,
1988.

Were the group members excited or disappointed at this prospect? One participant offered this comment: "We're ready for the
rapture. My little one sort of wants a three-wheeler before it
happens, but we're ready to go."[1]

Both dates Maupin calculated have long since come and gone.
But the phenomenon of predicting the date of Christ's return
continues. One of the most recent timetables, well-covered by
the media, was that of radio evangelist Harold Camping of Family
Radio Inc. Camping forecast a September 1994 date for Jesus'
return in his book *1994?*[2] That specific date, of course, like the

others before it, is past and "the end" is still not here.

As the more recent examples of this phenomenon of forecasting dates suggest, the sense that the end could come soon remains strong. And rightly so. The Bible clearly declares that one day God will bring down the curtain on human history.

But when and how will this happen? Will we destroy the planet, perhaps by igniting a destructive nuclear war or by producing an ecological disaster? And how should we respond to the prospect of an imminent end? These questions take us into a realm commonly called "eschatology."

When you hear the word "eschatology" perhaps you immediately think about predictions about the end times. Your mind may be drawn to these popular questions about future dates and events:

☞ *Can we anticipate being "raptured" out of the world soon?*
☞ *Is a seven-year tribulation period coming?*
☞ *Who is the Antichrist?*
☞ *Will Christ reign a thousand years in Jerusalem?*

And perhaps you are reading the newspaper with these questions in mind:

☞ *Are supermarket scanners and the move toward a cashless society paving the way for "the mark of the Beast"?*

☞ *Is the European Community the precursor of a revived — and evil — Roman Empire?*

☞ *Is the ongoing strife in the Middle East paving the way for Armageddon?*

These matters are indeed among the topics *some* Christian theologians and teachers treat under the heading "eschatology." Yet the crucial issues lie deeper. Eschatology pursues questions of *telos,* of goal or purpose:

• Eschatology inquires about our *corporate* human *telos:* Where are *we* going? That is, does history have a goal? Or is human existence in the end meaningless, merely the chance result of some unguided — or *mis*guided — evolutionary process?

• Eschatology inquires about our *personal* purpose: Where am *I* going? Does my life have a goal? Or is my existence ultimately meaningless, destined in the end only for death?

• And eschatology inquires about the goal of the *cosmos:*
Where is *creation* going? Does the universe have a *telos?* Or is
everything here by accident — merely an unstable interlude between some cosmic Big Bang and Big Crunch?

In short, eschatology asks:

☞ *What — if anything — is the meaning of history?*
    Of my life?
    Of the universe?
☞ *Why are we here? — why is* anything *here?*

Christian eschatology explores the biblical answers to these
questions. In so doing, we speak about *God's* purpose. We articulate what the Bible says — and therefore what we must say —
about God's *telos* ("goal") for creation, for human history, and for
our personal existence. In this chapter and the next, we seek to
offer a Christian perspective on these questions:

☞ *Where are* we *going?*
☞ *Where am* I *going?*
☞ *Where is* creation *going?*

WHERE ARE WE GOING?

On their afternoon stroll Blondie and Dagwood came upon a
street corner preacher. With a thick Bible tucked under his arm,
he was haranguing the passersby from his soap box. "The world
is coming to an end," he announced, pointing his finger at the
surprised couple. But then Dagwood interrupted the monologue:
"You've told us that a dozen times." On cue Blondie completed
the sentence: "And it hasn't happened yet." As this broadside
sank in, a downcast look came over the preacher. "I know," he
stammered, "I'm really on a losing streak." And with a brisk
movement he picked up his soap box, declaring optimistically as
he made his exit, "Maybe I'll get lucky tomorrow."

The preacher's approach was, of course, misguided. But his
message was basically sound. The world is coming to an end. Yet
acknowledging the imminent end of the world does not automatically make us doomsayers. Our focus is not on the end of the

world, but on the end (i.e., *telos)* of human history. As Christians, we affirm that history has an "end," that is, a goal or purpose toward which it is moving. We explore this claim by posing two related questions:

☞　*What is the meaning of history?*
☞　*How will history end?*

The Meaning of History

One of the hallmarks of life today is the widespread conviction that our world is ending.[3] We are witnessing the shattering of the unbridled optimism that dominated the attitudes of our culture for over a hundred years.

What do we have to say in the midst of this situation? What message can we offer to a generation raised under the specter of nuclear war, the menace of worldwide famine, and dire predictions that overpopulation and commercial exploitation will strain our environment beyond its capacities? What hope can we offer to a world in the throes of unrelenting crises? What dare we say to people living under the shadow of economic chaos and portents of ecological disaster? In the midst of the gloom rampant today can we still claim that history has a unifying meaning? And if so, what is the *telos* toward which human history is moving?

History is "his story." The Bible itself informs us that "the end of all things is near" (1 Peter 4:7). But in contrast to the "doom and gloom" that haunts people around us, we believe that history is going somewhere. And this "somewhere" is glorious. As trite as it may initially sound, we believe that history is "his story."

This phrase embodies a great truth: the human story is not meaningless. God is at work directing history to a glorious goal. The world as we know it will soon come to an end. But the curtain of our age will be brought down by nothing less than the return of the risen and exalted Lord Jesus Christ.

This promise lies at the heart of Scripture. The Bible presents the human story as the acts of the sovereign Lord of history accomplishing his goal. This biblical understanding stands contrary to two other widely held outlooks.

• The first alternative has no actual sense of history. Rather, it views time as cyclical. Life follows a rhythmic pattern, a circle of a finite number of events that occur repeatedly and with observable regularity. Indeed, life repeats itself in a never-ending circle, the "circle of life."

Israel's neighbors accepted this cyclical understanding of time.[4] And their religious rituals reflected their belief in the circle of life. In early summer as the coming drought began to dry out the vegetation, the Canaanites lamented the death of the fertility god Baal and the triumph of Mot, the god of death. Then as the winter rains began to replenish the dry ground bringing the promise of good crops, they celebrated Baal's rebirth.[5]

God directed Israel to view time in a different manner: time is linear, not cyclical. Events don't merely follow a repeatable pattern. Rather, each occurrence is ultimately unique. Taken together, events form a trajectory that moves from beginning to end. Hence, occurrences form a history—a narrative. And this history is the activity of the one God asserting divine rulership over all the nations. God's actions move from creation to final redemption, from the primeval garden to that day when the earth will be "filled with the knowledge of the glory of the Lord as the waters cover the sea" (Hab. 2:14; cf. Ps. 102:15; Isa. 66:18-19).

• A second alternative, "secular progressivism," builds from the biblical idea of linear time. But it makes humankind, not God, the subject of history.[6] Rather than being "his story," history is "our story." It is merely the narrative of human progress. And the goal of this secularized history is the construction of a human utopia on earth.

The results of this innovation have been disastrous. The secular progressivists brought the goal of history into the historical process itself. However, when clouds began to darken the horizon of the future, belief in human progress faltered. With no vision of God establishing a glorious goal beyond time, pessimism loomed as the only possible response.

We declare, in contrast, that history is not our story—it is not the story of the progress of humankind. Rather, history is the narrative of God at work bringing creation to a divinely intended goal. And the unity of history lies ultimately in the activity of the one God.

This understanding of history as "his story," as the story of the unfolding of God's purposes for humankind, offers a message of hope in the midst of a pessimistic world. The Bible presents history as meaningful, for it is directed toward a goal; it is going somewhere. This "somewhere" is not an illusive human utopia which we are ultimately powerless to create. Rather, history's goal is nothing less than the realization of God's purposes for creation. The grand culmination of history arrives only because God stands at the end of the human story. By grace, God is ordering our story to its intended goal. And this *telos* will be realized when Jesus returns in glory.

But what exactly is that goal?

History is God at work establishing community. The Bible leaves no doubt as to the actual content of God's goal for human history. God is directing history toward the fulfillment of Jesus' petition: "your kingdom come, your will be done on earth as it is in heaven" (Matt. 6:10). And God's reign — God's will — is reconciliation and fellowship — "community." The Scriptures assert that God's goal is a redeemed people living within a renewed creation enjoying fellowship with the Triune God.

John describes this future community. The seer pictured a new heaven and the new earth beyond the present age. He envisioned the new order as a human society, a city, the New Jerusalem (Rev. 21:9-21). Its inhabitants will be those whom Christ purchased for God "from every tribe and language and people and nation" (Rev. 5:9). Nature will again fulfill its purpose of providing nourishment for humans (Rev. 22:1-4). Most glorious of all, *God* will dwell with us on the new earth (Rev. 21:3; cf. 22:3-5).

In our closing chapter we will look more closely at our eternal home. Here we need only add that although the fullness of community comes only at the culmination of history, we can enjoy fellowship in the present as well. Such experiences of community are a foretaste of the complete fellowship we will enjoy with God, one another, and the renewed creation in eternity.

This means that we ought to join with others in seeking to promote the goal of community on a variety of levels. We can seek to foster fellowship in our families and even in human society. Wherever people are promoting wholesome relationships in the midst of a fallen world, Christians should be providing active assistance, for this is "kingdom work."

But as was implicit in chapters 9 and 10, the focal point of God's work in establishing of community is the church, the fellowship of Jesus' disciples.

> ✍ *Where can you find God at work in our world? Wherever genuine "community" is being established.*

How Will History End?

We know that history is not the story of human progress toward a utopia on this earth. Instead, it is the story of God at work bringing creation to its goal—the eternal community for which we were created.

What marks the transition from this age to the age to come? We have already mentioned the central event—the return of the risen and exalted Christ. But can we say more? Is the Second Coming one aspect of a series of events which together mark this transition?

In one sense, the answer is yes. Connected to Jesus' return are the resurrection of all humans, the last judgment, and the inauguration of eternity.

But in what order do these events occur? And does the Bible describe a host of other events which must transpire as we move toward the consummation of history? About these matters—matters relating to the exact "chronology of the end"—Christians differ.[7]

Many of the differences revolve around a central question: What is the significance of John's vision of "a thousand" year reign of Christ? (Rev. 20:1-8) That is, do the second coming of Christ and the resurrection of all humankind, together with the judgment and the inauguration of the eternal kingdom, occur as one grand event? Or are they separated by an earthly rule of Christ lasting 1,000 years? In other words, does eternity arrive as the catastrophic end to human history? Or are time and eternity separated by a thousand-year golden age on earth (the millennium)?

Competing visions of the millennium. The question concerning the correct interpretation of John's vision of the 1,000 years has intrigued and exercised Christians since the second century. The basic answers have solidified around three major positions. Although there are differences of detail within each, we may designate the positions as "premillennialism" (which may be subdivided into two types), "postmillennialism," and "amillennialism." Each view offers a specific answer to the question of when Christ will return relative to the 1,000 years of John's vision.

• If you have heard any detailed "end-times" chronology, it has likely been the *premillennialist.*

As the name suggests, premillennialists declare that Christ's coming is "pre-millennial." They expect the return of the Lord *prior* to the thousand-year period, during which time Jesus will be physically present and exercise dominion over the entire earth. Only afterward will God inaugurate eternity.

Premillennialists anticipate that the present age will climax with a period of tribulation, when the world will languish under the sway of the Antichrist, until Christ interrupts the rule of this "man of lawlessness," binds Satan, and commences his reign of peace and righteousness. After the millennium, Satan will be freed from his prison to gather the unbelieving nations in a rebellion against Christ's government. Satan's treason will be short-lived, however, for it is squelched by fire from heaven. Then will follow the general resurrection (including the resurrection of the unrighteous), the judgment, and eternity.[8]

All premillennialists agree on these general features. They disagree, however, on certain particulars surrounding the tribulation and the millennium.

"Historic" premillennialists[9] assert that both the tribulation and the millennium focus on the church. The Antichrist will direct his persecution against Christ's disciples. But during the millennium our Lord's faithful followers will be the recipients of God's blessings.

"Dispensational" premillennialists, in contrast, view the future tribulation and millennium as stages in God's purposes for national Israel, rather than the church. Many dispensationalists teach that the church age will climax in the "rapture,"[10] when Christ meets his faithful followers "in the air" and takes them to heaven to celebrate "the marriage supper of the Lamb" (Rev. 19:6-9).[11] With the true church out of the picture, the way is open for the Antichrist to launch his seven-year diabolical rule, while God pours out wrath on the earth. The tribulation will climax with a military conflagration in Palestine,[12] in the midst of which Christ will return with the armies of heaven and rout his enemies.[13] Israel will then acknowledge Jesus as Messiah, and the thousand-year kingdom will be established. During the millennium, Israel will enjoy presence in the land of Palestine and prominence among the nations.[14]

The premillennial chronology embodies an underlying pessimism concerning the role we play in the culmination of history. Despite all our attempts to convert or reform the world, the church age closes with the Antichrist in control of human affairs. Only the catastrophic action of the returning Lord will bring about the glorious age of blessedness and peace. In this manner, premillennialism is a stark reminder that ultimately the hope of the world rests in God, and not in our feeble actions.

• Adherents of postmillennialism anticipate that Christ will return only after a thousand-year earthly golden age. (Hence, they hold to the "post-millennial" return of Christ.)

Postmillennialists anticipate that the church age will witness the spread of the gospel throughout the earth. As this happens, evil (and perhaps its personal representation in the form of the Antichrist[15]) will eventually be routed, and the millennium then arrives. The 1,000 years will be a period of time much like our own, but with a heightened experience of goodness. Because of the pervasive influence of Christian principles throughout the world, the nations will live in peace.

After the 1,000 years have ended, the devil will launch the final conflict of evil with righteousness.[16] Satan's rebellion, however, is short-lived. Jesus will return in triumph, followed by the general resurrection, the judgment, and eternity.

Postmillennialism embodies a basically optimistic outlook toward history and our role in the attainment of God's program. Despite Satan's seduction, treachery, and persecution, we will be successful in the completion of our divinely given mandate. And the principles of peace and righteousness will permeate the whole earth.

The postmillennial worldview leads to engagement in the world.[17] It forms a reminder that before we can become the church triumphant, we must be the church militant. Through Christ, our sovereign God has commissioned us to participate in the divine work in the world. En route to the end of the age there are battles to be won. And our ultimate victory is assured, because the divine power is now at work through the church. This should motivate us to redouble our commitment to work and pray, in order that God's will might be done on earth as it is in heaven.

● The word *amillennialism* literally means "no millennium." Its proponents do not anticipate an earthly golden age in the future. Instead they find some other significance to the symbol in John's vision.

Some amillennialists see the 1,000 years as a symbol for the church age in its entirety. It refers to the victory the church experiences now.[18] Others believe that John had conversion in view. Through the new birth, we come to life and reign with Christ over sin, temptation, and the devil.[19] Or the 1,000 years might refer to the reign of departed saints in the heavenly realm during this age.[20]

Regardless of their actual interpretation of John's vision, all amillennialists anticipate that the second coming of Christ will mark the beginning of eternity without an intervening thousand-year period. Amillennialists, therefore, propose a simple chronology.[21] The time between the two advents will be characterized by a mixture of good and evil. At the close of the age, this conflict will intensify as the church completes its mandate of evangelism and the forces of evil coalesce (perhaps in the appearance of the Antichrist). In the midst of a final, intense time of persecution, Christ will return[22] to complete his redemptive work[23] by routing the forces of evil. Also connected with his return are the general resurrection, the last judgment, and the inauguration of eternity.

The amillennialist chronology is neither overly optimistic nor radically pessimistic about our role in God's program. Victory and defeat, success and failure, good and evil will coexist until the end. This means that we cannot inaugurate God's reign by our efforts to cooperate with the divine power currently at work in the world. But neither should we simply wait expectantly for God to act to bring history to a close.

Amillennialism calls the church to realistic engagement in the world. Under the guidance and empowerment of the Holy Spirit the church can be successful in its mandate; yet ultimate success will come only through God's grace. Therefore, God's people must expect great things in the present; but they must never forget that the *telos* of history will never arrive in its fullness within history.

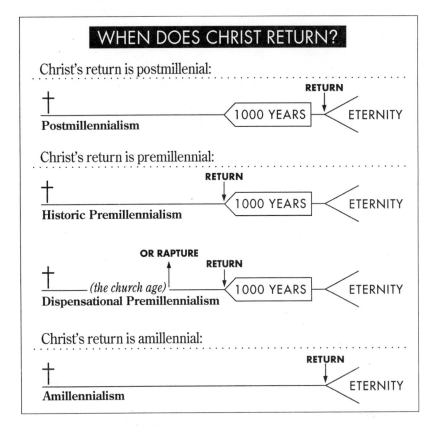

What can we conclude from the debate among the classical millennial viewpoints? In the end, we must lift our gaze beyond the specific question of the thousand years. Regardless of the exact chronology of the end, our ultimate goal is not a golden age on earth, whether preceding or following the return of Christ. Rather, we await with eager anticipation the eternal community God promises us in the new heaven and new earth. This alone forms the final fulfillment of God's promises to his people. This alone marks the fullness of our participation in eternal life—full community with nature, with each other, and most importantly with God our Creator and Redeemer—as proclaimed in the New Testament. Indeed, it is for this community that we were created.

To this we must add an additional note. Although its fullness lies in the future, God has already inaugurated the eternal community.[24] Despite the brokenness of the present, through Christ and because of the presence of the Holy Spirit we now can enjoy a foretaste of the complete fellowship that will one day be ours.

> ✍ *Regardless of your millennial view, eagerly anticipate above all the coming of God's eternal community.*

But what about the end of the age? We still haven't addressed the questions of when and how. Does the Bible have nothing to say about these matters? To respond to this question, we must inquire about the New Testament conception of the end of the age.

The era of the imminent end of history. We may capsulize the biblical understanding with one terse statement:

We are living in the age of the imminent consummation of history.

The biblical writers repeatedly speak about the end of history. One day, God will bring the divine program for humankind to completion in the glorious return of Christ. But what events must transpire en route toward that day? What we may say with certainty arises from the biblical understanding of our era as the age of the imminent end, the epoch of the consummation of history.

According to the New Testament, we are living in a special, "eschatological" era. This age is bounded on the one side by Christ's first coming and the outpouring of the Holy Spirit. It is bounded on the other side by the return of Christ in victory and judgment. When viewed from the Old Testament perspective of promise, *this* is the time of fulfillment (1 Peter 1:10-12). These are "the last days," the final era before the consummation of God's activity in the world.

The biblical writers suggest that the era between the ascension and the consummation is filled with tension. On the one hand, it is marked by the onslaught of evil. Persecution, heresy, deception, and seduction will increase as the Evil One attempts to neutralize the gospel message. Satan's efforts are partially effective, for many fall away, become deceived, or lose heart. On the other hand, the New Testament indicates that our era is also marked by the progress of the gospel. The Spirit-empowered church will complete its mandate before the end comes.

The early Christians themselves experienced both dimensions. They knew firsthand the onslaught of the forces of evil, even as the gospel was spreading throughout the world. To them, this was the sign that the eschatological age had indeed dawned. The last days were already upon the world (1 John 2:18-19). And these believers anticipated the day when Christ would return to vindicate those who acknowledge his lordship. On that day he would exercise dominion over every cosmic power, including our great cosmic enemy, death. For this reason, the apostles saw Christ's return to raise the dead as *the* crucial future event.

What does all this say about how history will come to an end? The Bible clearly declares that the central event with which the human story closes is the final triumph of good over evil. One day the forces of evil will regroup for one last onslaught. But they will be routed by the victorious return of Jesus Christ himself. On that day we will be united with our Lord through resurrection. And this union will be the doorway to our enjoyment of eternal fellowship with our God.

Beyond this basic sketch, the Bible does not intend to provide dates and detailed sequences. We cannot glean from the Scriptures a group of isolated incidents that together form a series of mileposts from which we can construct an "end-times check-list." Nor can we determine what length of the distance from the first to the second advents which the world has traversed. On the contrary, we say with John the seer, "The time is near" (Rev. 22:10).

WHERE AM I GOING?

In the minds of many people, discussions of the end of history only lead to speculation about some distant future day. Of greater immediate concern to them is the question of the end of personal life. "Where am I going?" they (and we) wonder.

In an uncharacteristically sober installment of the famous comic strip bearing his name, Garfield reflected on this question. "Good heaven!" he thought as he stared at the calendar. "I'm going to be eight years old this Thursday!" Turning to the viewer, he remarked, "I hate birthdays. They're a lot like calendars." Then placing his head in his hand, he sighed, "They remind you your days are numbered."

Garfield is not far off track. His candid musings remind us of the words of the psalmist: "The length of our days is seventy years—or eighty, if we have the strength; yet their span is but trouble and sorrow, for they quickly pass, and we fly away." Then the inspired writer adds, "Teach us to number our days aright, that we may gain a heart of wisdom" (Ps. 90:10, 12).

But what does it mean to "number our days aright"? And why should we bother? Isn't life in the end meaningless? Do I not simply live my days and then die? Doesn't life simply culminate in death?

Indeed, we all wonder, does death end it all, or does God have a purpose for me? Is there a divinely intended goal to my existence that extends beyond death? Does my earthly sojourn culminate in some higher life that overcomes death?

Life Beyond Death

The place to begin our inquiry is with death itself—with that abrupt end to life that stalks us throughout our days. Death marks the end of life. But is death life's end *(telos)?*

The Christian faith answers this question with a resounding no! The gospel declares that death need not speak the final word. It is not the goal of our existence. This is good news!

What is death? As we all know, death is universal. All people die. Although we all know *about* death, it remains a great mystery— perhaps the greatest mystery of human existence.

Death is not merely the cessation of biological functioning; it marks the end of personal life. Death means the end of *my* life. Death calls *my existence* into question.

Because we know that we will die, death — so it seems — undermines all our attempts to find meaning in and for life. The inevitability of death suggests that life is a meaningless absurdity. As the preacher concluded: "All share a common destiny — the righteous and the wicked, the good and the bad, the clean and the unclean, those who offer sacrifices and those who do not" (Ecc. 9:2). They all "join the dead" (v. 3).

Does our Christian faith shed any light on the apparent absurdity of death? Yes! To discover this, we must look to the Bible and see how death is ultimately understandable only in the light of God's purposes as revealed in Jesus Christ, for Jesus has gone through death on our behalf.

In contrast to life, which is connected with God (1 Sam. 2:6; Job 1:21), the Hebrews viewed death as ambiguous. On the one hand, it is the inevitable result of the aging process (1 Sam. 2:6). Therefore, to die "old and full of years" is one of the highest blessings God could bestow upon the righteous person. On the other hand, the Old Testament speaks of death as an evil, alien power over which humans have no control (2 Sam. 22:6; Ps. 89:48).

What happens when we die? Like death itself, the Hebrews viewed the situation of the dead as ambiguous. To die is simply to be gathered to one's people (cf. Gen. 49:33). Yet, to die is also to descend into *sheol* (Job 21:13; Ps. 55:15; Prov. 15:24; Ezek. 31:15-17).[25] In *sheol* the dead cannot praise Yahweh (Ps. 6:5) or see him (Isa. 38:10-11), for they "go down to silence" (Ps. 115:17). We can well understand why the Old Testament saints raised the question, "If a man dies, will he live again?" (Job 14:14)

Although the Old Testament hints at the answer to this question,[26] the grand event that shattered death and unleashed a new hope came later: God's power raised Jesus of Nazareth from the dead! Jesus' resurrection eliminates death's ambiguity. He has unmasked death, showing it to be a sinister force (Heb. 2:14).

Death gains this sinister power, because it is the outworking of sin (Rom. 5:12; 6:23). In fact, sin and death form a law at work in us, an alien power to which we are slaves (Rom. 7:21-25; 8:2; cf. 7:5; James 1:15). Sin reigns through death (Rom. 5:21) and gives death its sting (1 Cor. 15:56).

Hope in the face of death. But *sheol* (Gk.: *hades)* does not speak the last word. Christ "has destroyed death" (2 Tim. 1:10), demonstrating thereby that God is greater than death's power. And his resurrection shows that God's goal for us is not death, but life — eternal life — life in fellowship with him. We are created for community!

We now bring this into sharper focus. Like sin, death is contrary to our divinely given destiny, namely, that we enjoy eternal fellowship with God, one another, and our environment. Death marks a breach in this community. Biological death functions as a vivid sign of this breach. Even though a person may die surrounded by a crowd of people, in the end each human goes through death totally alone. No one can experience death for us; nor can anyone travel through death accompanied by another. And death calls into question whatever meaning we seek to devise in life, thereby casting the shadow of meaninglessness over our entire existence. Death, therefore, is a breach of community, a fall into isolation, a loss of identity.

Through Christ, however, we can look beyond death to the eternal community God promises us. One day we will join Christ and enjoy fellowship with him forever.

Because we have this hope beyond death, we also have hope in the face of death. The prospect of dying and the thought of our own death need no longer hold terror for us. Death is no longer the isolating, solitary experience it once was. On the contrary, because Jesus has tasted death for us, we do not die alone. We are not abandoned in death. Instead, even in death we enjoy community. We are surrounded by God's love in Christ (Rom. 8:34-39); indeed, we are "with Christ" (Phil. 1:23).

Having lost its ultimacy, death can even carry positive significance. Divested of its sting, the last enemy of humankind is now a picture of the transformation that occurs through conversion. In baptism we "died to sin" (Rom. 6:2-4), that is, we laid aside the old estranged manner of living. Further, our old foe now marks the completion of our earthly vocation in service to God (2 Tim. 4:7). And the sinister power which led to the shadowy realm of *sheol* marks our entrance into rest (Rev. 14:13).

Because of Christ, death can even become a special way of sacrifice. For those who are martyred because of their testimony to their Lord, death is the means through which they give their own life in praise to the one who suffered for us all (2 Tim. 4:6; Phil. 2:17; Rev. 6:9).

Overcoming Death in the Resurrection

Death is a defeated foe. Indeed, because we experience community with God, we have in a sense already passed from death to life (John 5:24; 8:51; 1 John 3:14). Nevertheless, our final victory over death lies in the future. Death, our "last enemy" (1 Cor. 15:26), will only be fully overcome when our mortal bodies are clothed with immortality (vv. 54-55). Then God will banish death from our experience (Rev. 21:4, 8), for "death and Hades" will be "thrown into the lake of fire" (Rev. 20:14).

But how does this happen? In what manner do we finally overcome death? What event will inaugurate our eternal participation in community? People today have varying opinions about this topic.

Competing visions of life beyond death. We must place the biblical answer to this question in the context of three contemporary conceptions of life after death.

• The first view, which we might call "monism," anticipates that through death each of us is united with the divine.

Monism does not view God as personal, but speaks of the divine in impersonal terms — as "the Absolute," for example. Union with the divine, therefore, means the dissolution of all personal distinctions. At death, we lose our personal identity. As a drop of water disappears into the vast ocean, so also we dissolve into the Absolute, of which we are already a part.

• "Reincarnation," the second alternative, does not anticipate an immediate blending into the divine at death. Rather, the deceased person reemerges. We are reincarnated in a new earthly form.

This chain of death and rebirth continues indefinitely as the soul either progresses or regresses from one earthly life to the next. Eventually, however, sufficient progress allows the cycle to end and the soul to merge with the divine as in monism.

• The third view builds from the idea that the soul is immortal. Death, in turn, marks the culmination of life. At death, the soul discards the body that housed it. It departs the material realm to attain its eternal blessedness.[27]

The Christian vision. The Bible answers the question as to how we overcome death with the word "resurrection." We will overcome death on that great future day when we join Christ in the resurrection. Through this event we will share together in the eternal community God has in store for us.

Can we say more? What exactly is this experience the Bible calls "resurrection"?

• As the word itself suggests, "resurrection" has to do with the body and by extension with personal existence.

This reminds us that God does not intend to "rescue" us from the body or the earth as each of the alternative visions suggests. Rather, we will participate in the eternal community as the embodied, earthly creatures we are.

• At the same time, "resurrection" points out that our future also involves a fundamental discontinuity with our current existence.

We enter into the fullness of God's design only as we undergo a radical change. This change is, of course, ethical. Our susceptibility to sin ("flesh") must be rooted out. And we will be completely conformed to Christ. But this change is likewise physical. Our mortality — our susceptibility to disease and death — must be transformed into immortality (1 Cor. 15:42-43). For this reason, the Bible declares that through the resurrection we will be changed into a "spiritual body" (1 Cor. 15:44), that is, a body transformed by God's Spirit so as to fit it for the new creation where God will dwell.[28]

Beyond this, however, the Bible does not take us. It does not speculate on exactly *how* God will bring us into fullness of life. Although God's precise method remains unknowable, *that* God will do so is clearly evident in Scripture. In addition to the written promise, we also have an internal witness. As believers we already experience the foretaste of the resurrection. The Holy Spirit dwelling within is the "down payment" guaranteeing our future fullness of life (cf. Eph. 1:14; Rom. 8:23). And this Spirit testifies to the truth of the biblical promise.

Our Situation in Death

We believe that one glorious day we will join Christ in the resurrection. This hope offers us solace in the face of death. One question remains, however. What happens immediately at death? Do we "go" somewhere when we die? Once again, people have differing opinions.

Competing visions. Some Christians believe that death is the doorway to eternal life; at death we enter the fullness of God's eternal community.[29] Others offer a diametrically opposite vision often called "soul sleep." On the basis of biblical references that speak of death as "sleep" (e.g., 1 Kings 2:10; John 11:11; Acts 7:60; 13:36; 1 Cor. 15:6, 18, 20, 51; 1 Thes. 4:13-15), they suggest that at death we enter an unconscious state of existence.

More widely held than either of these is a third expectation. At death we experience continued personal, conscious existence beyond death, albeit in a disembodied state. But *where* do our disembodied souls *go* when we die?

The most obvious possibilities are a place of bliss (e.g., "heaven") and a place of torment (e.g., "hell"). Many Christians, therefore, believe that after death the righteous consciously experience God's presence, whereas the unrighteous know the pain of retribution.

Some believers offer further speculations about this "intermediate state." After death, believers are able to converse with the saints of ages past, as well as with deceased loved ones. And we are able to view events transpiring on earth from the vantage point of heaven.

If death is the gateway to the realm of disembodied conscious existence, there might be additional repositories of the souls of the dead. Perhaps at death the vast majority of people enter "purgatory," a place where we are purified—fitted for heaven by undergoing disciplinary suffering.[30]

In the face of these varying opinions, what can we confidently conclude from the Bible?

The Christian hope. We know that death does not simply mark the end of personal life, because every human will be present at the final judgment (Rom. 14:10; 2 Cor. 5:10; 2 Peter 2:9). As Christians, however, our hope does not focus on any conception of life after death. On the contrary, our hope is directed toward the promise of resurrection. Therefore, anything that we say about the status of the dead must arise out of our hope for resurrection. The Christian hope of the resurrection leads to three central statements about the situation of Christians who die.

• Whatever may be our situation when we die, death does not elevate us into the fullness of God's eternal community.

Death is not the entrance into the "higher" existence God intends for us. Only when we are resurrected at the consummation of history will we enter into the fullness of our salvation (Matt. 25:34; 1 Peter 1:4-5), for God's intention includes the physical or bodily aspect of human life.

• While not the fullness of salvation, our situation after death ought not to arouse anxiety and fear in us.

Because we know that at Christ's return we will be united with our Lord, we may rest assured that even in death we are secure. Our greatest enemy is powerless to separate us from the love of God in Christ. Even in death, we remain surrounded by God's loving presence (Rom. 8:35-39).

• This assurance leads to a third statement. The righteous dead are at "rest from their labor" (Rev. 14:13). Resting "blissfully," we should say, for we know that at the resurrection the fruit of our labors will be revealed.

What, then, can we conclude about the situation of the dead? Simply stated, they are "held by God." God "holds" us — that is, our personhood — until the final judgment. On that day, each one appears before God bearing the marks of personal continuity — bodily identity, memory, and similarity of character or mental characteristics. Until that day, the unrighteous are kept *by* God unto judgment and eternal death. But the righteous are kept *with* God unto resurrection and eternal life.[31]

One question still begs to be answered. Are the dead who are held by God aware of earthly events? Here we can only *conjecture.* From the perspective of those who remain on earth, the dead appear to be "sleeping." This picture language means that they are no longer participants in the ongoing flow of earthly time. But this does not mean they have no cognizance of these occurrences.

It would seem that the dead are aware of what is happening on earth, yet not like we are — not as those who move from a known present to an unknown future. They perceive events from the vantage point of the glorious completion of God's program in the resurrection. They are cognizant of earthly events in their unity and interconnectedness.[32]

> ✍ Regardless of what actually "happens" at death, you can face death with confidence, knowing that even then you are not separated from Christ and his eternal love.

A specific situation may serve to illustrate this. When my father died over twenty years ago, my mother often asked whether or not he was conscious of events surrounding his family. The possibility that he remained cognizant of her offered my mother comfort, for thereby she sensed that she was somehow still connected to her husband despite their physical separation. But this also had a "down" side. If he were aware of us, then he was also aware of her grief. And seeing her grieving would surely cause him pain.

So I have asked a number of time through the years, "Does my deceased father know what has transpired in our lives?" And my speculation is, "Yes, in a certain sense." He is aware of earthly happenings, but not as isolated events in the process of time. He is conscious of them, but not as one who moves with us from the present into an uncertain future. Hence, he saw our grief — yes — but in the context of the interconnectedness of events which culminate in the joy of our reunion with him in the resurrection.

So what is the bottom line? The Christian hope of resurrection means we have good news to proclaim in the face of the apparent meaninglessness of our existence, which tragically ends in death. Just as history will one day culminate in Jesus' triumphant return, so also we are destined to share one great day in Christ's resurrection.

Therefore, we can confidently sing:

I know where I'm goin', and I know who's goin' with me;
I know why there's music in the quiet summer morning. . . .
I'm goin' where He goes, and He'll be there beside me,
The love for which He died is all I need to guide me. [33]

FOR CONNECTION AND APPLICATION

1   Why are so many people today interested in predictions about the imminent end of the world?

2   Some people suggest that we should "read the Bible in one hand and the newspaper in the other." Do you agree with this advice? If so, how do we best do so?

3   What practical difference does it make whether we are *pre*millennialists, *post*millennialists, or *a*millennialists?

4   Paul declares that Christians should not mourn as those who have no hope (1 Thes. 4:13). In what way should our beliefs about death and resurrection affect how we mourn? What about how we respond to those who have lost family or friends?

5   For what would you be willing to die, if called upon to do so? How would you view your death in such a situation?

6   How ought the Christian teaching about death and resurrection guide us as we seek to respond to contemporary issues of life and death, such as abortion and euthanasia?

TWELVE

God's Community — Our Eternal Home

"Then I saw a new heaven and a new earth;
for the first heaven and the first earth had passed away,
and the sea was no more. And I saw the holy city, the
new Jerusalem, coming down out of heaven from God,
prepared as a bride adorned for her husband. And I heard a
loud voice from the throne saying, 'See, the home of God
is among mortals. He will dwell with them as their God;
they will be his people, and God himself will be with them' "
(Rev. 21:1-3, NRSVB).

"Hmm . . ." Lucy mused, as she was reading a page fresh from Snoopy's typewriter. Handing the paper back to the budding writer, she commented, "I don't think your subject is serious enough." Making a sweeping gesture, she advised the perplexed dog: "You should write something that is really thought-provoking." Then as she walked away she added, "Write about something that has been a puzzle since the world began." Snoopy pondered the counsel and then returned to his work. "Are there dogs in heaven?" began his new literary piece.

In his own way Snoopy had indeed captured the question that has loomed since the world began. Where is the universe going? What is our eternal home?

Our answer to this query comes in two words: "God's community." According to the Bible, God's purposes go beyond our individual existence or even the human story. The divine goal is ultimately cosmic in scope. It envelops all creation. God's program is nothing less than the bringing to pass of an eternal community encompassing a new creation. We conclude our study, therefore, by looking at this great biblical hope as the answer to three questions:

☞ *What event marks the transition from now to eternity?*
☞ *Will everyone participate in God's eternal community?*
☞ *What will our eternal home be like?*

THE JUDGMENT

God is at work bringing to pass an all-encompassing goal. His intention is to transform creation into the glorious eternal community of the new creation. What precipitates that transformation? What event forms the boundary between our present and God's future?

The Bible answers this question with the word "judgment." Creation becomes new creation only as it passes through judgment.

Actually, judgment is one of the most pervasive themes in all of Scripture. God is not only the Creator; God is also the Judge. But exactly who—or what—comes under divine judgment? The Scriptures speak of two aspects of this future reality.

☞ *A cosmic judgment.*
☞ *A judgment of humankind.*

God Will Judge the Cosmos

The Bible teaches that all creation will come under God's scrutiny. Of course, this includes the cosmic powers, the spiritual hosts. In fact, the New Testament indicates that those who rebelled against God have already been judged (2 Peter 2:4; Jude 6). Indeed, in his death Jesus "made a public spectacle" of the powers and authorities (Col. 2:15).

Nevertheless, Scripture also speaks about a future judgment involving both demons and angels (Matt. 25:41), in which we too will participate (1 Cor. 6:3). Above all, however, God will bring the devil to the day of reckoning. On that day, our foe will be banished from God's eternal community (Rev. 20:10).

The future judgment will not be limited to moral creatures, however. The material creation itself will undergo judgment. Peter declares, "The heavens will disappear with a roar; the elements will be destroyed by fire, and the earth and everything in it will be laid bare" (2 Peter 3:10).

But why? We can readily understand that God must judge Satan and the spiritual hosts. But what possible purpose could a cosmic judgment serve? Why must the physical universe undergo judgment?

Judgment is necessary for the liberation of creation from its present situation. You see, humans are not the only aspect of creation that has not yet reached perfection. Even the physical world does not now fully reflect God's intention (Rom. 8:20-22). Contrary to what several philosophers have claimed, this is *not* the best of all possible worlds.

In what sense is creation not yet perfect? One central aspect is the pervasive presence of the power of decay at work in creation. Of course, viewed as a universal process, decay and death are a natural part of the cosmos. But if we view things from the perspective of God's ultimate purpose and desire, we come to a different conclusion. Decay and death are not "natural." They are not part of the eternal realm that God intends to create.

The present creation can become God's new creation only as it is liberated from the power of decay. And this liberation occurs through judgment. One day, the Creator will transform this universe. To do so God will purge from the physical realm all decay-producing elements. By means of this judgment, the cosmos will be freed from bondage.

But we must probe deeper. Why must decay and death be purged from the cosmos? God desires to create an eternal home for his redeemed people. We can enter into eternal fellowship with him only through resurrection. This event marks the transformation of our perishable, mortal bodies into the likeness of Christ's immortal body. Consider that glorified immortal persons cannot inhabit an earth characterized by decay and death. Therefore, for it to become a fitting environment for us, the earth must undergo judgment and transformation.

This answer is still incomplete, however. Our complete response takes us to the very heart of God's plan. Judgment is necessary to prepare the physical realm for the fellowship God intends to share with all creation!

As we will see later, one day God will leave his lofty home beyond the world and dwell within creation (Rev. 21:1-3). Then we will finally enjoy immediate, unending fellowship with our

Creator. In its current state, however, the cosmos cannot serve as "home" to this new community. Rather, it must first be freed from decay and death: the presence of the eternally unchanging God requires that the physical realm be cleansed from the power of decay. And the presence of the God who is life itself requires that the cosmos be purified from the power of death.

As the home of the Triune God, the entire cosmos will one day join in glorifying the Creator. But this, too, requires transformation. Only when it has been changed—liberated from everything that stands contrary to God's own nature—can all creation offer complete and worthy praise to the perfect and holy Creator.

We can now summarize our response. The judgment is God's act of transforming the old cosmos into the new. God does this so that creation might become "home" to the eternal community of redeemed humans enjoying the presence of the Triune God and living in harmony with the renewed creation.

God Will Judge Us

Although cosmic in scope, God's activity in the world focuses on humans. As the perpetrators of sin, we are the ones in all creation needing reconciliation. It comes as no surprise, therefore, that we are the focus of the judgment as well. And like the cosmos in general, our judgment marks the transition from the old to the new creation.

The certainty of our judgment. The Bible is clear that all people will one day face divine judgment (Matt. 11:24; 12:36; Acts 10:42; Rom. 14:10; 2 Cor. 5:10; 2 Tim. 4:1; Heb. 9:27; 1 Peter 4:5; 2 Peter 2:9; 1 John 4:17).

But how can this include believers? Doesn't the Bible indicate that we are no longer under condemnation, for we have passed from "death" to "life"? How, then, could we possibly be present at the final judgment? (1 Cor. 11:31)

Yet, Scripture is adamant: we will all face God's judgment. Everyone will give an account to the righteous Judge.

Of course, as believers we face judgment with one crucial difference. We know the Judge. The one who calls us to account is the God whom we have come to know in Christ. The one before whom we will stand on the last day is the one who has extended saving love toward us. Our Judge is the God who has already judged our sins in Jesus' death (Rom. 3:21-26; 8:1). Consequently, we can face the day of reckoning without fear of condemnation (Rom. 8:31-34).

Yet the question remains: Why must we stand before our Maker? What is the purpose of the judgment?

The purpose of our judgment. We often picture the great judgment day as a vast line of individuals passing by a judge's bench where they await the verdict—either "condemned" or "acquitted." This, however, is not the scene painted by the Bible.

The judgment will occur swiftly, even instantaneously. More significantly, it doesn't so much entail a pronouncement of some previously unknown verdict, but the making public of hidden realities (Luke 8:17).

Why is this important? Why must God bring these hidden realities to light? And exactly what will be revealed on that great day?

This public disclosure will involve God's vindication of himself. Evil, not God, appears to be in control of the world. The wicked prosper and the righteous suffer (see Ps. 73:1-16). Most tragic of all, the Righteous One suffered at the hands of the wicked. And his followers continue to suffer at the hands of God's enemies. In all of this, God appears slow to act in the cause of justice. This apparent slowness leads us to question the divine power, God's willingness to act, even God's existence.

One day, however, God will overturn this situation. God will pass judgment on behalf of the righteous (Luke 18:1-8). Thereby he will vindicate himself (Eph. 3:10). God will show that he is the one who does indeed bring about justice in creation (2 Peter 3:3-10).

The judgment will also vindicate Jesus and his followers. Through the ascension, God declared Jesus to be the Lord of the cosmos. Our Lord's return will mark his universal, public vindication. But we will share in that glorious event. The public day of judgment that vindicates Jesus will likewise vindicate all those who have confessed his name. For us, therefore, the return of Christ in judgment should be a source of hope (1 John 4:17).

This public disclosure will also affect human social conditions. At the present time the powerful appear to be in control. On that day, however, all will see that the sovereign God has sided with the powerless, for the Lord will champion the cause of the downtrodden. That is, all will see that God does not measure success as power and earthly prestige, but in accordance with humble servanthood, ministry to one another and service to the needy (Matt. 25:31-46; Mark 10:35-45). Then the first will indeed be last and the last first.

This public disclosure will also reveal the underlying unity of the cosmic story. What now appears to be a fragmented flow of disconnected events actually hides a unifying thread. On that day, all humankind will see plainly that Jesus of Nazareth is the *logos*, the one who gives unity to all of life.

Not only will Jesus be *publicly* displayed as the meaning of history, *each* human *life* will be scrutinized in accordance with the unifying principle of all history as revealed in Jesus. The comparison of how we have lived with the revelation of the unity of life will result in a "shrill dissonance." We will see plainly the great gap between God's pattern for our lives and the actual way we lived.

But we still may raise the question of why believers must stand before God. We can understand the presence of the wicked at the judgment. But why us?

For Christians the day of reckoning will complete the sanctification process. In a sense, our judgment will be a purging. God will test our works so that he might remove all the dross (1 Cor. 3:13-15). In so doing, God will fit us for eternity. For us, judgment will mark the transition into an eternal fellowship with God.

At the same time, the judgment will be a day of surprises. Jesus warned that not all who call him "Lord" will enter the kingdom. To some he will respond, "I never knew you" (Matt. 7:21-23). Simply offering "lip service" to God is insufficient. The judgment day will reveal who truly are Jesus' disciples.

The shock of judgment will extend into the believing community as well. Some will discover that although they are saved, they rendered only meager service to the Lord (1 Cor. 3:15).

Obviously God's standard of judgment differs radically from that of the world. What will form the criterion for this scrutiny?

The basis of our judgment. The Bible consistently declares that we will be judged according to our "works" (Gen. 2:15-17; Jer. 17:10; 32:19; Matt. 16:27; Rom. 2:6; 2 Cor. 5:10; Gal. 6:7-8; Rev. 20:11-15; 22:12). Among the works which Jesus cited as leading to condemnation include the accumulation of earthly possessions to the exclusion of true wealth (Mark 10:17-31; Luke 12:13-21), a lack of care for the disadvantaged (Matt. 25:31-46), and an unwillingness to forgive (Matt. 18:21-35).

But this doesn't yet give us the final standard for judgment. Our foundational answer to this question can only be "the divine will." We are judged according to the extent to which our lives have measured up to God's intention for us.

This focus takes us back to the idea of "community." As we have been arguing, God desires that we live in fellowship with him, with each other, and with all creation, and thereby live according to our own true identity. To the extent that we pursue godly community, our lives glorify God and, therefore, are consistent with God's divine standard. The Lord greets such consistency with "glory, honor, and peace," even "eternal life" (Rom. 2:7-10).

This focus leads us to realize that Christ is the standard for judgment. As we noted in chapter 5, Jesus revealed the divine design for humankind—that we are created for community. We are designed to live in fellowship with and obedience to God. Because he shows us what it means to be human, our Lord is the standard in comparison to whom our lives will be measured.

This emphasis suggests how it is that we will be involved in God's act of judging (Matt. 19:28; Luke 22:30; 1 Cor. 6:2; Rev. 20:4). We are those in whom and among whom the Holy Spirit is creating obedience to God's intent to establish community. As a result, our lives bring to light the failure of moral creatures who do not live in accordance with God's purpose.

While conformity to God's will is the standard of judgment, those who incur condemnation do so in accordance with the light they have received. Jesus declared that the servant who knowingly disobeys his master will suffer greater punishment than the one who disobeys in ignorance. Indeed, "From everyone who has been given much, much will be demanded; and from the one who has been entrusted with much, much more will be asked"

(Luke 12:48; see also John 12:48; Rom. 2:12-16; Heb. 10:28-29).

The rewards resulting from our judgment. Will the judgment have consequences in addition to determining our eternal destinies? More specifically, will we receive divine rewards at the judgment? Simply stated, the answer is yes (Matt. 25:14-30; 1 Cor. 3:10-15).

But how can this be? Should not God's eternal community be devoid of the distinctions among people so prevalent in this age? (Matt. 20:1-16) Will the eternal kingdom be ruled by the privileged few — the "rewarded" — just as human societies are? And doesn't the expectation of rewards lead us to serve Christ for personal benefit — to be exalted above others — rather than out of love for the one who saved us?

In contemplating eternal rewards, we must keep in mind that the judgment will be a day of surprises. Our Judge's criterion differs greatly from the world's standard. The Lord may elevate those who appear to be lowly and unimportant above others whom we esteem as the most prominent.

This principle applies to motives as well. Those whose labors have been motivated by purely selfish ends will be surprised when the Lord rewards others who simply served him without expecting anything in return. As Jesus repeatedly declared, the path to greatness in the kingdom follows the route he himself pioneered, self-sacrificial service to others. As a result, the prominent persons in God's new order will be those who are servants of all.

> ✍ *Live each moment conscious of the glorious reality of a coming day of judgment.*

Let's now summarize. The judgment is the public, cosmic revealing of the truth of reality. This revelation will bring surprise and joy to some, as they are welcomed into eternal bliss and receive the rewards of their labors. For others, this day will come as a shock, for they will see clearly the "ultimate failure" of their lives.

THE DARK SIDE OF THE JUDGMENT

"Ultimate failure." This is an ominous phrase. Is ultimate failure truly possible? Will the judgment result in some being excluded from the eternal community? The Bible responds with a resounding yes (Matt. 22:13; Luke 13:25-29; Rom. 6:21; Phil. 1:28; 3:19; 1 Thes. 5:3; 2 Thes. 1:8-9).

But perhaps the answer is more complicated than it appears on the surface. Perhaps this failure is not beyond repair. Let's look at this possibility.

Will All Eventually Come "Home"?

Justice requires that the divine Judge not overlook human failure, of course. But perhaps the sentence of condemnation God speaks on the day of judgment is not irrevocable. Indeed, perhaps it is remedial, intended merely to bring the prodigal to return to the Father's waiting arms. Perhaps God is a great pedagogic; God condemns so that all persons might come to salvation. Those who fail to do so in this life will be gathered in sometime in eternity.

The belief that in the end God will gather every person into his eternal fellowship is known as "universalism." Your first response might be to ask, "How could anyone come to this conclusion?"[1]

Universalists are convinced that the Bible itself teaches their view. The God of the Bible, they argue, loves all creation so much that he is unrelenting in pursuing the wayward.[2] The God who is long-suffering and desires that all "come to a knowledge of the truth" (1 Tim. 2:4) could not rest in the enjoyment of eternity until he had brought the last human into the fold.

In addition, universalists argue that Christ's lordship over the cosmos is so complete that there can be no enclave lying outside his reign. There can be no realm to which his death for sin and his triumph over the evil powers does not extend. An eternal hell would be just such a place — a realm beyond the reach of Jesus' reconciling work, a sphere over which sin (and not Jesus) rules.

Hell cannot be an eternal fate, universalists add, because God desires that all be saved (1 Tim. 2:4; 4:10; 2 Peter 3:9). And Christ's death is the atonement for all (2 Cor. 5:19; Titus 2:11; Heb. 2:9; 1 John 2:2). Didn't the Second Adam win justification for all humankind by his obedience, proponents ask, just as the first Adam brought sin and death to all? (Rom. 5:12-21) And doesn't the Second Adam bestow resurrection life on all, just as the first Adam brought death to all? (1 Cor. 15:20-26) Therefore, universalists conclude, the God who will bring all creation to its fullness in Christ (John 12:32; Eph. 1:10; Col. 1:15-23) will also restore all persons to himself (Acts 3:19-21; Phil. 2:9-11).

Universalists raise another significant theological point. Isn't it inconceivable that earthly choices should determine an irrevocable eternity apart from God, when so many people do not respond to the gospel in this life? The God who is just, proponents demur, must continue to draw all people to himself in the next life, until everyone freely responds to his invitation and so participates in God's eternal community.[3]

The hope that in the end all will be saved resonates well with our sympathies as Christians. Do we not long that everyone join us in eternal praise to God? And can we speak about the prospect of anyone going to hell except with tears in our eyes?

The Bible, however, simply does not support universalism. Scripture declares that God's *intent* is universal. But as we noted in chapter 8, salvation requires *personal* appropriation.[4] In creating humankind, God has imposed a certain limitation on himself. God takes us so seriously as to allow us to absent ourselves from the eternal fellowship for which we were created.[5]

Will the Unrighteous Simply Cease to Exist?

If some will not enjoy God's eternal community, then perhaps their fate is extinction. Perhaps God will destroy them at the judgment. Or perhaps God simply withdraws the Spirit's life-giving presence so that they simply pass out of existence. This suggestion is known as "annihilationism" or "conditional immortality."

While acknowledging that some people are eternally lost, annihilationists find the traditional doctrine of conscious suffering problematic. They claim that it came about through the intrusion of the Greek idea of the soul's immortality into the church.[6] According to the Bible, in contrast, we must receive immortality from God—specifically, through participation in the resurrection.

In addition, like universalists, annihilationists find the idea of hell repugnant. The presence of people in hell contradicts both

Christ's victory and God's intention to reconcile all things in Christ, they argue.[7] Likewise, rather than serving a useful purpose, eternal torment exhibits a vindictiveness incompatible with the loving God revealed in Jesus. It makes God act in a manner that contradicts his own revealed goodness and offends our God-given sense of justice.[8]

More importantly, annihilationists find their view to be the explicit teaching of the Bible: the end of the wicked is destruction (Ps. 37:2, 9-10, 20, 32; Mal. 4:1-3). The unrighteous will be cast into the smoldering garbage heap of *gehenna* (Matt. 5:30) where they will be burned up (Matt. 3:10, 12; 13:30, 42, 49-52) and destroyed in both body and soul (Matt. 10:28). They will experience "the second death" (Rev. 20:14-15; cf. Rom. 1:32; 6:23; 1 Cor. 3:17; Phil. 1:28; 3:19; Heb. 10:39; 2 Peter 2:1, 3, 6; 3:6-7; Jude 7).

But doesn't the Bible speak about eternal damnation? Doesn't Scripture describe hell as an eternal reality, a place of never-ending torment?

Not when properly understood, annihilationists reply.[9] These texts refer to the permanence of the *result* of judgment, not the continuation of the *act* of punishment.[10] "Eternal punishment" means that the results of judgment "cannot be reversed."

Upon closer inspection, however, we conclude that such passages of Scripture simply cannot be read in the way annihilationists prefer.[11] Unfortunately for their position, the very word the biblical authors use to speak of the eternal bliss of the righteous is the one they also choose to describe the punishment of the lost (Matt. 25:46) and even the fate of Satan and his cohorts (but see Matt. 8:29; Mark 5:7; Rev. 14:10; 18:7-8). Just as we await an "eternal" bliss, so also will they suffer a punishment that is "eternal."

In addition, the idea that all the wicked suffer an equal punishment for their crimes — annihilation — violates our sense of justice. Does my "morally upright" but unbelieving neighbor face the same fate as a man like Hitler or even the devil himself? Do they receive an undifferentiated sentence — "mere" extinction for each of them? No! The Bible indicates that the unrighteous will suffer varying degrees of punishment (Matt. 10:15; 11:20-24; Luke 12:47-48).

Although insufficient, annihilationism does caution us against becoming too graphic in describing the fate of the lost. Just as we cannot envision what conscious bliss will mean to us who have been transformed into resurrected, spiritual bodies, so also we do not know what punishment will feel like to those eternally outside God's community.

What Is Hell Like?

The Bible explicitly teaches that there are two eternal possibilities. And according to Scripture, hell is not a happy fate (Dan. 12:2; Matt. 13:42, 49-50; 22:13; 24:51; 25:10-30, 46; John 5:29; 2 Thes. 1:9; Heb. 6:2; Jude 7; Rev. 14:10-14).[12]

Most people today continue to give at least passing acknowledgment to this biblical truth. Results from a 1990 Gallup Poll indicate that 60 percent of Americans still believe in hell. But who will be there? Interestingly enough, while the same poll found that 3 percent of church-going people believed they had an "excellent or good chance of going" there, only 7 percent of nonmembers felt they were hell-bound.[13]

Why hell? The reality of hell is a great mystery. And we dare never claim to understand it completely. But whatever we say about hell, we must understand it from the perspective of the character of God.

The Bible teaches that God is an eternal lover. In keeping with the divine nature, he loves creation eternally. God desires that we respond to the divine love — that we enjoy eternal community with him, one another, and creation, and thereby truly be the image of the Triune God.

We noted in chapter 2 that we dare not confuse God's love with sentimentality. As the great Lover, God is also the avenging protector of the love relationship. Consequently, God's love has a dark side.

Some may spurn God's love or seek to destroy the holy love relationship God desires to enjoy with creation. Those who do experience the divine love as protective jealousy or wrath. Because God is eternal, our experience of God's love — whether as fellowship or as wrath — is also eternal. Just as the righteous enjoy unending community with God, so also those who set themselves in opposition to God's love experience this holy love (wrath) eternally. This is hell.

What more can we say about this awful reality? Only that hell is the eternal tragedy, the eternal human failure.

● Hell is failure.

The tragic truth is that some creatures simply refuse to live in accordance with God's intention. Those in hell suffer gnawing despair as they realize that they missed the purpose—the community—for which God created them. The judgment brings to light the "shrill dissonance," the discrepancy between their lives and the wonderful destiny God intended for us all. And they know this dissonance throughout eternity.

● Hell is "burning fire."

Many Christians interpret the biblical images of hell as burning fire literally.[14] However, the Reformers were surely correct in understanding "fire" as a metaphor. "Fire" refers to the anguish generated by the awareness that a person has invested his or her entire life in what is perishable and temporal, rather than imperishable and eternal (Matt. 6:19-20; Luke 12:16-21).[15]

● Hell is isolation.

God's purpose for humans is community—the enjoyment of fellowship with the Creator, with one another, and with creation. The lost, however, fail to realize this destiny. Rather than living in fellowship with God through obedience to the divine will, they have remained alienated from him.

> ✍ The Bible's picture of hell is a sad state. Only talk about hell with tears in your eyes.

This is the "second death" (Rev. 20:14). Alienation from God is now eternal. The lost are forever separated from our human destiny in the eternal divine community.

● As isolation, hell is estrangement and loneliness.

Hell is "outer darkness" (Matt. 8:12; 22:13; 25:30). Banished from the realm where believers bask in the light of God's presence, the unrighteous are shut up into themselves where they can only grope in darkness.

A cartoon pictures Satan conducting an orientation session for people who have just entered hell. "Try to think of this as a support group for the eternally damned," he glibly states.

Were it only true, then the lost might find some consolation! But hell offers no support for the damned. Shut out from fellowship with the God of all comfort and the community of the saints, they experience only the pain of isolation.

In short, then, there is a dark side to eternity. The other side of the good news is bleak. Some will not participate in the eternal community God wills for us all. But thanks be to God, the divine patience is not yet exhausted. The God who does not delight in the death of the wicked (Ezek. 18:23; 1 Tim. 2:4) continues to offer pardon and grace to wayward humans. And the Holy Spirit continues to call sinful humans to enter into a fellowship that will continue throughout all eternity.

OUR ETERNAL HOME

One day God will bring to pass a glorious new situation. Then the entire universe will conform to what has been the Creator's purpose from the beginning. This new situation God is creating will be our eternal home.

But how can we even talk about this reality? We can only do so by invoking the images the Bible uses.

To help us understand what God is planning to do, the Bible speaks about God fashioning a "new creation." Through Isaiah, for example, God declares, "Behold, I will create new heavens and a new earth. The former things will not be remembered, nor will they come to mind" (Isa. 65:17). And John's vision of the future concludes in a similar manner: "Then I saw a new heaven and a new earth, for the first heaven and the first earth had passed away" (Rev. 21:1).

The New Creation Is the Renewed Cosmos

Christians throughout the ages have wondered what our eternal home will be like. The phrase "the new creation" offers an important clue. The glorious future reality that God promises is "the creation." It is none other than this very universe, the cosmos that we know. But it is not merely *this* universe. That future reality is also the *new* creation. Our eternal home, therefore, is the renewed cosmos, the purified and transformed universe.

To see how this is so, we must return to chapter 11. There we spoke about the resurrection as the means whereby we enter God's eternal community. As such, it marks the culmination of our personal stories. We likewise indicated that Christ's return forms the culmination of history. It lies at the boundary between our experience of linear time and God's eternity.

This suggests yet one more connection. The judgment marks the transition from creation to new creation. But as we noted earlier, the judgment is both cosmic and personal. It involves each of us, as well as the spiritual beings and the physical universe. This judgment, therefore, lifts human life in all its dimensions (both personal and social) into the life of the entire cosmos.

For this reason, the hope of God's renewal of all creation stands at the apex of our vision. But what does this hope entail? How can we describe the future renewal?

The renewal is the completion of creation. The place to begin is with a reminder as to what "creation" is all about. And to get a handle on this we need to ask a question. When did God create the world? Of course, the answer is obvious: "In the beginning God created the heavens and the earth" (Gen. 1:1). God called the universe into existence "in the beginning."

Yet, this is not the entire story. God brought the cosmos into being in the distant past. Nevertheless, God's purpose in creating and for creation has not yet been attained. In fact, it remains unrealized until the end, until God fulfills his promise to "make all things new." Indeed, why would God make this promise, if creation were already what God intends?

The cosmos does not yet conform to the Creator's design. In this sense, it is not yet completely created.

One day, however, this will change. The Creator will liberate the cosmos from its present incompleteness. God will bring it into conformity with the divine design.

What will the renewed cosmos look like? The picture the Bible presents differs greatly from what we often imagine. We describe our eternal home as an entirely "spiritual" (i.e., nonmaterial) place, a realm far away from the earth. For indeed, our eternal home is inhabited by purely spiritual beings. And to distinguish it from earthly, physical existence, we commonly call it "heaven."[16]

The biblical vision, in contrast, anticipates a physical place. It is a new earth blanketed by a new heaven (Isa. 65:17; Rev. 21:1).

Don't we go to live with God for all eternity? Not exactly. The Bible doesn't speak of resurrected believers being snatched away to some heavenly world beyond the cosmos where God waits. John, the seer of Revelation, envisions exactly the opposite. The home for the citizens of God's eternal community will be on the renewed earth. And God will take up residence with us! The Triune God will dwell in the new creation (Rev. 21:3).

How can this be possible? Surely the Creator can't simply leave heaven behind and move in with creatures. What kind of "creation" must the new creation be? That is, what is the relationship between creation as we know it and the new creation?

The relationship of the new to the old. The eternal God plans to dwell with his saints within creation. But as we noted earlier, for this to occur, God must inaugurate certain changes in the cosmos. Therefore, the new creation both is and is not like the creation we know. We must speak of both continuity and discontinuity between the old and the new.

First, let's examine the discontinuity. The new creation will differ greatly from the cosmos as we know it. The basic difference is obvious. Everything we find in creation that is harmful or stands counter to God's perfect design is banished from the new creation.

• Above all, our eternal home is a sin-free realm.

God will root sin out of our hearts. The Spirit will purge us of the sinful disposition with which we struggle in this life. He will expunge every trace of the alien power that now keeps us in bondage.

God will also cast out sin as a network or menacing power in the cosmos. No longer will the tempter, the architect of wickedness, be able to buffet us. No longer will demonic powers plague human relationships and social structures. Peace and harmony will reign everywhere.

• Our eternal home will also be free from the vestiges of fallenness.

We will enjoy an environment free from decay, disease, and most importantly death (Rom. 8:21; Rev. 21:4).

• Incompleteness will likewise be absent from God's new world.

We will no longer yearn to experience the fullness of life. Gone will be all uncertainty and insecurity (Heb. 11:10; 12:28) and any sense of anxiety or despair. Relegated to the past will be all suffering. And no one will ever again go wanting for the necessities that sustain life (Rev. 22:1-3).

Second, let's look at the continuity. While differing greatly from creation as we now know it, the new creation will nevertheless be the renewed creation. God promises to make all things new, not to begin anew. The Creator will not totally destroy the old creation and then once again begin from scratch. Only once does God create out of nothing.[17] Rather than the total destruction of creation, our vision is of its renewal and liberation (Rom. 8:20-22). The best of human culture may even flow into God's new world (Rev. 21:26).

Perhaps we can understand this idea of continuity and discontinuity by comparing it to the Resurrection. To do so, consider Christ's resurrection. The resurrected Lord was the same person as the crucified Jesus. His disciples knew this, for they recognized him. Yet he was also different. He had been transformed into a new existence. Consider as well our future resurrection. Each of us will also be the same, yet different. We will recognize each other (sameness). But we will be transformed and perfected after the likeness of Jesus (difference).

The same will characterize the entire creation. The old will give way to something radically new. Yet it is *this* universe that God will transform into the new creation.

But what difference does this make? Why does it matter whether God starts again from scratch or transforms the present creation into the new creation? God's promise that he will transform the physical world into our new dwelling means that the material universe in which we now live is important — it is eternally significant. And this in turn means that the so-called "material dimension" of life is likewise important.

In chapter 11, we spoke about the importance of our being embodied creatures. We noted that death is not the glorious moment when the soul is liberated from its bodily prison. Death is not the point when we shed the body and float off into the better realm beyond. You see, the "real" me is not my soul. We are not created for death—for the separation of the soul from the body. Rather God created us for resurrection, for embodied existence in the new creation.

In the same way, God did not create the universe for annihilation. God does not intend to replace the cosmos in its physicality for some purely nonmaterial, "heavenly" realm.

For this reason, we rightly engage in "material" ministries in the present. Feeding the hungry—just as "saving souls"—is "kingdom business." Indeed, our task is not an either-or matter. Rather we are to engage in both simultaneously; we must minister to whole persons. And our concern extends beyond human needs to include all creation. Our mandate as Christ's community includes seeking to model the future. As far as is possible in the present age, we are to be a fellowship of redeemed people living in harmony with creation.

The New Creation Is Fullness of Community

Our eternal home will be on this earth—that is, on the earth as it is transformed through the renewing action of the Creator God. But this declaration has not yet taken us to the heart of our description. What will our new home be like? What will characterize life in the new creation?

Of course, we cannot answer this question to our satisfaction. It is similar to asking a baby developing in the womb what life will be like after birth. Nevertheless, we can offer one word which capsulizes for us in the present what our future will be like. That word is "community." Our eternal home will be characterized by the fullness of community.

Community means God is present. Above all, God will be present in our eternal home. John reports, "And I heard a loud voice from the throne saying, 'See the home of God is among mortals. He will dwell with them' " (Rev. 21:3, NRSVB).

The eternal community is the complete fulfillment of the promise running throughout the Bible, namely, that God will be present among his people. But the fulfillment John saw is grander than any earlier prophet could have imagined. At the end of time, the transcendent Creator of the universe willingly and graciously chooses to leave the lofty realm beyond the world to become fully immanent in creation.

Our eternal home, therefore, will be characterized by community in the highest sense. It will be home not only to creatures but to the Triune God. The one who throughout eternity is the community of Persons — Father, Son, and Holy Spirit — will grace the new community with the divine presence.

> ✍ *Our eternal home will be characterized by the fullness of community.*

Because God will choose to dwell with us, we will enjoy complete fellowship with the Triune God. John described this in the poignant statement, "and there was no longer any sea" (Rev. 21:1). Here the "sea" represents the distance between God and creation. Indeed, we now sense a great gulf separating us from God: God is in heaven and we are on the earth (Ecc. 5:2). On that day, however, we will no longer be estranged from God's presence. Just as we will see our Lord "as he is" when he returns (1 John 3:2), so also we will enjoy a relationship of immediacy with the Triune God throughout eternity.

This does not mean, however, that the distinction between God and creatures is erased.[18] We are not advocating monism. God will remain eternally God. And we will always be God's creatures, albeit creatures who now bathe in the radiance of the divine presence.

Community means fellowship. Our eternal home will likewise be a place of fellowship. Peace, harmony, love, and righteousness will reign throughout the new creation.

• Fellowship will be our experience as humans.

Above all, we will enjoy fellowship with the Triune God. God will dwell among us. And we will gaze on the face of our Lord and Savior.

We will enjoy fellowship with each other as well. In the realm beyond the resurrection we will recognize each other. We will know each other for who we are.

Does this mean that we will remember the connections that had characterized our earthly lives, including family ties? Will we know each other as parent, spouse, or offspring?

The answer is a qualified yes. We will recall the earthly connections. But these former roles will not govern our relationships in the new community. Thus, we will not be married in eternity (Matt. 22:30), despite what the followers of Joseph Smith and others teach. Instead, we will remember the former relationships and rejoice in how God used others to influence our lives for his glory.

And we will enjoy fellowship with all other creatures. Our eternal home will be the new *earth*. We will live in the transformed and renewed universe. According to John, the new creation will rival the Garden of Eden which was home to our first parents before the Fall. John saw the tree of life in the middle of the New Jerusalem, yielding a bounty of fruit and providing leaves for healing. This bounty was possible because the curse caused by our sin had finally been lifted (Rev. 22:2-3). In short, the discord between humankind and nature will come to an end. God's intention that Adam (and hence humankind) live in harmony with nature will finally be fulfilled.

• Fellowship will not only be our experience, however, it will also mark all creation.

The prophets anticipated a realm where even the animosity within the animal world will give way to harmony. Isaiah, for example, looked to a day when the wolf would learn to feed with the lamb (Isa. 65:25), when God's creatures would never again know fear or competition. In our eternal home all creation will enjoy the peace that comes when God liberates the cosmos from the effects of our sin.

Does this provide an answer to Snoopy's question? Are there dogs in "heaven"? Of course, the Bible doesn't respond to the question itself. But it does answer the desire which often motivates our query. We long for complete fellowship in the universe. We groan for a day when all creatures can dwell together in full harmony. We can even envision a place where creatures in some sense "know" each other—perhaps even actually communicate with one another—just as occurs in some of the animated movies Hollywood produces.

The Bible promises just such a situation. That day is coming. We don't know what other beings will populate the new heaven and the new earth. But we do know that our eternal home will be a place of fellowship, and this fellowship will encompass all inhabitants of the new creation. This too belongs to the fullness of community.

Community means glorification. Our eternal home will be a glorious place. It will not only be glorious in appearance, however. It will be glorious because all creation will participate in an eternal glorification.

- Of course, in eternity *God* will be glorified.

What will we be doing in our eternal home? Glorifying God! In the eternal community we will glorify God as we offer him our praise. In fact, we will join all creatures in this act. On that great day, the Spirit will mold us into one great chorus of praise to the eternal Creator and Savior.[19]

- *We* will also experience glorification.

We already spoke about glorification as the end product of the sanctification process (chap. 8). On that day, the Holy Spirit will transform us, bringing us into perfect conformity with Christ.

Eternal glorification involves more than the perfecting of the saints, however. As we glorify God, we also experience glorification.

Why is this? Ultimately we do not glorify God merely on our own. Rather we serve and praise God through the power of the Holy Spirit within us. But in bringing us to offer our praise and service to the Father, the Spirit actually places us alongside Jesus. As the eternal Son, our Lord glorifies the Father throughout eternity, just as Jesus glorified the Father on earth through the completion of his mission (John 17:4).

But as the Son glorifies the Father, so the Father also glorifies the Son. And because we are united to Jesus Christ, the Father's lavish glorification of the Son overflows to our benefit as well (John 17:24).

In short, as the Spirit leads us to glorify the Father *through* the Son, the Father glorifies us *in* the Son. As we offer our eternal praise *to* our God, we receive the very goal of our existence, the praise *of* our God.

- All *creation* experiences glorification.

The dynamic of glorification is not limited to us. Nor does our glorification involve us in isolation from the rest of creation. Rather, the experience of glorification through the act of giving glory to God encompasses all creation, and all creation together. We are glorified together with creation.

And as we have seen, this glorification occurs *through* the Son—through the union of all creation in the Son (Col. 1:15-20). In the dynamic of glorification we actually participate in the eternal relationship between the Father and the Son—who is the Spirit within us bringing us to glorify the Father through the Son. Therefore, the eternal community ultimately means the participation of creation through the Spirit in the glory of—even in the life of—the Triune God (2 Peter 1:4).

This participation of creation in the Son's glorification of the Father and in the Father's glorification of the Son marks the consummation of the Spirit's work. As the Spirit of the relationship between the Father and the Son, he is the completer of both the dynamic within the Triune God and God's work in the world. In this way, the Spirit eternally glorifies the Father and the Son both within the divine life and by completing the mission of God in bringing creation to share in this eternal glorification.

What the Holy Spirit effects at the consummation is but the heightening of what he is already accomplishing in the brokenness of our present experience. Ultimately, therefore, the eternal community is the renewal of our earthly enjoyment of fellowship, the Spirit's radical perfecting of the community we now share. Seen in this light, our glorious future does not come as a stranger, but as a mysterious, yet welcomed friend.[20] The eternal glorification in which we participate is nothing else but the community for which we were created.

No wonder Paul declared, " 'No eye has seen, no ear has heard, no mind has conceived what God has prepared for those who love him'—but God has revealed it to us by his Spirit" (1 Cor. 2:9-10).

Shall we gather at the river,
Where bright angel feet have trod;
With its crystal tide forever
Flowing by the throne of God?

On the bosom of the river,
Where the Savior-King we own,
We shall meet, and sorrow never,
'Neath the glory of the throne.

Soon we'll reach the shining river,
Soon our pilgrimage will cease;
Soon our happy hearts will quiver
With the melody of peace.

Yes, we'll gather at the river,
The beautiful, the beautiful river,
Gather with the saints at the river
That flows by the throne of God.[21]

FOR CONNECTION AND APPLICATION

1 Is the Christian teaching about the judgment good news or bad news?

2 How ought knowledge of the judgment affect the way you live? How *does* it affect your life?

3 Is either universalism or conditional immortality more "Christian" than the doctrine of hell?

4 How would your presentation of the gospel differ if you came to embrace universalism? If you came to embrace annihilationism?

5 What practical difference does it make whether we conceive of our eternal home as a heavenly realm beyond the universe or a new earth enveloped by a new heaven?

6 What does it mean for you to live in the light of our future glorification? In what ways can we glorify God in this life?

Making the Connection

As Christians we share certain basic theological beliefs. These beliefs focus on God, ourselves as God's special covenant partners, and God's program for creation. In the pages of this book, we have outlined these beliefs in view of God's overarching goal which we described as the establishment of an eternal community of redeemed people inhabiting a renewed creation and enjoying the presence of the Triune God. Using the theme of "community" as a guide, we have viewed how the Christian beliefs we share lead to the conclusion that we are "created for community."

Our exploration began with our foundational Christian belief about God. We believe in the God of the Bible, the one God who throughout all eternity is the social Trinity—the fellowship of Father, Son, and Holy Spirit. This God is the Creator of the universe. And the Triune God created us so that we might reflect his own divine character. Therefore, as we live in fellowship with God, each other, and our environment—as we live as "community"—we show what God is like.

Christian belief then moves to our human failure. We have failed God. Rather than reflecting the divine love, we exploit others for our own ends or allow ourselves to be exploited. We are alienated from God, each other, our environment, and even ourselves. We stand condemned before our righteous Judge. We find ourselves enslaved to sin. And, try as we will, we cannot remedy our hopeless situation, for we are depraved.

But our Christian belief does not end here. God did not leave us on our own nor forsake us to wallow in our own failure. Throughout history the Triune God has been at work. Central to our faith is the coming of Jesus Christ, "the Word made flesh." In Jesus' life, death, and resurrection, the Father has provided the antidote for our hopeless situation, which the Holy Spirit applies to our lives through his indwelling presence.

As those who have come to know the life-giving grace of God, we now participate together in the great community of Christ's disciples. And we anticipate the completion of our salvation one glorious future day when our Lord returns to consummate God's program for creation. Then we will enjoy community on the highest plane, as we join all creation in glorifying the Triune God forever.

In this way, then, the common thread of community has run through our entire discussion. The presence of this thread suggests that our beliefs are not merely a collection of unrelated postulates. In fact, instead of beliefs (plural) we do well to speak of Christian *belief* (singular), as in the subtitle of this book. At the heart of our faith is a unified vision. This vision focuses on who God is, who we are as the recipients of God's grace, and what God's purposes are for creation.

Further, this vision affects life. Of course, it would be possible to speak of Christian belief as a body of intellectual or "heady" statements we hold to be true. Yet, to isolate our beliefs into some purely intellectual realm would be to misunderstand the point of believing. Instead of simply "confessing our common faith," we must act upon our faith. We must allow the central vision of our faith, as outlined in these pages, to spill over into life.

Actually, it simply cannot be otherwise. If we *truly* believe — if we acknowledge that the biblical vision is true — Christian belief *will not* be content to remain solely on the intellectual level. If the Christian vision of God, ourselves as God's creatures, and God's purposes for creation truly shape the way we view life, it will also begin to color the way we live. As we come to view God, ourselves, and our world in the light of the Christian gospel, this vision will not only mold how we think, it will come to expression in how we speak and how we act. It will restrain us to measure our words and season them with divine grace. It will embolden us to testify forthrightly in speech and conduct to the reality of the God who has called us into his family. It will motivate us to live in a manner that brings honor to the God whom we confess with our mouths.

Above all, the understanding of the Christian vision outlined in these pages—focusing as it does on the central truth that we are created for community—should motivate and stimulate us to respond to God's call to community in every aspect of our lives. It should draw us into fellowship with God by leading us to pray more effectively and to seek to reflect with greater clarity the character of the Triune God. At the same time, this vision ought to draw us into fellowship with one another, as our awareness that "community" lies at the center of God's intention for us begins to shape our actions toward others and even toward the universe around us. Finally, this vision should lead us to a new sense of personal identity, as we discover that living in fellowship with God and others is the pathway to finding our true selves.

In short, "head," "heart," and "hand" are forged together in an unbreakable chain. What begins in our "head" will soon find its way into our "heart" and eventually come to be expressed through our "hand." Consequently, as we come to clarify and understand the foundational vision that comprises Christian belief, our intellectual reflections ought naturally to rekindle our devotion to God, leading to a renewed vitality in our service in the name of the one who "loved us and gave himself up for us" (Eph. 5:2; cf. Gal. 2:20; 2 Thes. 2:16). Thus, as we discover anew that God created us for community, God's Spirit will lead us to desire even more sincerely that the light of God's word shine through us to others to the praise of the Triune God.

Shine, Jesus, shine, fill this land with the Father's glory;
blaze, Spirit, blaze set our hearts on fire.
Flow river, flow, flood the nations with grace and mercy;
send forth your word, Lord, and let there be light![1]

NOTES

Introduction

1. Frank Whaling, "The Development of the Word 'Theology,' " *Scottish Journal of Theology* 34 (1981): 292–300.

2. Friedrich Schleiermacher, *A Brief Outline of the Study of Theology* (Atlanta: John Knox, 1966).

3. Emil Brunner, *The Christian Doctrine of God* (Philadelphia: Westminster, 1950), 93–96.

4. For a more detailed discussion, see Stanley J. Grenz, *Revisioning Evangelical Theology* (Downers Grove, Ill.: InterVarsity, 1993), 87–108. See also Stanley J. Grenz and Roger E. Olson, *Who Needs Theology?* (Downers Grove, Ill.: InterVarsity, 1996).

5. For a similar delineation, see Gabriel Fackre, *The Christian Story* (Grand Rapids: Eerdmans, 1984), 40.

6. The Westminster Confession of Faith, which formed the apex of Puritan efforts to delineate a proper recounting of biblical doctrine, declares that the final authority in the church is "the Holy Spirit speaking in the Scriptures." See "The Westminster Confession of Faith," 1:10, in John H. Leith, ed., *Creeds of the Churches,* 3rd ed. (Atlanta: John Knox, 1982), 196.

7. For a discussion of theological use and study of culture, see Robert J. Schreiter, *Constructing Local Theologies* (Maryknoll, N.Y.: Orbis, 1985), 39–74.

8. For a lengthier discussion, see Grenz, *Revisioning Evangelical Theology,* 137–64.

9. Mark Pendergrass, "The Greatest Thing."

Chapter 1

1. Anselm, *Prosloquim,* in *St. Anselm: Basic Writings,* 2nd ed., trans. S.N. Deane (La Salle, Ill.: Open Court, 1962), 7.

2. Ibid., 8.

3. René Descartes, *Discourse on Method and the Meditations,* trans. Laurence J. Lafleur, Library of Liberal Arts edition (Indianapolis: Bobbs-Merrill, 1960), 120.

4. G.W.F. Hegel, *The Phenomenology of Mind,* trans. J.B. Baillie, Harper Torchbooks/The Academy Library edition (New York: Harper and Row, 1967), 207–13. For a discussion of Hegel's thinking, see Wolfhart Pannenberg, *Basic Questions in Theology,* 2 vols., trans. George H. Kehm (Philadelphia: Fortress, 1970), 3:84–86.

5. Norman Malcolm, "Anselm's Ontological Arguments," in *Knowledge and Certainty: Essays and Lectures* (Englewood Cliffs, N.J.: Prentice Hall, 1963), 20–27.

6. Thomas Aquinas, *Summa Theologica* 1.2.3, in *Introduction to St. Thomas Aquinas*, ed. Anton C. Pegis (New York: Modern Library, 1948), 24–27.

7. William Paley, *Natural Theology* (New York: American Tract Society, n.d.), chaps. 1–6.

8. F.R. Tennant, *Philosophical Theology*, 2 vols. (Cambridge, England: Cambridge Univ. Press, 1928–1930), 2:78–104.

9. Robert Jastrow, *God and the Astronomers* (New York: Norton, 1978).

10. Immanuel Kant, *Critique of Practical Reason*, trans. Lewis White Beck (Indianapolis: Bobbs-Merrill, 1956), 114–15, 126–39.

11. Hastings Rashdall, *The Theory of Good and Evil*, 2 vols. (Oxford: Clarendon, 1907). 2:189–246.

12. C.S. Lewis, *Mere Christianity*, Macmillan Paperbacks edition (New York: Macmillan, 1960), 17–39.

13. John Calvin, *Institutes of the Christian Religion*, 1.1.2, in volume 20 of the *Library of Christian Classics*, trans. Ford Lewis Battles, ed. John T. McNeill, (Philadelphia: Westminster, 1960), 37.

14. For a discussion of the development of the Israelite concept of monotheism, see Walther Eichrodt, *Theology of the Old Testament*, 2 vols., trans. J.A. Baker (Philadelphia: Westminster, 1961), 1:220–27.

15. Elmer A. Martens, *God's Design: A Focus on Old Testament Theology* (Grand Rapids: Baker, 1981), 43.

16. Ibid., 41.

17. Ibid., 197.

18. Eichrodt, *Theology of the Old Testament*, 1:226–27.

19. Ibid., 219–21.

20. John Baillie, *The Idea of Revelation* (New York: Columbia Univ. Press, 1956), 19–40.

21. J.I. Packer, *Knowing God* (Downers Grove, Ill.: InterVarsity, 1973), 37.

22. For a discussion of history as the focus of divine revelation, see Wolfhart Pannenberg, "Hermeneutic and Universal History," in *Basic Questions in Theology*, 1:96–136; and Wolfhart Pannenberg, ed., *Revelation as History*, trans. David Granskou (New York: Macmillan, 1968), 3–21, 125–35.

Chapter 2

1. J.N.D. Kelly, *Early Christian Doctrines*, rev. ed. (San Francisco: Harper & Row, 1978), 258.

2. Paul Tillich, *A History of Christian Thought*, ed. Carl Braaten (New York: Simon & Shuster, 1968), 77.

3. Augustine, *The Trinity* 6.5.7, trans. Vernon J. Bourke, vol. 45 of *The Fathers of the Church*, ed. Hermigild Dressler (Washington: Catholic Univ. of America Press, 1963), 206–7; see also 15.17.27 (491–92); 5.11.12 (189–90); 15.19.37 (503–4). For the connection of this Augustinian idea to the Greek tradition, see Yves Congar, *I Believe in the Holy Spirit*, 3 vols., trans. David Smith (New York: Seabury, 1983), 3:88–89, 147–48. For a contemporary delineation of this position, see David Coffey, "The Holy Spirit as the Mutual Love of the Father and the Son," *Theological Studies* 51 (1990): 193–229.

4. Packer, *Knowing God*, 154.

5. Edwin Hatch, "Breathe on Me, Breath of God," 1878.

6. Rosemary Radford Ruether, *Sexism and God-Talk* (Boston: Beacon, 1983), 258.

7. Wolfhart Pannenberg, "The Question of God," in *Basic Questions in Theology*, 2:226–33; Wolfhart Pannenberg, "Speaking about God in the Face of Atheist Criticism," in *The Idea of God and Human Freedom* (Philadelphia: Westminster, 1973), 112.

8. Jacques Guillet and E.M. Stewart, "Yahweh," in the *Dictionary of Biblical Theology*, 2nd ed., ed. Xavier Leon-Dufour, trans. P. Joseph Cahill, et al. (New York: Seabury, 1973), 690; Alexander Harkavy, *Students' Hebrew and Chaldee Dictionary to the Old Testament* (New York: Hebrew Publishing, 1914), 122; J. Philip Hyatt, *Exodus*, in the *New Century Bible*, ed. Ronald E. Clements (London: Oliphants, 1971), 76; Martin Noth, *Exodus: A Commentary*, trans. J.S. Bowden (Philadelphia: Westminster, 1962), 45.

9. Paul Fiddes, *The Creative Suffering of God* (New York: Oxford Univ. Press, 1988).

10. For a further discussion of this theme, see Stanley J. Grenz, *Prayer: The Cry for the Kingdom* (Peabody, Mass.: Hendrickson, 1988).

11. H. Kleinknecht, *"lego,"* in the *Theological Dictionary of the New Testament*, 10 vols., ed. Gerhard Kittel and Gerhard Friedrich, trans. Geoffrey Bromiley (Grand Rapids: Eerdmans, 1967), 4:80–86.

Chapter 3

1. Ashley Montagu, *Man in Process* (New York: Mentor, 1961), 17–18.

2. Wolfhart Pannenberg, *What Is Man?* trans. Duane A. Priebe (Philadelphia: Fortress, 1970), 3.

3. Augustine, *Confessions* 1.1, trans. Vernon J. Bourke, vol. 21 of *The Fathers of the Church*, ed. Roy Joseph Deferrari (Washington: Catholic Univ. of America Press, 1953), 4.

4. "The Westminster Shorter Catechism," question 1, in *Creeds of Christendom*, ed. Philip Schaff, 3 vols. (Grand Rapids: Baker, 1977; reprint), 3:676.

5. For a more detailed discussion, see Stanley J. Grenz, "Abortion: A Christian Response," *Conrad Grebel Review* 2/1 (Winter 1984): 21–30. See also Stanley J. Grenz, *Sexual Ethics* (Dallas: Word, 1990), 135–41.

6. See, e.g., Phyllis A. Bird, " 'Male and Female He Created Them': Gen. 1:27b in the Context of the Priestly Account of Creation," *Harvard Theological Review* 74 (April 1981): 137–44.

7. Gerhard von Rad, *"eikon,"* in the *Theological Dictionary of the New Testament*, 10 vols., ed. Gerhard Kittel and Gerhard Friedrich, trans. Geoffrey W. Bromiley (Grand Rapids: Eerdmans, 1964), 2:392. See also Henri Blocher, *In the Beginning: The Opening Chapters of Genesis*, trans. David G. Preston (Leicester, England: Inter-Varsity, 1984), 81.

8. Gerhard von Rad, *Genesis*, trans. John H. Marks, in the *Old Testament Library*, ed. G. Ernest Wright (Philadelphia: Westminster, 1972), 58.

9. For a development of the philosophical basis for the social understanding

of personhood, see Alistair I. McFadyen, *The Call to Personhood: A Christian Theory of the Individual in Social Relationships* (Cambridge: Cambridge Univ. Press, 1990).

10. For a fuller discussion of the relationship of sexuality and community, see Grenz, *Sexual Ethics,* 35–37.

11. Hendrik Berkhof, *Christ and the Powers,* trans. John H. Yoder (Scottdale, Pa.: Herald, 1962), 30, 33.

12. John Howard Yoder, *The Politics of Jesus* (Grand Rapids: Eerdmans, 1972), 145.

13. Berkhof, *Christ and the Powers,* 22, 37.

Chapter 4

1. Gottfried Quell, *"hamartano,"* in the *Theological Dictionary of the New Testament,* 10 vols., ed. Gerhard Kittel and Gerhard Friedrich, trans. Geoffrey W. Bromiley (Grand Rapids: Eerdmans, 1964), 1:271.

2. Karl Menninger, *Whatever Became of Sin?* (New York: Hawthorn, 1973).

3. Karl Barth, *Church Dogmatics,* trans. Geoffrey W. Bromiley (Edinburgh: T & T Clark, 1956), 4/1:358–413.

4. Isaac Watts, "At the Cross."

5. Louis Berkhof, *Systematic Theology,* rev. ed. (Grand Rapids: Eerdmans, 1953), 215.

6. The idea of a primordial covenant of works has been a controversial thesis within Reformed theology. It was articulated at length by the great Dutch theologian Herman Bavinck. It has been defended in North America by many of the leading lights of the old Princeton school. See, e.g., Charles Hodge, *Systematic Theology* (New York: Charles Scribner, 1871), 2:117–22; William G.T. Shedd, *Dogmatic Theology* (1888; Grand Rapids: Zondervan, n.d.), 2:152–53; Berkhof, *Systematic Theology,* 211–18. Several recent proponents have proposed substituting the designation "covenant of creation." E.g., Meredith Kline, *By Oath Consigned* (Grand Rapids: Eerdmans, 1968), 27–29, 32, 37. For a recent rebuttal of the viewpoint, see Anthony A. Hoekema, *Created in God's Image* (Grand Rapids: Eerdmans, 1986), 119–21.

7. Berkhof, *Systematic Theology,* 215.

8. Friedrich Schleiermacher, *The Christian Faith,* ed. H.R. MacKintosh and J.S. Steward (Edinburgh: T & T Clark, n.d.), 296, 299–304; Paul Tillich, *Systematic Theology,* 3 vols. (Chicago: Univ. of Chicago Press, 1951), 1:255–56; Søren Kierkegaard, *The Concept of Dread,* trans. Walter Lowrie (Princeton: Princeton Univ. Press, 1957); Reinhold Niebuhr, *The Nature and Destiny of Man,* 2 vols. (New York: Charles Scribner's, 1941), 1:269.

9. Donald G. Bloesch, *Essentials of Evangelical Theology,* 2 vols. (San Francisco: Harper and Row, 1978), 1:107–8, 118 n.63.

10. Augustus Hopkins Strong, *Systematic Theology,* 3 vols. (Philadelphia: Griffith and Rowland, 1907), 2:661.

Chapter 5

1. Schleiermacher, *Christian Faith*, 362, 385; Gordon R. Lewis and Bruce A. Demarest, *Integrative Theology*, 3 vols. (Grand Rapids: Zondervan, 1990), 2:336–38.

2. Adolf von Harnack, *What Is Christianity?* trans. Thomas Bailey Saunders (New York: G.P. Putnam's, 1901), 55.

3. Jürgen Moltmann, *The Crucified God*, trans. R.A. Wilson and John Bowden (New York: SCM, 1974), 243–44.

4. Strong, *Systematic Theology*, 2:681–82; Millard Erickson, *Christian Theology*, 3 vols. (Grand Rapids: Baker, 1984), 2:684–88.

5. John R.W. Stott, *Basic Christianity*, 2nd ed. (London: Inter-Varsity, 1971), 21–34.

6. Schleiermacher, *Christian Faith*, 417; Rudolf Bultmann, "New Testament and Mythology," in *Kerygma and Myth: A Theological Debate*, ed. Hans Werner Bartsch (New York: Harper and Row, 1961), 39–42.

7. Wolfhart Pannenberg, *Jesus – God and Man*, 2nd ed., trans. Lewis L. Wilkins and Duane A. Priebe (Philadelphia: Westminster, 1977), 88–106.

8. Hugh J. Schonfield, *The Passover Plot* (New York: Bantam Books, 1967), 151–62; "Christ Could Have Faked Death on Cross, Article Purports," *Vancouver Sun*, 27 April 1991, sec. A3.

9. For a concise discussion of the prayer life of Jesus, see Grenz, *Prayer: The Cry for the Kingdom*, 11–18.

10. Lewis and Demarest, *Integrative Theology*, 2:336–38.

11. Erickson, *Christian Theology*, 2:718–21. Erickson cites Leon Morris, *The Lord from Heaven: A Study of the New Testament Teaching on the Deity and Humanity of Jesus* (Grand Rapids: Eerdmans, 1958), 51–52.

12. H. Kleinknecht, *"logos,"* in the *Theological Dictionary of the New Testament*, 10 vols., ed. Gerhard Kittel and Gerhard Friedrich, trans. Geoffrey W. Bromiley (Grand Rapids: Eerdmans, 1967), 4:80–81.

13. See, e.g., E.W. Hengstenberg, *Christology of the Old Testament and a Commentary on the Messianic Predictions*, 2 vols. (Grand Rapids: Kregel, 1970; reprint).

14. For an example, see Jerry Falwell, "The Revelation of the Incarnation," *Fundamentalist Journal* 7/11 (December 1988): 10.

15. "Fairest Lord Jesus," from the German, 17th century.

Chapter 6

1. Phillip Brooks, "O Little Town of Bethlehem."

2. J. Ramsey Michaels, *Servant and Son* (Atlanta: John Knox, 1981), 285.

3. Ibid., 289.

4. Sigmund Mowinckel, *He That Cometh*, trans. G.W. Anderson (New York: Abingdon, 1954), 187.

5. For a helpful survey of the Atonement in theological history, see Robert S. Paul, *The Atonement and the Sacraments* (Nashville: Abingdon, 1960), 35–281.

6. Ibid., 47.

7. Ibid., 52.

8. Origen, "An Address on Religious Instruction" *[Oratio Catechetical]* 24, in *The Christology of the Later Fathers*, vol. 3 of the *Library of Christian Classics*, ed. Edward Rochie Hardy and Cyril C. Richardson (Philadelphia: Westminster, 1954), 300–302.

9. For an important exception, see Gustaf Aulén, *Christus Victor*, trans. A.G. Hebert (New York: Macmillan, 1969).

10. Julia Johnston, "Jesus Ransomed Me."

11. Eugene M. Bartlett, Sr., "Victory in Jesus."

12. See Paul, *Atonement and the Sacraments*, 74; Aulén, *Christus Victor*, 84–92.

13. Calvin, *Institutes of the Christian Religion*, 2.12.3, volume 20 of the *Library of Christian Classics*, 466–67.

14. Paul, *Atonement and the Sacraments*, 109.

15. See, e.g., Millard J. Erickson, *Christian Theology*, 3 vols. (Grand Rapids: Baker, 1984), 2:815.

16. Many interpreters set Abelard's interpretation of the Atonement against that of Anselm. See, e.g., Paul, *Atonement and the Sacraments*, 80. See also, Kenneth Scott Latourette, *A History of Christianity* (New York: Harper and Brothers, 1953), 504.

17. Peter Abelard, "Exposition of the Epistle to the Romans" 2, in *A Scholastic Miscellany: Anselm to Ockham*, vol. 10 in the *Library of Christian Classics*, trans. Eugene R. Fairweather (Philadelphia: Westminster, 1956), 283.

18. Ibid.

19. Isaac Watts, "When I Survey the Wondrous Cross," 1707.

20. Jürgen Moltmann, *The Crucified God*, 2nd ed., trans. R.A. Wilson and John Bowden (New York: Harper and Row, 1974), 145–53.

Chapter 7

1. Friedrich Baumgaertel, *"pneuma* . . . : Spirit in the OT," in the *Theological Dictionary of the New Testament*, 10 vols., ed. Gerhard Kittel and Gerhard Friedrich, trans. Geoffrey W. Bromiley (Grand Rapids: Eerdmans, 1968), 6:359–62.

2. The orthodox teaching became dogma at the Council of Constantinople (A.D. 381). See J.W.C. Wand, *The Four Great Heresies* (London: Mowbray, 1955), 78.

3. Frank Bottome, "The Comforter Has Come."

4. Reginald Heber, "Holy, Holy, Holy."

5. According to Ramm, the "Protestant principle of authority" is "the Holy Spirit speaking in the Scriptures, which are the product of the Spirit's revelatory and inspiring action." Bernard Ramm, *The Pattern of Religious Authority* (Grand Rapids: Eerdmans, 1959), 28. See also *The Westminster Confession of Faith*, 1/10, in *The Creeds of the Churches*, 3rd ed., ed. John H. Leith (Atlanta: John Knox, 1982), 196.

6. For a more detailed discussion of the Spirit and Scripture, see Stanley J. Grenz, *Revisioning Evangelical Theology* (Downers Grove, Ill.: InterVarsity, 1993), 109–36.

7. Strong, *Systematic Theology*, 1:196.

8. C.H. Dodd, *The Authority of the Bible* (1929; reprint, New York: Harper and Brothers, 1958), 36.

9. Edgar V. McKnight, "Errantry and Inerrancy: Baptists and the Bible," *Perspectives in Religious Studies* 12/2 (Summer 1985): 146.

10. Thomas A. Hoffman, "Inspiration, Normativeness, Canonicity, and the Unique Sacred Character of the Bible," *Catholic Biblical Quarterly* 44 (1982): 457.

11. C. John Weborg, "Pietism: Theology in Service of Living Toward God," in *The Variety of American Evangelicalism,* ed. Robert K. Johnson and Donald W. Dayton (Downers Grove, Ill.: InterVarsity, 1991), 176.

12. Mary A. Lathbury, "Break Thou the Bread of Life," 1877.

13. David Kelsey, *The Uses of Scripture in Recent Theology* (Philadelphia: Westminster, 1975), 214.

14. Robert N. Bellah, et al., *Habits of the Heart: Individualism and Commitment in American Life* (New York: Harper and Row, 1986), 81.

15. James Barr, *The Scope and Authority of the Bible* (Philadelphia: Westminster, 1980), 126–27; William R. Herzog II, "Interpretation as Discovery and Creation: Sociological Dimensions of Biblical Hermeneutics," *American Baptist Quarterly* 2/2 (June 1983): 116.

16. Donald Bloesch, "In Defense of Biblical Authority," *Reformed Journal* 34/9 (Sept. 1984): 30.

17. Kate B. Wilkinson, "May the Mind of Christ, My Savior," 1925.

18. Rippon's *Selection of Hymns,* 1787.

Chapter 8

1. John Newton, "Amazing Grace! How Sweet the Sound," 1779.

2. William D. Chamberlain, *The Meaning of Repentance* (Philadelphia: Westminster, 1943), 41; J. Goetzmann, *"metanoia,"* in "Conversion, Penitence, Repentance, Proselyte," *The New International Dictionary of New Testament Theology,* ed. Colin Brown (Grand Rapids: Zondervan, 1981), 1:357–59.

3. Lewis Carroll, *Through the Looking Glass and What Alice Found There* (New York: Random House, 1946), 76.

4. See *Fides,* in Richard A. Muller, *Dictionary of Latin and Greek Theological Terms* (Grand Rapids: Baker, 1985), 115–16.

5. Karl Kertelge, *"dikaiosune,"* in the *Exegetical Dictionary of the New Testament,* 3 vols., ed. Horst Balz and Gerhard Schneider (Grand Rapids: Eerdmans, 1990), 2:331.

6. Gottlob Schlenk, *"dikaioo,"* in *The Theological Dictionary of the New Testament,* 10 vols., ed. Gerhard Kittel and Gerhard Friedrich, trans. Geoffrey W. Bromiley (Grand Rapids: Eerdmans, 1964), 2:215.

7. Berkhof, *Systematic Theology,* 517.

8. George A. Lindbeck, "Confession and Community: An Israel-like View of the Church," *Christian Century* 107/16 (9 May 1990): 495.

9. Bellah, et al., *Habits of the Heart,* 81.

10. Alisdair MacIntyre, *After Virtue,* 2nd ed. (Notre Dame, Ind.: Univ. of Notre Dame Press, 1984), 221

11. For a more detailed discussion, see Grenz, *Revisioning Evangelical Theology,* 33–35.

12. Otto Procksch, *"hagiazo,"* in the *Theological Dictionary of the New Testament,* 10 vols., ed. Gerhard Kittel and Gerhard Friedrich, trans. Geoffrey W. Bromiley (Grand Rapids: Eerdmans, 1963), 1:111.

13. For a discussion of Wesleyan perfectionism, see Melvin E. Dieter, "The Wesleyan Perspective," in *Five Views on Sanctification* (Grand Rapids: Zondervan, 1986), 15–32.

14. Newton, "Amazing Grace! How Sweet the Sound."

Chapter 9

1. Jüergen Roloff, *"ekklesia,"* in Balz and Schneider, *Exegetical Dictionary of the New Testament,* 1:411; Karl L. Schmidt, *"ekklesia,"* in the *Theological Dictionary of the New Testament,* 10 vols., ed. Gerhard Kittel and Gerhard Friedrich, trans. Geoffrey W. Bromiley (Grand Rapids: Eerdmans, 1964–76), 3:513.

2. For a discussion of the adoption of the term by the early community, see Roloff, *"ekklesia,"* in Balz and Schneider, *Exegetical Dictionary of the New Testament,* 1:412.

3. According to Kenneth Cauthen *(Systematic Theology* [Lewiston, N.Y.: Edwin Mellen, 1986], 296), the implicit trinitarianism of the choice of these metaphors and their significance as the three major motifs in the history of Christian thought dates to a book by Lesslie Newbigin, *The Household of Faith* (New York: Friendship, 1954). Millard Erickson, who employs them in his ecclesiology [*Christian Theology,* 3:1034–41] cites as the source of the idea, Arthur W. Wainwright, *The Trinity in the New Testament* (London: S.P.C.K, 1962).

4. Alex T.M. Cheung, "The Priest as the Redeemed Man: A Biblical-Theological Study of the Priesthood," *Journal of the Evangelical Theological Society* 29/3 (September 1986): 265–75.

5. Andrew Perriman, " 'His Body Which Is the Church. . . . ' Coming to Terms with Metaphor," *Evangelical Quarterly* 62/2 (1990): 123–42; Barbara Field, "The Discourses Behind the Metaphor 'the Church Is the Body of Christ' as Used by S. Paul and the 'Post-Paulines,' " *Asia Journal of Theology* 6/1 (April 1992): 88–107.

6. John D. Zizioulas, *Being as Communion: Studies in Personhood and the Church* (Crestwood, N.Y.: St. Vladimir's, 1985), 148.

7. Augustine, *The City of God,* 20.9, trans. Marcus Dods (New York: Random House, 1950), 725.

8. Lewis Sperry Chafer, *Systematic Theology,* 7 vols. (Dallas: Dallas Seminary, 1948), 4:385–86.

9. C. Rene Padilla, "The Mission of the Church in the Light of the Kingdom of God," *Transformation* 1/2 (April-June, 1984): 17.

10. For a discussion of this point, see Grenz, *Sexual Ethics,* 21–23.

11. Zizioulas, *Being as Communion,* 140.

12. Miroslav Volf, "Kirche als Gemeinschaft: Ekklesiologische Ueberlegungen aus freikirchlicher Perspektive," *Evangelische Theologie* 49/1 (1989): 70–76; Kilian McDonnell, "Vatican II (1962–1964), Puebla (1979), Synod (1985):

Koinonia/Communio as an Integral Ecclesiology," *Journal of Ecumenical Studies* 25/3 (Summer 1988): 414.

13. J.M.R. Tillard, "What Is the Church of God?" *Mid-stream* 23 (October 1984): 372–73.

14. Aristotle, *Metaphysics,* 12:1-10 (1069a18–1076a4), in *Great Books of the Western World,* ed. Robert Maynard Hutchins (Chicago: William Berton; Encyclopedia Britannica, 1952), 598–606.

15. "To pay divine honors to; to reverence with supreme respect and veneration; to perform religious service to; to adore; to idolize." *New Websters Dictionary of the English Language* (n.p.: Delair, 1971), 1148.

16. Ralph Martin, *The Worship of God* (Grand Rapids: Eerdmans, 1982), 4.

17. For an interesting, although overstated discussion of the significance of praise for spiritual living, see Paul E. Billheimer, *Destined for the Throne* (Fort Washington, Pa.: Christian Literature Crusade, 1975), 115–26.

18. See, e.g., Grenz, *Prayer: The Cry for the Kingdom,* previously cited.

19. Lukas Vischer, *Intercession* (Geneva: World Council of Churches, 1980), 25–27, 48–49.

20. In *The Problem of Christianity,* Josiah Royce (1855–1916) explored the idea of one vast "community of interpretation," not so much as a present reality but as a task to which we ought to be loyal. Anticipating contemporary writers such as Robert Bellah, he spoke of community in religious terms, as a community of memory and hope, faith, and redeeming grace. For a short overview, see "Josiah Royce," in the *Dictionary of Philosophy and Religion,* ed. William L. Reese (Atlantic Highlands, N.J.: Humanities, 1980), 498–99. Drawing from the work of earlier thinkers, including Royce, contemporary secular communalists acknowledge the presence in the wider society of such communities. For an example, see Bellah, et al., *Habits of the Heart.*

21. The World Literature Crusade, which has as its goal the blanketing of the earth with the gospel of Christ, suggests seven petitions appropriate for Christians to offer with respect to world leaders. See Dick Eastman, "The Sevenfold World Leaders Prayer Focus," in the pamphlet, "Kings and Presidents" (n.p.: World Literature Crusade, n.d.).

22. Eastman offers an alternate list of proper requests: workers for the harvest, open doors, abiding fruit, and strong suppport base. See Dick Eastman, *The Hour That Changes the World* (Grand Rapids: Baker, 1978), 153–57.

23. Vernon Grounds, *Evangelicalism and Social Responsibility* (Scottdale, Pa.: Herald, 1969), 8.

24. See Grenz, *Prayer: The Cry for the Kingdom.*

25. Mary A. Thomson, "O Zion, Haste."

Chapter 10

1. For an overview, see J.G. Davies, *The Early Christian Church* (Grand Rapids: Baker, 1980), 103–4. For a description of early church practices, see *Didache,* 7 (p. 19); Justin Martyr, *Apology* 1.61 (pp. 99–100).

2. The architects of the early Reformed tradition appealed to this understanding of the church in setting themselves apart from the Anabaptists. Second

Helvetic Confession (1566), 20, in John H. Leith, *Creeds of the Churches,* 3rd ed. (Atlanta: John Knox, 1982), 169.

3. For a discussion of this from a believer's baptist position, see Marlin Jeschke, *Believer's Baptism for Children of the Church* (Scottdale, Pa.: Herald, 1983).

4. Bellah, et al., *Habits of the Heart,* 152–54.

5. Alasdair I.C. Heron, *Table and Tradition: Toward an Ecumenical Understanding of the Eucharist* (Philadelphia: Westminster, 1983), 69.

6. J.N.D. Kelly, *Early Christian Doctrines,* rev. ed. (San Franciso: Harper and Row, 1978), 422–23.

7. As Calvin rightly declared, "they have been instituted by the Lord to the end that they may serve to establish and increase faith" (Calvin, *Institutes of the Christian Religion,* 4.14.9., in volume 21 of *The Library of Christian Classics,* 1284).

8. Calvin, *Institutes of the Christian Faith,* 4.14.4., in volume 21 of *The Library of Christian Classics,* 1279.

9. See Bo Reicke, *The Epistles of James, Peter and Jude,* vol. 37 of *The Anchor Bible* (Garden City, N.Y.: Doubleday, 1964), 106–7, 139.

10. For the development of this idea, see e.g., L. Gregory Jones, *Transformed Judgment: Toward a Trinitarian Account of the Moral Life* (Notre Dame, Ind.: Univ. of Notre Dame Press, 1990), 137–39.

11. "Eucharist" dates to the patristic era. E.g., *Didache* 6.5, trans. James A. Kleist, *Ancient Christian Fathers* (New York: Paulist, 1948), 6:20; Justin Martyr, *First Apology,* trans. Thomas B. Falls, *The Fathers of the Church* (Washington, D.C.: Catholic Univ. of America Press, 1948), 6:105–6.

12. "Mass" may originally have been derived from the closing words of the Latin liturgy. See Heron, *Table and Tradition,* xii.

13. For a discussion grounding the Lord's Supper in the Jewish Passover celebration, see Markus Barth, *Rediscovering the Lord's Supper* (Atlanta: John Knox, 1988), 7–27.

14. Ragan Courtney, "In Remembrance," 1972.

15. "Strong emphasis should be placed in the active participation of all members in the life and the decision-making of the community." *Baptism, Eucharist and Ministry,* Faith and Order Paper no. 111 (Geneva: World Council of Churches, 1982), 26.

16. Erickson rightly notes that the epistles addressed to individuals — Philemon, 1 & 2 Timothy, Titus — were intended primarily for these persons and not for congregations under their care. Erickson, *Christian Theology,* 3:1082, citing Edward T. Hiscox, *The New Directory for Baptist Churches* (Philadelphia: Judson, 1894), 155ff.

17. In certain New Testament texts, we find bishop and elder used interchangeably (Acts 20:17-28; Titus 1:5, 7). This suggests that in the early church they were likely not two offices, but merely alternate designations for the same position. See, Joachim Rohde, *"episcopos,"* in Balz and Schneider, *Exegetical Dictionary of the New Testament,* 2:36. Milne writes, "It is now generally accepted among scholars of all traditions that the Greek words *Episcopos* (bishop) and *presbyteros* (elder) are equivalents in the NT" (Bruce Milne, *Know the Truth* [Downers Grove, Ill.: InterVarsity, 1982], 241).

18. Rohde, *"episcopos,"* in Balz and Schneider, *Exegetical Dictionary of the New Testament,* 2:36.

19. Alfons Weiser, *"diakonos,"* in Balz and Schneider, *Exegetical Dictionary of the New Testament,* 1:302.

20. The consensus document put the point well: "ordained ministers must not be autocrats or impersonal functionaries." Rather they are to "manifest and exercise the authority of Christ in the way Christ himself revealed God's authority to the world, by commiting their life to the community." See *Baptism, Eucharist and Ministry,* 23.

Chapter 11

1. "Fifty Quitting Jobs, Getting Ready to Be Lifted to Heaven June 28," *Winnipeg Free Press,* 3 June 1981.

2. Gareth G. Cook and David Makovsky, "Radio Preacher Foresees Doom Soon," *U.S. News & World Report,* 19 Dec. 1994, 71.

3. Christopher Lasch writes, "Storm warnings, portents, hints of catastrophe haunt our times. The 'sense of ending,' which has given shape to so much of twentieth century literature, now pervades the popular imagination as well" (Christopher Lasch, *The Culture of Narcissism: American Life in an Age of Diminishing Expectations* [New York: Norton, 1978], 3).

4. Karl Loewith, *Meaning in History* (Chicago: Univ. of Chicago Press, 1950), 19.

5. Hans-Joachim Kraus, *Worship in Israel: A Cultic History of the Old Testament,* trans. G. Bushwell (Richmond, Va.: John Knox, 1966), 38–43.

6. For a discussion of the development of this historical shift, see Hans Schwarz, *On the Way to the Future,* rev. ed. (Minneapolis: Augsburg, 1979), 19–23.

7. For a fuller delineation and discussion, see Stanley J. Grenz, *The Millennial Maze* (Downers Grove, Ill.: InterVarsity, 1992).

8. J. Dwight Pentecost, *Things to Come* (Findlay, Ohio: Dunham, 1958), 547–83.

9. Historic premillennialists, writings include Clarence Bass, *Backgrounds to Dispensationalism* (1960; reprint, Grand Rapids: Baker, 1977); Millard Erickson, *Contemporary Options in Eschatology: A Study of the Millennium* (Grand Rapids: Baker, 1977); and D.H. Kromminga, *The Millennium* (Grand Rapids: Eerdmans, 1948).

10. Some dispensationalists, however, argue that the rapture is midtribulational, that is, that the first three and one-half years of the tribulation precede the rapture. For a presentation of this position, see Gleason L. Archer, "The Case for the Mid-seventieth-week Rapture Position," in Gleason L. Archer, et al., *The Rapture: Pre-, Mid-, or Post-Tribulational* (Grand Rapids: Zondervan, 1984), 113–45.

11. See Pentecost, *Things to Come,* 219–28.

12. The classical dispensationlist scenario is summarized by Dallas Seminary theologian Robert P. Lightner in the column, "Dallas Seminary Faculty Answer Your Questions," *Kindred Spirit* 15/1 (Spring 1991): 3.

13. Pentecost, *Things to Come,* 358. For detailed dispensationalist descriptions of the military intrigue at the end of the tribulation, see Pentecost, *Things to Come,* 318–58; see also Hal Lindsey, *The Late Great Planet Earth* (New York: Bantam, 1973). For a recent update of Lindsey's thought see, *Planet Earth — 2000 A.D.* (Palos Verdes, Calif.: Western Front, 1994) and *The Final Battle* (Palos Verdes, Calif.: Western Front, 1995).

14. See, e.g., Pentecost, *Things to Come,* 508–11.

15. Hence, e.g., Strong, *Systematic Theology,* 3:1008.

16. Ibid., 1009; For a lengthier discussion of this question, see Loraine Boettner, *The Millennium* (Philadelphia: Presbyterian & Reformed, 1957), 67–76. The expectation of a final apostasy is not universally held among postmillennialists.

17. It is no historical accident that by and large the great thrusts toward worldwide evangelistic outreach and social concern in the modern era were launched by a church imbued with the optimism that characterizes postmillennial thinking. See, e.g., the discussion of Puritan missions in Iain H. Murray, *The Puritan Hope* (London: Banner of Truth, 1971), 131–83, esp., 149–51, 178. See also, John Jefferson Davis, *Christ's Victorious Kingdom* (Grand Rapids: Baker, 1986), 118–19.

18. See G.C. Berkouwer, *The Return of Christ,* trans. James Van Oosterom (Grand Rapids: Eerdmans, 1972), 314–15.

19. See, e.g., William Cox, *In These Last Days* (Philadelphia: Presbyterian & Reformed, 1964), 68–71.

20. For a discussion of this position, see Oswald T. Allis, *Prophecy and the Church* (Grand Rapids: Baker, 1972), 5. See also Benjamin B. Warfield, *Biblical Doctrines* (reprint, Edinburgh: Banner of Truth, 1988), 649.

21. For the typical amillennial scenario, see Floyd Hamilton, *The Basis of Millennial Faith* (Grand Rapids: Eerdmans, 1952), 35–37.

22. See, e.g., Cox, *In These Last Days,* 59–67.

23. Louis Berkhof, *The Second Coming of Christ* (Grand Rapids: Eerdmans, 1953), 83.

24. This is the consensus reached by the newer research into the kingdom of God in the teaching of Jesus. See, Bruce Chilton, "Introduction," in *The Kingdom of God in the Teaching of Jesus,* ed. Bruce Chilton, *Issues in Religion and Theology* 5 (Philadelphia: Fortress, 1984): 25–26.

25. George Eldon Ladd, *The Last Things* (Grand Rapids: Eerdmans, 1978), 32.

26. God can save the righteous from its power and bring them into his own presence (Ps. 49:15; cf. 86:13). Hence, when Hosea voiced God's promise, "I will ransom them from the power of the grave *[sheol];* I will redeem them from death," he burst forth in praise: "Where, O death, are your plagues? Where, O grave, is your destruction?" (Hosea 13:14)

Similarly, Job confidently asserted: "I know that my Redeemer lives, and that in the end he will stand upon the earth. And after my skin has been destroyed, yet in my flesh I will see God; I myself will see him with my own eyes — I, and not another. How my heart yearns within me!" (Job 19:25–27)

And Daniel pointed to the resurrection as the means whereby death is overcome (Dan. 12:2).

27. The ancient Greek philosophers were imbued with this vision. Perhaps the classic statement is Plato's description of Socrates' death in the *Phaedo*. His thesis is that death merely completes the liberation begun through philosophical reflection. It frees the soul from the contaminating imperfections of the body so that it might penetrate the world of the eternal ideas to which it belongs. See, Plato, *Phaedo*, 64a–67b, in *The Collected Dialogues of Plato*, ed. Edith Hamilton and Huntington Cairns (Princeton: Princeton Univ. Press, 1961), 46–49.

28. Ladd, *The Last Things*, 83.

29. *Constitutio Benedictina*, in *The Church Teaches: Documents of the Church in English Tradition*, trans. John F. Clarkson, et al. (St. Louis: Herder, 1955), 349–51.

30. For a recent delineation of this view, see Zachary J. Hayes, "The Purgatorial View," in *Four Views on Hell*, ed. William Crockett (Grand Rapids: Zondervan, 1992), 93.

31. Thielicke noted, "The emphasis here is not on some quality of mine that outlasts death, but on the quality of my Lord not to desert me" (Helmut Thielicke, *Death and Life*, trans. Edward H. Schroeder [Philadelphia: Fortress, 1970], 215).

32. Schwarz declared, "Eternity is . . . the fulfillment of time in perfection." (Hans Schwarz, *On the Way to the Future*, rev. ed. [Minneapolis: Augsburg, 1979], 229).

33. Author unknown, "I Know Where I'm Going."

Chapter 12

1. For a summary of the threefold apologetic universalists devise, see Stephen Travis, *I Believe in the Second Coming of Jesus* (Grand Rapids: Eerdmans, 1982), 200.

2. Nels Ferré, *Christ and the Christian* (New York: Harper, 1958), 247; *The Universal World: A Theology for a Universal Faith* (Philadelphia: Westminster, 1969), 258.

3. John Hick, *Death and Eternal Life* (San Francisco: Harper and Row, 1976).

4. For the significance of this as an argument against universalism, see John Sanders, *No Other Name: An Investigation into the Destiny of the Unevangelized* (Grand Rapids: Eerdmans, 1992), 107–8.

5. Travis, *I Believe in the Second Coming*, 203; Hans Schwarz, *On the Way to the Future*, rev. ed. (Minneapolis: Augsburg, 1979), 262.

6. Clark Pinnock, "The Conditional View," in *Four Views on Hell*, ed. William Crockett (Grand Rapids: Zondervan, 1992), 147; Travis, *I Believe in the Second Coming*, 198.

7. Pinnock, "Conditional View," 154–55.

8. Ibid., 149–54.

9. See, e.g., Pinnock, "Conditional View," 145–46.

10. Travis, *I Believe in the Second Coming*, 199.

11. For a helpful discussion of the biblical materials, see Larry Dixon, *The Other Side of the Good News* (Wheaton, Ill.: Victor/BridgePoint, 1992), 74–95.

12. For a recent discussion of the relevant texts, see Dixon, *The Other Side*, 121–47.

13. "Hell's Sober Comeback," *U.S. News & World Report,* 25 March 1991, 57.

14. See, e.g., John Walvoord, "The Literal View," in *Four Views on Hell,* 28.

15. For a statement of this position, see William Crockett, "The Metaphorical View," in *Four Views on Hell,* ed. William Crockett (Grand Rapids: Zondervan, 1992), 44–76.

16. This tendency is visible in the title of a recently written "history of the images Christians use to describe what happens after death." Colleen McDannell and Bernhard Lang, *Heaven: A History* (New Haven, Conn.: Yale Univ. Press, 1988).

17. For a critic of the proponents of this disjunctive view, see Berkouwer, *Return of Christ,* 291–95.

18. Wolfhart Pannenberg, "The Significance of the Categories 'Part' and 'Whole' for the Epistemology of Theology," *Journal of Religion* 66 (1986): 385.

19. Wolfhart Pannenberg, "Constructive and Critical Functions of Christian Eschatology," *Harvard Theological Review* 77 (1984): 135–36.

20. Berkouwer, *Return of Christ,* 234.

21. Robert Lowry, "Shall We Gather at the River?" 1864.

Epilogue — Making the Connection

1. Graham Kendrick, "Shine Jesus Shine," 1987.

Resources for Further Study: One-Volume Treatments of Historical and Systematic Theology

Barth, Karl. *Dogmatics in Outline*. Translated by G.T. Thomson. New York: Harper & Row, 1959.

Berkhof, Hendrikus. *Christian Faith: An Introduction to the Study of the Faith*. Translated by Sierd Woudstra. Grand Rapids: Eerdmans, 1979.

Bilezikian, Gilbert. *Christianity 101*. Grand Rapids: Zondervan, 1993.

Bromiley, Geoffrey W. *Historical Theology: An Introduction*. Grand Rapids: Eerdmans, 1978.

Brunner, Emil. *Our Faith*. Translated by John W. Rilling. New York: Scribner's, n.d.

Conyers, A.J. *A Basic Christian Theology*. Nashville: Broadman & Holman, 1995.

Erickson, Millard. *Introducing Christian Doctrine*. Edited by L. Arnold Hustad. Grand Rapids: Baker, 1992.

Evans, James H. *We Have Been Believers: An African-American Systematic Theology*. Minneapolis: Fortress, 1992.

González, Justo L. *Mañana: Christian Theology from a Hispanic Perspective*. Nashville: Abingdon, 1990.

Grenz, Stanley J. *Theology for the Community of God.* Nashville: Broadman & Holman, 1994.

Grenz, Stanley J., and Roger E. Olson. *Twentieth Century Theology: God and the World in a Transitional Age.* Downers Grove, Ill.: InterVarsity, 1992.

Grenz, Stanley J., and Roger E. Olson. *Who Needs Theology?* Downers Grove, Ill.: InterVarsity, 1996.

Johnson, Alan E., and Robert E. Webber. *What Christians Believe: A Biblical and Historical Summary.* Grand Rapids: Zondervan, 1989.

Leith, John. *Basic Christian Doctrine.* Louisville: Westminster/ John Knox, 1993.

Migliore, Daniel L. *Faith Seeking Understanding: An Introduction to Christian Theology.* Grand Rapids: Eerdmans, 1991.

Milne, Bruce. *Know the Truth.* Downers Grove, Ill.: InterVarsity, 1982.

Pannenberg, Wolfhart. *The Apostles' Creed in the Light of Today's Questions.* Philadelphia: Westminster, 1972.

Placher, William C. *A History of Christian Theology: An Introduction.* Philadelphia: Westminster, 1983.

Shelley, Bruce L. *Theology for Ordinary People.* Downers Grove, Ill.: InterVarsity, 1993.

Smith, David L. *A Handbook of Contemporary Theology.* Wheaton, Ill.: Victor/BridgePoint, 1992.

Wainwright, Geoffrey. *Doxology: The Praise of God in Worship, Doctrine, and Life.* New York: Oxford, 1980.

Scripture Index

Genesis
1:1 *59, 63, 287*
1:2 *46, 62, 156*
1:26 *76, 79*
1:27 *74, 79*
1:28 *51*
2 *79*
2:7 *53, 62, 156*
2:15 *51, 76, 92,
185*
2:15-17 *279*
2:16 *92*
2:16-17 *76*
2:17 *93*
2:19-20 *92*
2:25 *92*
3:1-7 *92*
3:8 *92*
3:8-19 *93*
3:14-15, 17-19 *93*
3:19 *93*
3:23 *93*
6:3 *62, 156*
6:17 *62, 155*
7:15 *155*
7:22 *62, 155*

8:1 *155*
9:6 *77*
49:33 *265*

Exodus
3:14-15 *55*
4:22 *124*
10:13 *155*
15:1-18 *219*
15:11-16 *34*
19:3-6 *166*
24:1-11 *167*
31:1-5 *156*
35:31 *156*
34:6 *59*

Levitcus
1:1 *166*

Numbers
7:89 *166*
12:8 *166*
14:29-31 *102*
24:2-3 *156*
27:18-23 *248*

Deuteronomy
1:39 *102*
6:4-5 *16, 43*
26:5 *16*
32:36-39 *43*

Joshua
5:1 *34*

Judges
3:10 *156*
6:34 *156*
14:6, 19 *156*
15:14 *156*

1 Samuel
2:6 *265*
9:15 *166*
10:6, 10 *156*
19:19-24 *156*

2 Samuel
7:14 *124*
7:22 *43*
22:6 *265*

Subject Index

J

Jastrow, Robert   *31*
judgment   *93, 101–2, 187, 257, 259–60, 270, 274–80, 287*
justice   *51, 59, 74, 84, 224–25, 277, 282–83*
justification   *191, 281*

K

Kant, Immanuel   *31*
kingdom of God   *209–12, 225, 240, 256–57, 260*

L

Lewis, C.S.   *32*
liberation   *100, 133, 159, 190, 192–93, 275–76, 287, 289, 292*
Lord   *24, 115–16, 183, 197, 210, 213, 218, 224, 236, 254, 281*
Lord's Supper   *220, 232–35, 238–42, 245*
love   *20, 24–25, 47–48, 51, 59–62, 75–77, 80, 84, 114–15, 121, 142,
    147–48, 150, 160–62, 169, 191, 195, 198, 214–15, 217, 224, 232,
    266, 277, 281, 284, 291*
Luther, Martin   *104, 238*

M

Malcolm, Norman   *30*
Mass   *239*
Messiah   *133, 136, 157, 210*
millennium   *257–59*
monism   *267, 291*
moral influence theory   *142*
music   *219*
mutuality   *221, 248*

N

natural headship   *95*
new creation   *261, 273, 275–76, 286–90, 292–93*
notitia   *182*

O

offering   *220*
omnipotence   *57–58*
omnipresence   *57–58*

omniscience   *57–58*
ordinances   *233*
ordination   *248*
orthodoxy   *21*
outreach   *221–23, 238, 246*

P

Packer, J.I.   *37*
paedobaptists   *231*
Paley, William   *30*
parish   *231*
pastor   *247–48*
penal-substitution theory   *141–42*
Pentecost   *157–58, 171, 211, 213*
perfection   *201–2, 220, 275, 293*
personhood   *54–55, 154–55, 161–63*
plenary inspiration   *172*
positional sanctification   *199–200, 202*
postmillennialism   *259*
prayer   *49–50, 58, 200, 219, 221–25, 299*
preaching   *221, 247*
   See also: proclamation, sermon
predisposition   *192*
preexistence   *127–29*
premillennialism   *258*
presence   *223*
priesthood   *207–9, 222, 244*
procession   *45, 160*
proclamation   *194, 223–24, 237*
   See also: preaching, sermon
prophetic utterances   *219*
pure church ideal   *230*
purgatory   *269*

R

racism   *74*
ransom theory   *137–39*
rapture   *258*
Rashdall, Hastings   *31*